Leo —

To my friend — and the best lawyer in the universe — he brought Shell Oil Co to its knees!

Best always —

Tom

5/14/09

"Momma, Don't Ya Want Me to Learn Nothin?"

Reflections on a Young Man's Life

Eugene M. Munger, Jr.

Center for Regional History
Southeast Missouri State University
Cape Girardeau, Missouri

green
press
INITIATIVE

Southeast Missouri State University is committed to preserving ancient forests and natural resources. We elected to print this title on 30% postconsumer recycled paper, processed chlorine-free. As a result, for this printing, we have saved:

6 Trees (40' tall and 6-8" diameter)
4 Million BTUs of Total Energy
531 Pounds of Greenhouse Gases
2,204 Gallons of Wastewater
283 Pounds of Solid Waste

Southeast Missouri State University made this paper choice because our printer, Thomson-Shore, Inc., is a member of Green Press Initiative, a nonprofit program dedicated to supporting authors, publishers, and suppliers in their efforts to reduce their use of fiber obtained from endangered forests.

For more information, visit www.greenpressinitiative.org

Environmental impact estimates were made using the Environmental Defense Paper Calculator. For more information visit: www.edf.org/papercalculator

Southeast Missouri State University
Center for Regional History
One University Plaza
Cape Girardeau, MO 63701

Printed in the United States

ISBN:1-890551-14-7

Dedication

This book is dedicated to Ms. Alene Sadler,
my Central High School English Teacher.

Contents:

Editors' Preface

Dick, Rin Tin Tin, Cotton, Apples, Topper, Roundball, and War. These are just a few of the titles of stories that you'll find in *Momma Don't Ya Want Me to Learn Nothin?* Through entertaining anecdotes of his childhood, Gene Munger reflects on the way things used to be in the 1940s and 50s in southeast Missouri.

Gene takes readers from his early days in Chaffee, Sikeston, and Benton through his growing up in Cape Girardeau, Missouri. Tales of activities like Boy Scouts, picking cotton, tornadoes, playing basketball and Indian ball, and attending Cape Central High School and Southeast Missouri State College fill his stories. A lot has changed since 1957, the year Gene left Cape Girardeau to attend Navy Officer Candidate School, but some things are still the same.

Even if we grew up in southeast Missouri years later, we can still relate to the places and activities that Gene shares. I know I did. As a young girl, I attended Girl Scout Camp Cherokee Ridge, right across the St. Francis River from Boy Scout Camp Lewallen that Gene recalls so fondly. My parents were raised in the Bootheel communities of New Madrid and Wilhelmina and I often traveled through the locations of Gene's stories on the way to my grandparents' homes. Like Gene and my parents before me, I will soon be a graduate of Southeast Missouri State University. Not only could I relate to his stories, but as I read them, I felt as though he was a friend telling the anecdotes of his childhood years before in the region where I grew up.

Following months of preparing this book for publication and compiling images from yesteryear, I spoke with Gene Munger. Having read his stories, I felt as though I already knew him. I hope you feel the same when you reach the last page.

Hallie Fieser
Research Assistant
Center for Regional History

Acknowledgements

The idea of writing a series of short stories covering "my growin' up" in southeast Missouri came to me few months after I had retired from Shell Oil Company in December 1991. With Shell, my writing, for the most part, had been wrapped around corporate reports, memorandums, etc. Creative writing, had I tried, was definitely not the proper format, and management would have soon relegated me to other opportunities, but not with Shell.

My first effort at creative writing was "Dick," a story about my shoe shining career, albeit one day, in Benton, the county seat of Scott County. Friends who had never been to Benton, much less anywhere in Missouri, read and liked it. They encouraged me to write more. Such encouragement gave me the impetus to do just that, and over the years, my stories scanned a period from 1940, living in Chaffee, Sikeston, Benton, and Cape to my leaving there in 1957 to go to the Navy Officer Candidate School.

As I have written these stories, the editing support and memory refreshment of events that took place more than 50 years ago was invaluable and I believe, added significantly to the book. If in those stories, I have offended anyone, I deeply regret that. I meant no harm nor harbor any ill feeling toward those appearing in the stories.

To those who took the time and interest to edit my offerings, I salute the following and will hold them as always in respect. I will never be able to thank them enough. Without their support and objective views, this book would never have been published:

Dr. Jeanette Baker, Ph.D., Northern Arizona University's Associate Vice President of Enrollment Management and Student Affairs

John Jacobson, Retired Vice President, Northern Arizona Healthcare, Public Affairs and Marketing

Holly Taylor, former Administrative Manager, Flagstaff Symphony Orchestra

Dr. Frank Nickell, Director of the Center for Regional History at Southeast Missouri State University and Hallie Fieser, Research Assistant, Center for Regional History

To write stories of events and people who were a big part of my life more than 50 plus years ago, I fortunately had the following that refreshed and corrected my memory, added their thoughts and reflections of that period, and contributed beautifully to the overall writing. In my view, their input added credibility and sparkle to my stories.

John Brussman, retired Vice President and General Manager, Busch Agricultural Resources, Inc., who I first met when I was six years old; we were classmates in Benton, Cape and State College, and he remains a close and loyal friend forever.

Dr. Richard Eichorst, retired Assistant Superintendent, Hancock Place School District, a true friend and former college basketball teammate whose recall of our college days continues to amaze me.

Jeanette and Andy Juden, Central High School classmates and long-time Cape Girardeau residents, with whom I could always count on in those early days.

Dr. John B. Hinni, retired Director of University Studies, Southeast Missouri State University, who I have known since my scouting days, my soul mate and brother.

To all of those who encouraged, supported and loved me through the good and bad times of my youth, I shall forever be indebted to you.

In closing, I must add that without Molly, my beloved wife and most constructive critic, who continuously urged me to continue writing, I would not have finished this book. She will always be "the straw that stirs my drink." I love her madly!

Map of Southeast Missouri

Early Days
Chaffee, Sikeston, and Benton, Missouri

1934-1946

*An eager Gene Munger posing for his
first grade school picture in September
of 1940 in Chaffee, Missouri.*

Beginnings

My first six years were spent in the small railroad town of Chaffee, Missouri. We lived in a two-story white house next to the Christian Church when I started to grade school. I remember the story my mother always liked to tell of my first day of school.

I was dressed in short pants, a short-sleeved white shirt and a light blue beanie when I tramped down the steep front steps to walk to school only two short blocks away. My mother sat on the bottom step and waved good-bye. Tears eased down her soft face as her little boy started his formal education.

Seeing her cry alarmed me. I looked back and asked "What's 'da matter, Momma? Don't ya want me to learn nothin'?" That was the beginning. I never forgot what I asked her. Mother never failed to teach me.

The next spring, in 1941, we moved to Sikeston, a town of about 8,000 people. My father's law practice was not that good and a larger town offered better prospects. He rented a new house at the terminus of Scott Street with Murray Lane, an unpaved country road leading over to Highway 61. Our house stood at the southern-most point of the city limits. Across Murray Lane, a huge uncultivated field lay silent adjacent to a heavy stand of oak and maple trees that gave clear evidence that the town's growth went no further.

A few months later, Mother was diagnosed with tuberculosis by local doctors. In those days, total bed rest was ordered. For nearly a year, her bedroom was her world. I was only six years old, but I was allowed to bring her meals. Our housekeeper would fix her food and place it carefully on a bed tray. I would then walk proudly into her space. An English butler could have done no better. Finished, she would ring a tiny bell that I found fascinating. She would read to me constantly as I sat quietly by her bedside. I never heard her complain. She didn't appear sick, but my father explained that she was and that she'd have to rest in bed for awhile before she could get up and be with us. I accepted that, but didn't quite understand.

Ruth Humphreys Munger—1900-1992
Photo of Gene's mother taken in 1941.

Later that year, the spot on Mother's lung had not decreased and her doctors suggested she go to the sanatorium in Mount Vernon, Missouri. Unknown to me, going there was the last resort. This was incurable tuberculosis and Mount Vernon was the place to die.

We made the cross-state journey in Daddy's four-door 1939 Plymouth. It was my first trip out of southeast Missouri. Unlike the flat and virtually treeless landscape of the land in the state's Bootheel where we lived, the bountiful green forests and the clear flowing streams along the highway leading westward opened up a different world to me. I loved the trip. I had no idea that it could be the last time that I would ever see my mother alive.

We arrived at the sanatorium just before noon the next day after spending the night at a motel (my first motel experience) in the little town of Mansfield, about 90 miles or so from Mount Vernon.

The sanatorium sure didn't look like a place for someone to go when they were sick. It reminded me of a giant park, where people sat on benches on grassy knolls or picnicked freely with their families.

Mother's check-in was brief and efficient. A petite nurse's aide escorted us to Mother's room, a cheerful, almost homey setting shaded by giant white oak trees outside her window. In my view, it was much better than she had had at home. But it wasn't. It was not the same.

"Are we going to spend the night here, Daddy?" I asked. "It's really nice."

"No, Son. We're going on back. Your mother's tired from the trip." Daddy sounded tired, too.

"How long are you going to have to stay here, Mother?" I asked.

"I'll stay here as long as it takes me to get well, Son," she said as she held out her long, thin arms motioning for me to come close.

I bounded forward eagerly, hugging her warmly as she sat quietly on the edge of the single bed. Remaining silent, my father stood at the door rocking back and forth on his heels. He watched and listened to a mother and son saying what could have been their last good-bye. Tears flowed heavily down his strained face. His right hand tried valiantly to wipe them away.

"Did I remember to tell you that . . . ?" That was my mother's recurring and favorite question to me when we were together. My response was always the same.

"That I adore you," I said as I giggled softly. We both held each other with no further words. It was her way of saying good-bye. She was keenly aware that she might never see her son again. For me, her absence was only temporary. We'd be back soon and bring her home. I had no doubt.

Then Dad came over and held both of us as we stood pressing against the tiny bed. I could feel their bodies quivering. They were both tuned into the reality of what could happen. I didn't quite understand why they were so sad. We'd be back soon to take her home. I had just turned seven years old.

Our drive back to Sikeston was mostly silent. My father was essentially non-communicative as the car moved back

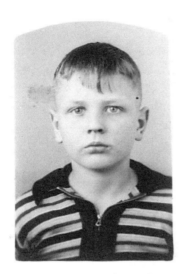

Gene, a second-grader in Sikeston, Missouri, poses for his school picture in the fall of 1941.

along the scenic highway. He announced that we would drive straight through which meant that we wouldn't be back to Sikeston until way after dark.

We stopped outside of Mount Vernon to get my dad a bottle of Coca-Cola, me an orange soda. As we drove away, he confused me with a strange order, "Hand me the baby." Hand me the baby?

"Whaddaya mean Daddy?" I asked.

He pointed to the car's glove compartment and said, "Get me the bottle in there." I handed him the pint of Seagram's 7.

During the ride home, I'd hold his coke while he'd take a long drink of whiskey. Then, we'd exchange and he'd chase his whiskey with another long swig of the cold soda. This sacrament continued throughout the trip. The baby was never far away from him. My father seemed to show no effect from his drinking that day as the torment burned in his soul. The longing he had for his wife, my mother, became a solid deterrent to any kick that he would ever receive from the alcohol.

I began to feel grown-up. After he purchased each soda, Daddy would give me his loose change. My pockets began to bulge. Since any money I ever received before was placed into my piggy bank, I had never experienced the feeling of carrying money around with me. The increasing load in my pocket gave me a feeling of power. I could count and with that much money, I began to feel rich.

We arrived home just before midnight. It had been an exhausting long day for both of us. Daddy arranged for a babysitter to stay with me until school started the next month. She came early the next morning. Life became normal again except I missed my mother deeply.

About a week later, my father came home in a joyous mood. He had gotten a phone call from the sanatorium, "Come get your wife, there's nothing wrong with her!" Doctors had examined her and found that she did not have tuberculosis. The diagnosis by local doctors had been wrong. The spot on her lung was a genetic thing. It had no relationship to the fatal disease.

I, too, was ecstatic. First, my mother was coming home. Second, we would be returning to Mount Vernon along that beautiful highway. And lastly, I'd be able to get more change to fill my pockets. We departed for Mount Vernon the next day.

The drive westward was upbeat. There was no exchanging of bottles between him and me on this trip. Baby was no where to be found. The few stops we made were brief, ordering hamburgers from a roadside restaurant and with my own money, a Pepsi Cola and a Moon Pie. The power returned. We spent the night at the same motel in Mansfield and left early in the morning to pick up Mother by 9 am.

Seeing her again, even though it had been barely more than a week, was very exciting. She was obviously anxious to leave, her bag was already packed and she waved to us from the wide front porch of the main building as we drove up. Mother looked beautiful that warm summer morning. Her cotton dress clung tightly against her thin, graceful body as she skipped excitedly down the gently rolling lawn to our car. Her blue eyes danced with eagerness as we jumped from the car to greet her. My mother was coming home. She was well again!

As we motored home, I was simply beside myself with happiness. All I could say over and over again from the back seat was "I love my Mummy Dud . . . I love my Mummy Dud." Mother smiled and looked at me with love and affection. My father grinned all the way home. It was a very special day and time for all of us. There were few other moments of such parental togetherness and happiness in my life, but these were remembered with great affection.

Topper

It was early fall in 1940. I was six years old and like all boys that age, I was begging my parents to get me a dog.

We had visited my father's aunt and uncle in Little Rock over the weekend and were heading home back to Chaffee along the meandering and narrow Route 67 out of the city. Just before we reached the Missouri line, our 1937 Plymouth suddenly slowed and suddenly came to an abrupt stop just off the highway.

I had been sleeping and the car's jerky movement awakened me. Daddy got out of the car, crossed the road and started walking briskly up a gravel road toward a white house with a green roof.

Watching my father through a pair of sleepy eyes, I turned to my mother and asked, "Where is Daddy going?"

She smiled and said, "See the sign there across the highway? What does it say?"

I squinted at the small sign perched unevenly on a whitewashed post and saw in large, uneven letters the word P-U-P-P-I-E-S. I didn't know what the word was; I was only six years old.

"I can't read it," I replied. "What does it say?"

"Try again, Gene. What does the sign read?"

I spelled the word "P-U-P-P-I-E-S," slowly and out loud, but I still couldn't understand it. "Tell me, Mother. Please tell me."

"What do you think it is, Gene? Guess."

"I give up," I sighed and turned away from the sign. I didn't care anymore.

"Oh, look! Here comes Daddy! What does he have with him?" Mother's anxious voice brought me out of my blue funk as I pressed my nose against the car's back window.

"Daddy's got a doggie! Daddy's got a doggie! He's got me a doggie!" I quickly opened the back door, dashed out across the highway and reached for the small bundle of black and white fur held closely in my father's arm. "Lemme have him, please, lemme have him!" I cried as I kept trying to pull the small puppy from my father's grasp.

"Here he is. Here's your puppy, Gene. He's all yours. He's your dog."

Very gingerly, he handed me the puppy as we crossed the highway. "Gene, this is a bulldog, a Boston bulldog. What do you want to name him?"

"Doesn't he have a name yet?" I asked as I opened the car's back door and carefully lifted my new pet inside with me. One would have thought I was carrying and protecting the queen's crown jewels.

"No name yet, but you can name him," replied my father. "Do you have a name in mind?"

"No, let's let Mother name him. She's a good namer, I bet."

Mother smiled again and said, "No, that's your job. You name him."

"Please, Mother. You do it," I pleaded. "Please."

"Well, if you want me to, I'll try. How about Topper? Is that a good name?"

"Topper? What's a topper?" I asked.

"A topper is, well, something like, uhhh, well, a topper is a dog that's smart. One who is the smartest." Mother's hesitating explanation appeared to be made up for the moment, as she, too, had no idea what a topper was.

"Yes, that's what we'll call him. Topper. And he's my dog," I said as I continued to hold and caress him.

And so Topper became my dog, really the first one that I could remember ever having. We were inseparable as he grew from puppyhood to a full-sized male. At only about 18 inches high, he was an adorable, loving dog. He slept with me, was always at my side when we frolicked indoors and out and, of course, shared many of my meals as I would slip food to him as he waited patiently beside me. Yes, he was the smartest and also the most handsome pet in the world! My mother had named him well.

We relocated from Sikeston to Benton in early 1942. Rather than living in a house like we had in Sikeston, a second story duplex apartment became our home. Steep stairs, at least 25 in number, provided our access. It didn't bother Topper and me. We would go up and down quickly and with no fear. Besides, there were nearby woods where we'd go and play. I'm not sure whether woods were the most natural place for bulldogs, but it didn't matter, Topper went where I went.

Gene playing with his sister's bulldog, Lady in 1946. After the loss of Topper, Gene did not have another dog throughout the 1940s and 1950s.

And then along came Coalie. Coalie was a mixed breed, solid black male Collie, a little larger than most pure breeds. He suddenly appeared in the neighborhood one day and started running and playing with me and my friends. No one owned the dog, but he seemed to always find a meal somewhere and quickly became the neighborhood's dog. But, he certainly was no friend of Topper's. The feeling was mutual.

Time after time, these two dogs would engage in fierce combat with Topper always coming out on the losing end. One would think that after getting whipped again and again, his ears nearly chewed in half, he would choose to avoid his menace. But, those defeats seemed to give him more resolve to attack Coalie anytime he saw him. Topper may have been the smartest, but he certainly wasn't the most sensible.

Topper's continuing aggressiveness toward Coalie continued. My friends would alert me yelling, "Coalie's out," which prompted me to take all steps to keep Topper inside the apartment. Before he and I would go outside, I'd scour the neighborhood to see if Coalie was around. But, just as Topper and I would go down the steps, his antagonist would appear out of nowhere, make a bee-line toward my dog and before I could gather him up in my arms, the battle would start again, always with the same result.

Every now and then, Topper would slip out of the apartment and ultimately become ambushed by his ever vigilant enemy. Seeing him drag his tortured body up the long steps after another defeat would be so depressing. Would he ever learn? Topper's continuing losses took their toll, leading to the loss of one eye and two ears that looked like he had been boxing Joe Louis, the then heavyweight boxing champion of the world.

Then one day, Topper strangely disappeared. I presumed that someone had let him out of the apartment without me, and perhaps he had wandered away into the woods. Maybe, someone had stolen him. Could it be Coalie had finally lent a life-ending blow to him? I looked all over the town, knocking on neighbor's doors to inquire as to whether someone had seen my dog. My search proved fruitless.

Night after night I would cry myself to sleep grieving for Topper, my best friend. Little did I know that one morning when I was in school, my mother had taken him to the veterinarian to "put him down." It was time. They never told me and I never forgot him.

Pearl Harbor

It was December 7, 1941. We lived in Sikeston, Missouri, a town of about 8,000 essentially midway between St. Louis and Memphis, a distance of about 250 miles. I was seven and one-half years-old and had started to get excited about Christmas.

After playing outside with my friends most of the afternoon on that cold and windy day, the sound of my mother's familiar police whistle was more than enough to make me bid farewell to the gang and scurry home to dinner. Entering the house on Murray Lane, I ripped off my hooded mackinaw and cried out to the seemingly empty rooms, "Where's everybody at?" I gazed anxiously around the living room thinking nobody was home.

"In here." Mother's strong voice reassured me. "We're in here listening to the radio."

I moved quickly to the small room where the small radio's loud, gravelly sounds were filling the air. I sensed something was wrong. Mother was sitting totally erect on the couch with her long, slender hands shielding her face as if she had just seen the specter of some evil demon. The dull glow of the room's only lamp cast a funereal shadow on her. She appeared almost petrified.

Like a hungry bear ready to strike down and maul some unsuspecting creature of the forest, my father sat hunched by the radio concentrating completely on every word coming from the announcer's tense sounding mouth. Dad seemed to be in pain. His normally smooth face showed heavy lines of stress.

"I can't believe this. I just can't believe it. Why would they do this to us?" I had never heard such an anguished voice from my father. I still had no idea as to what was wrong.

"What is it, Daddy? What is it? Is someone hurt?" My voice cracked as I strained forward to hear his answer.

"The Japs have bombed Pearl Harbor, Son. The Japs have bombed Pearl Harbor. We're going to war." His explanation completely puzzled me. Who were the Japs?

Where was Pearl Harbor? Where were we going to war? Who? When? Why?

Sensing my anguish and concern, my father left his chair to approach me to try to explain what was happening on this dreary, cold afternoon. I was totally sheltered and ignorant about world events and geography. It didn't make much sense to me why our country was being bombed by another country on a Pacific island more than 6,000 miles away.

"But, Daddy, isn't Hawaii the place where they grow pineapples and do the hula?" I asked. "Wouldn't it be better if they bombed us in New York City?"

My ignorance and lack of understanding of the gravity of the situation caused my father to break off his attempts to explain. He was too overcome with grief and anger to spell it out more clearly to his seven-year-old son.

Turning to my mother, he said, "I wonder how soon it will take me to get back in uniform? I'm ready to fight!" I was certainly old enough to understand what he meant by that. My father was going to war. He would be shooting a gun and killing people. I started crying uncontrollably as I rushed to my mother's waiting arms.

"Daddy's not going to die, is he? He's not gonna get shot, is he? I hate the Japs! Kill 'em all. Kill 'em all." My mother's soothing and reassuring voice calmed me down, but losing my father was more than I could bear to grasp.

My parents had already decided to move to Benton, in the spring of 1942. A small southeast Missouri town of only 408 residents, it served as the county seat of Scott County. Other than for county business and the only movie theater between Cape Girardeau and Sikeston, the town wasn't much to get very excited about. That wasn't true, however, for the cotton, beans, and watermelon farmers and their families who lived outside of town and came in on Saturdays to do their shopping. They enjoyed coming to town to break the monotony of working 12-15 hour days.

We moved where my father anticipated his law practice would thrive. He felt that having a law practice in the county seat made a lot of sense. There'd be no more round trips to court and he believed he could pick up a lot of business from folks going to the courthouse. His office was part of an extended building containing Miller's, a general store.

However, the next several weeks brought very tense times for my father as he tried desperately to join the Army. He was too old, at least according to government records. During World War I, he lied about his age and joined the Army. Rising from a private to a commissioned officer, he fought with the 138th Infantry and was decorated for his service in France. He was fiercely proud of his military duty.

Dad tried every avenue, any means to open any door that would enable him to get back into his beloved Army to defend his country. In a last ditch effort, he traveled to Washington D.C., lobbied his congressman and camped out on the War Department's front steps until he could get an audience with a bureaucrat who had the power to say yea or nay. Unfortunately, the final response was nay.

Returning to Benton after his futile trip, my Dad's spirits were never lower. He sat for hours at the small kitchen table, softly sobbing, nursing his ever omnipresent elixir of comfort, Seagrams 7 and Coke, swearing loudly about the gross injustice of rejection the War Department had cast upon him. There was never a worse time in his life. He had failed his country and, to his way of thinking, he had failed himself.

Bicycle

The Christmas of 1941 came despite our country's being at war and Santa brought me a bicycle. It was a *Challenger*, the one I wanted. It was white, with distinctive red stripes going down the fenders and had big white-walled balloon tires. It sported a large, wire basket firmly anchored in front of the handle bars. I was so pleased, so proud.

In mid-February, a terrible thing happened. My friends and I were riding our bicycles on Scott Street in front of my house. Winter had taken a brief respite and we had shed our mackinaws for light sweaters. Suddenly, a Western Auto truck pulled up at the curb.

A man dressed in gray coveralls over a soft wool plaid shirt jumped from the truck's cab, looked rather sadly at me on my bicycle and yelled, "Hey, Kid, is that your bike?"

"Yes Sir, it is. Santa Claus brought it to me for Christmas. It's a *Challenger*!" I replied wondering what this stranger was doing on our street.

"Well, I've got to take it back to the store," he replied in a soft southern twang as he walked over to me.

Frightened, I leaped off the bicycle, placed my foot hard against the kickstand and stepped cautiously away from the approaching man. Tears welled up in my eyes. I didn't understand what was going on. "You're going to take my bike, Sir? Why?"

"Sorry, Kid, but I got to take it." With a quick snatch, he picked the bicycle up over his head and threw it unkindly into the truck's empty bed. My friends stood there gawking at him. They didn't understand either and were speechless.

The driver pulled away from the curb and made a quick U-turn on Murray Lane as gritty sand flew wildly from the truck's tires. I ran into the house crying uncontrollably. "Mother, Mother, a man took my bicycle," I yelled. My screaming voice jostled Mother from her afternoon nap.

"What's the matter, Gene? What's the matter?" I tried to recreate the traumatic scene at the curb. My heavy sobbing made it almost impossible for her to understand. After a few weeping, almost unintelligible starts, she began to piece out what I said. She told me gently to go to my room while she got my bicycle back.

I made a brief detour into the adjoining kitchen to get a drink of water. I could hear mother's voice on the telephone with somebody. Her voice, while agitated, was crisp and firm. I couldn't exactly hear the conversation except for her repeated words, "I want that bicycle back here today. Do you understand? Today! Do you hear me? Today!"

Sure enough, the man in the truck reappeared two hours later. He honked twice as he parked his truck in front of the house. I ran outside and there it was, my beautiful bicycle standing curbside. My mother was a magician. I never expected to see it again. Through magic, she had made my treasure reappear.

Yes, she had been on the phone to my father and read him the riot act. It obviously made an impression because he settled the account in full and ordered the bicycle to be returned. I'm sure he raked the store manager over the coals for such an intemperate and unnecessary action. To my father, paying bills was never a high priority.

Lynching

The Christmas season of 1941, like my parents, like all of us, was severely dampened by the dark shadow of the Japanese December 7 attack on Pearl Harbor and our country declaring war. Our parents, friends, families and our nation were placed in a state of anxiety, of animated suspension not knowing who would be drafted, who would enlist or would we be attacked? Indeed, it was a most troubling time.

The following January was unseasonably cold. We moved from Chaffee the previous year and settled into a new house at the dead-end of Scott Street and Murray Lane. There was no break from the raw north wind blowing at us from an open field directly across from our house. Consequently, my new bicycle received very little use as I preferred to stay inside to escape the weather.

On the Sunday morning of January 20, one of my friends, Bubba Shy, who lived only a block away, knocked at our door. It was around 9:30 am, and we were preparing to go to church. For Bubba to be knocking on my door on a Sunday morning was very unusual.

My father answered Bubba's persistent knocking, greeted the boy at the door and said, "Bubba, don't you think it's a little early for you to be coming over? It's Sunday and we're getting ready to go to church."

"I know, Mr. Munger, but my folks just heard the police caught a nigger who cut up a white woman and a big mob is down at the jail, and they're gonna get him."

That word was not considered politically incorrect in those days. Southeast Missourians and those from other southern states used it as common language, with no serious thought of being racist or demeaning. "What are you talking about, Bubba? Settle down and tell me what you've heard."

My mother and I listened intently just away from the front door. I was not quite sure what Bubba was saying, but I did understand there seemed to be a lot of trouble taking place in town.

"Well, Mr. Munger, what my daddy heard was this guy broke into the woman's house last night around midnight and cut her up real bad. The police caught him and he told 'em what he had done, and they put him in jail. Now, a bunch of men are meetin' around the jail, and they're really mad."

"Well, thank you, Bubba. Now you go on home back to your parents."

"But, Mr. Munger, aren't you and Gene goin' down there to the jail to watch?"

"No, Bubba, we're not and I hope you and your folks don't go down there, either. Now, go on home."

My father was stunned with the news. He knew that for the most part, whites and blacks got along pretty well in Sikeston, but there was an underlying racial prejudice there like so much of the South those days. The blacks lived in Sunset Addition, about a quarter-mile west of downtown. They kept to themselves in their tight community, worked as field hands, domestic servants, or as common laborers at places like Sikeston's cotton oil mill. Wages for these people were sub-standard and for the most part, dead-end jobs.

Both of my parents, reared as southerners, had no negative feelings or prejudices against the Negro. One might say they were liberal in their way of thinking, but they were both keenly aware of the economic and social injustices afforded them in society. As a lawyer, my father had no problem defending them in court, but in those days, a Negro client was few and far between and representing a black man brought no accolades from his legal colleagues, only personal contempt for such representation.

"Oh, Daddy, let's go down to the jail. I wanna go. Can we? Can we?"

My father's sober face winced at me and in a direct, authoritative voice, responded, "No, Gene, we're not going down there, and I don't want to hear any more from you about it!" He never talked to me in that manner. Obviously, he was completely upset at what he heard and didn't need me talking or urging any trip to go downtown. My mother said nothing. She, too, was totally distraught with the news.

Dad had many friends in Sikeston, and he knew the one person who would be able to give him an accurate account of what was going on. The friend was R. D. Clayton. R. D., a land owner of immeasurable financial worth, or at least in my eyes, he must have been very rich, was bigger than life in my small world. He rode around town in the newest model Cadillac, dressed fashionably in a close to 300 pound body, always gave me a dime when he saw me and appeared to listen closely as I would tell him about my new bicycle or whatever. Yes, someday, I wanted to be just like R. D. Clayton! I was seven years old.

After a few short rings, R. D. answered followed by my father saying, "R. D.? This is Gene. I just heard there's trouble going on down at the jail. What do you know?"

In his loud, robust voice, R. D. recounted what he did know. With her ear pressed closely to the telephone, my mother heard the conversation. She said nothing, just looked so sad at what she heard. I still had not fully comprehended what was going on.

As R. D. summarized what he knew, they listened and I could tell it was not a very pretty story. It seemed that this young Negro, probably around 25 years old, forced himself into this woman's house on the southeast side of town around 1:30 am, took a knife and slashed her up pretty bad. Later, the cops stopped him, and tried to arrest him. He had blood all over his clothes. While in the car, the man used his knife again and stabbed one of the officers. The officers then shot the man a couple of times and then took the wounded deputy and the accused to the hospital. The docs treated them there, and then the cops drove him down to the jail. There appeared to be no question that the man was guilty. He had already confessed twice to his crime.

"R. D., thanks for the information. My son's friend tells me there's a mob down at the jail. Do you know anything about that?"

"No, Gene, I hadn't heard that, but if there's a mob down there, it won't be good. I'm afraid unless the police stop 'em, they're goin' to take the law into their own hands. I'm not goin' down there, but as soon as I hear something, I'll call you back."

Both parents huddled together in the living room, speaking softly and both visibly distressed about the whole thing. They were aware that Negro lynchings were not that uncommon in the deep South, but based on what R. D. had said, it looked like that was what was going to happen. It had never happened in Sikeston.

Dad stood listening to R. D.'s return phone call for another hour or so. He became even more agitated as I tried to ask him more questions. I asked, "Did you know the lady who was knifed? Do you think they'll ask you to be the man's lawyer?"

"No, Son, we're just not going to talk about this right now. I don't have the answers so, please no more questions."

Around 1 pm, R. D. called. My father grabbed the phone and with an urgent, trembling voice, said, "R. D., what's happened since we last talked?"

"It's really bad, Gene, really bad. Here's the latest." In a slow, deliberate voice, R. D. brought my father up-to-date with a brief summary of what he had just learned.

"Well, when the guy got placed in jail, this mob wasn't about to let him get off with what he had done to that white woman. So, they forced themselves into the jail, literally breaking the bars, jerked him out of there, tied him to the back of a car, and dragged him out to the Sunset Addition. I've been told that neither the police chief nor his deputies did anything to keep them from taking him out of his cell.

When they finally got him out to Sunset, they dragged him over to the dump and while the mob and many of the folks living there watched in horror, they doused him with gasoline, set him on fire, and burned him to a crisp. Just like that, Gene, they burned him, like firewood."

My mother and I couldn't hear the final, sordid details, but it was apparent that hearing this from R. D. had a most dramatic effect on my father, as he turned ashen-white. "Thanks, R. D., I appreciate hearing from you. I don't know what to say. This is terrible."

Off the phone, he asked me to leave the room while he told Mother the gory details of the lynching. In time, hearing my father talk about it with Mother and listening to what my friends had heard from their parents, I began to understand.

This lynching had a profound effect on Sikeston and area residents and certainly my parents and me. Sikeston, the new

South, had never been the subject of such violence up to that time. Other lynchings, mostly hangings, had taken place in the Deep South, but no one in southeast Missouri had probably ever expected such a lawless and brutal event to take place there. It did happen when I was six years old, and I never forgot it.

Author's Note:

In Dr. Dominic J. Capecci's book, *The Lynching of Cleo Wright*, Dr. Capecci wrote, "Similar to traditional lynchings, yet unique in itself, Wright's execution revealed much about the evolution of black-white relations in changing southeast Missouri and even more about the roles of local, state and federal authorities in stemming future racial violence. Thus it bears greater significance than most lynchings."

Dick

Dick Harrison was my best friend. I was ten, he was twelve, but we were about the same size. He was two years ahead of me in school. Aside from the time he would visit his grandparents on their farm east of Sikeston a few weeks every summer, we were almost always together. Dick was also the best shoe shine boy in town and the only one.

Because of his toe hold on the market, Dick was getting rich. At least, he was getting rich by my standards. On Saturdays he'd tote his shoeshine box around town and hustle every man in sight wearing shoes, regardless of their condition, and offer his special services at a steady, convenient price of ten cents a shine. Some Saturdays, when the town was particularly crowded, like a Fourth of July weekend, he would pull in as much as four dollars, but usually it was around two dollars. For a twelve year old kid in 1944, that was a lot of money.

But the real secret of Dick's success was not his ability to turn the working farmer's shoes to a gentleman farmer's finely buffed footwear; it was his pleasing and jaunty manner. Actually, as a shoe shiner, he was only ordinary, but by the time that he went through his friendly, schmoozing greeting and responded to his customers with well-spaced polite and timely "Yes, Sirs" and "Thank you, Sirs," the shine on their shoe was secondary. For that short time, he would bring back a renewed spirit and feeling to a group of folks who only received flatteries and courtesies from their ministers and priests who honored them at their funerals.

Gene's Benton friends posing for a picture in 1945. Pictured from left to right are John Brussman, Dick's sister, Mary Harrison, Gene, and Dick Harrison.

Dick was a handsome kid with coal black hair, always neatly combed. His dark eyes and heavy eyebrows were a perfect complement to his olive complexion. While he was barely five feet tall, he walked much taller and always seemed to be in a hurry, a trait probably picked up from watching his county surveyor dad walking at mercurial speed between the house and the courthouse.

The combination of Dick's personality and his knack for making it work for him put him into the entrepreneurial class. His buddies and I were much more interested in playing baseball, hanging around the soda fountain at Frobase's Drug Store and reading *Captain Marvel* comic books.

But after a while, watching Dick work, doing his magic, and making all that money got me to thinking. When my dad let me shine his shoes, I thought I did a pretty fair job. He always thanked me, but I never knew whether he liked the shine, or was just happy with only being charged a dime. If I did it well for Dad, why couldn't I go out on the street and do it like Dick?

I approached Dick about the idea of getting into his business, but he was less than encouraging. He gave me some good reasons why it wouldn't work. "First, you're too young. Second, you don't have a box. And last, there's not enough business around here for both of us."

But I quickly countered his reasons. "Hey, you're only two years older than me . . . and I'm just as big as you are. Besides, you could help me make a box. I bet 'ya could. We could be partners, and at the end of the day, we could split up what we made."

"Look, Gene, I don't want to be your partner. Like I told you, there's not enough business here in Benton for the two of us. You'd only ruin it for me. Why don't you think of something else? How about goin' over and ask Jimmy Riles for a job washing cars? Heck, you don't need to make money. Your pop's a lawyer."

Dick's attitude puzzled me. We did everything together, and why couldn't we shine shoes together? I tried a different angle. "Dick, you can teach me. I'd pay you one-half of what I make. You see, you can't lose. You'd get half."

"Nope, I don't wanna do that," Dick replied, "I just don't wanna do that. You go ahead if you want to, but not with me." His black, piercing eyes stared right through me. I'd never seen him act that way. He was clearly mad. He had made his point.

That evening, I discussed it with my Dad. He thought it was a great idea and even offered to help me build the box. We went down to the lumber yard the next Saturday, bought a few white pine boards, and while I watched, he built me my box.

My dad was a total perfectionist, and his approach to my project was intense. You would have thought that he was designing and building a king's castle. It took him most of the afternoon, but it was a real beauty . . . probably one of the classic shoe shine boxes of all time, and it definitely was just as good as Dick's.

I carefully painted it a bright Cardinal red, and with a small loan from Dad (to be repaid, of course from my future earnings) I scooted down to Miller's General Store and bought my supplies: black, brown, and neutral paste, liquid polish for sole dressing, and a soft brush. I was really excited when Dad came home later and presented me with the ultimate in shoe shining paraphernalia, some discarded pool table cloths from Andy's Tavern.

I didn't tell Dick what I had in mind. He was going to Scout Camp for the first time the following Sunday, and I would have the whole town to myself the next Saturday. I was down at the courthouse square when he and the rest of Troop 25 headed out to Camp Lewallen. Since I was only ten, I couldn't join the troop, the legal age being 12. I desperately wanted to become a scout, since all my friends had joined Benton's first troop only a year before. I acted like I was sad to see them go. I guess I was because I wouldn't have anybody to play with for the whole next week. Of course, the thought of having the lock on the town's shoeshine business was pretty heady stuff to me.

With Dick and the boys gone, I practiced all week to hone my skills for the next Saturday. I shined Dad's shoes at least six times, getting accustomed to having a real foot and a shoe placed in front of me on my new box.

Saturday finally came. I was up early and out on the street before 8 o'clock. It was a clear, typically humid June day for southeast Missouri. I knew right off that it would be beastly hot, and my best bet would be to hang around the court house where it was always cool, shaded by the elm trees surrounding the outside front along Route 61, the main road between St. Louis and Memphis.

Benton's courthouse was built near the turn of the century. It was rectangle in shape, supported with Corinthian columns stretching two stories high. The main entry was up a long, shaded walk where three wide doors presented a majestic access to the sacred halls inside. We kids would sometimes slip into the huge courtroom on the second floor and watch Dad in action. He always seemed to enjoy seeing us there, and occasionally would introduce me and Dick to his fellow lawyers and the presiding judges.

Its high, cavernous walls and marble floors gave us kids great pleasure as we occasionally gathered inside at night to shout and hear our echoes resound throughout the building. We'd do it now and then during the weekdays, but this would usually upset some of the workers inside. Afterwards, we'd scurry towards home because some who worked there knew our folks, and we certainly didn't need to be discovered to ruin our good time.

To my disappointment, I wasn't able to attract one customer; it was nearly 2 pm. I heard the same line often that day, "Where's Dick? Isn't he here today? He always shines my shoes."

"Oh, Dick's at Scout Camp . . . but I'm taking his place. Can I shine your shoes, Mister?" I replied.

"Naww, that's okay, Son. I'll just wait 'til he comes back." This continuing tide of rejection was not uplifting, and although I was trying to stay mostly in the shade, the searing, humid heat was making me uncomfortable. I was soon thinking about abandoning this venture and finding something else more fun to do.

Then I spotted Harry Cane straightening up after getting a drink from the World War I Memorial Fountain that stood at the far southwest corner of the courthouse property. Harry, tall and erect, was a mysterious man in our young lives. He just appeared in town one day and without being asked, started buying us candy, soda, ice cream, anything we wanted to eat. He always dressed in heavily starched khaki work clothes which looked like he'd never even worked in them. We kids never knew what Harry did or where he got his money, but we could always count on him for a handout.

He was soft spoken, about 45 years old, I guess, and a real gentleman.

"Hi, Harry. How are you?" I greeted him real friendly. "How about a shine?"

"Shine? Where's Dick? I didn't know you shined shoes." His questioning caused me to hesitate a beat before answering his questions.

"Oh, he's at scout camp, but he put me in charge of his business," I said. "He'll be back tomorrow." Harry's long look down at me was not very consoling. "Shine?" I said again.

"Well, if Dick put you in charge, that'll be fine with me. Go to it." Harry's acceptance of my offer brightened my spirits.

I asked him to put his left foot on my well-crafted box. He cautiously placed his tan, high-topped work shoe on the top board, quite a contrast to the only other shoes that I had ever shined, my Dad's wing-tips. With my skinny knees digging evenly into the cool concrete of the shaded sidewalk, I stared hot and heavy on the task before me. Actually, Harry's shoes didn't need much of a shine. It was apparent that he only wore them when he came to town, and I could see that Dick's past work was lasting. I figured that if I did better than Dick, then Harry would start asking for me every Saturday, and that thought was very appealing to me.

My fingers dug deeply into the silky smooth brown paste. I spread it evenly and lightly all over the right shoe, then the left. My rhythm was right, and the past week's practice was paying off. When finished, I whipped out Andy's pool cloth rag and in a brisk, snapping motion, laid it on Harry's shoes. The leather responded positively to my deft touch. His shoes had never looked that good. I finished off the job with an even coat of brown polish around the soles and heels of both shoes. My work was sheer artistry.

"How's that, Harry?" My expectations had never been higher, as I gazed directly into the man's eyes.

"Pretty good, Gene. When did you say Dick would be back?" Harry asked.

I was shattered. How could he say a thing like that? I had given him my best. He had *never* had a shine like that in his life. And all he could say was, "When's Dick coming back?"

Harry reached into his pocket and pulled out a handful of change. Carefully, he selected a dime from among the many coins held in his long, thin hand and said, "Here, son, you did a good job. Not as good as Dick does, but a good job anyway."

"Thanks, Harry. Thanks a lot. I know Dick will appreciate that. I'll sure be glad when he gets back. I've missed him," I said as I picked up my box and moved slowly towards the courthouse entrance. I wished the day would hurry up and end.

Although I managed to shine a few more shoes that embarrassing Saturday afternoon, I ended my shoe shining career with a total take of forty cents. As for Dick, he got back from camp the next day and quietly resumed his tight and exclusive hold on the market. For me, I looked forward to that coming fall and the opportunity to pick cotton at Herman Schwartz' nearby fields. There I knew I wouldn't have Dick to contend with. There was plenty to pick, and Mr. Schwartz was paying two cents a pound, and for a ten year-old kid in 1944, that was a lot of money.

■ ■ ■ ■ ■

Rin Tin Tin

Summer in Benton, Missouri, a small rural town of only 408 residents, was always an engaging time for me when I lived there during the early 1940s. Despite the high heat and humidity, it never bothered me. I just assumed that there was no better place on earth!

I could play Army, always the private, with Dick as the sergeant. Further, I could play baseball and root for my beloved Cardinals when my folks would take me to St. Louis to see them play.

But fishing was my first love, my passion. My dad started taking me fishing when I about five and I always begged him to take me again and again. But when I discovered Scott's Pond, it became Dick's and my place. He and I would ride our bicycles about a mile south of town down a gravel road, climb a barbed wire fence, work our way through the high weeds and tall oak trees over to the pond. We never knew why it was there, something about the "WPA did it," but by our youthful standards, it was just fine—big and deep with lots of fish, mostly perch and a few bass.

Fishing was always good, although Dick usually caught more than I, at least until my dad discovered that my pole was just a limb taken from some downed tree. He was aghast that his son was so ill-prepared and without a word, presented me with one of his fly rods including an automatic reel. Dick scoffed at such elaborate trappings and resolved to continue his mastery over me. He did.

And of course, our summer Saturdays were really special. Benton would come alive as the area farmers came to town, bought their groceries at Miller's General Store, ate a $.50 plate lunch at Cannon's Restaurant, got their horses shoed over at Dewey Miller's black smith shop, and stayed around for the "free show."

There were no movies between Cape Girardeau and Sikeston, a distance of about 35 miles. Cape had three, the Broadway, the Rialto and the Orpheum. Sikeston had only one, the Malone. Having lived in Sikeston between the ages

Nine year old Gene Munger in 1944, at the start of the fourth grade in Benton.

of five and six, I had gone there many times on Saturday afternoons, to revel in the hilarious antics of Abbott and Costello and wish that I could ride a horse and shoot a gun as well as Hopalong Cassidy and Charles Starrett, the Durango Kid.

But, the free show was always the highlight of every summer Saturday evening. I never knew who sponsored it, maybe the Chamber of Commerce, but Benton didn't have one as I recall. Perhaps, the merchants, what few they were, pooled their resources and provided the entertainment. We didn't care . . . we didn't know. We only knew that there was always going to be a free show.

Directly behind Miller's was a huge open field with a fairly good gathering of grass, a few weeds here and there, but just right for showing outdoor movies during the summer. Someone had placed two telephone poles sans wires, so that a screen, probably a white sheet, could be stretched between them. Directly behind the screen a few yards away, there was a makeshift wooden stand erected there to hold the projector. And that was it. From that layout, some nameless person showed cartoons and movies every Saturday night . . . all summer long.

Long before the sun went down, folks would gather in the field spreading their blankets in places where they would have a full and unobstructed view of the pleasures to be seen. Many, I suppose, had never been to a "real moving picture show", but it didn't matter. As far as they were concerned, Radio Center Music Hall wasn't as good as that!

One Saturday, the word spread that the show that evening was going to feature Rin Tin Tin, a German Shepherd who had already starred in many movies. I had seen this dauntless dog once before at Sikeston's Malone

Theatre, but Dick had never seen him carry out his fearless ways of always conquering the bad guys despite being shot at, trampled, knocked out and left for dead.

"Dick, you're really going to like *Rin Tin Tin, the Lightning Warrior*! I don't think you've ever seen him. The free show's gonna have him tonight and we want to get over there early," I exclaimed.

"Who's Rin Tin Tin?" Dick asked.

"You don't know Rin Tin Tin? I can't believe that you haven't seen him," I replied in an all-knowing voice and proceeded to extol the dog's many virtues and deeds.

Dick mumbled under his breath something like, "Well, I was hopin' that the Durango Kid was gonna be on this evenin', but all right, if you say I'm gonna like Rin Tin Tin, I guess I will."

The day wore on as the streets filled around the court-house with Saturday's usual summer crowds. It was a blistering hot July day, but spirits were high, the area's cotton fields were looking good and our troops seemed to be getting the upper hand in the war. Besides, there was going to be the usual free show that evening and for most, it would be the high point of their week.

My mother fixed us a picnic dinner to take over to the show. His mother supplied our blanket and fixed some lemonade in a huge Mason jar. As we strolled over to the show, an ominous black cloud showed its ugly head. It looked like it might rain, but, we quickly discounted that. After all, Rin Tin Tin was playing, and the show would surely go on.

Arriving at the field, there was an energetic buzz emanating from the heavy throng of folks waiting for the show to start. We found a spot just to the right of the projectionist, eagerly spread our blanket down on the grassy field, and dug into our peanut butter sandwiches. Mother had even placed a couple of Twinkies into our large paper sack. We were sitting pretty.

At just about dark, a few heavy drops of rain began to fall. The crowd suddenly grew quiet. All looked apprehensively toward the heavy, thick rain-filled clouds swirling toward us. Some picked up their blankets, snatched their small infants swiftly into their arms and headed back to their cars and trucks.

Dick shrugged his head and said, "Gene, do you think that it's gonna rain? If so, we better get outta here. Since you're spendin' the night with me, maybe my mother will have something for us to eat."

"No, we're not . . . Rin Tin Tin is gonna be playin' and besides, it won't rain long. Let's just wait it out." While I sounded confident, I wasn't really sure. Summer storms with lots of lighting and thunder were pretty common in this part of the country, and this one coming looked like it was going to be a dandy.

Then, the rain started, coming down in wind-blown sheets, driving hard against all of us still unwillingly to move. And it did come down . . . really hard. I looked up as the projectionist swaddled his projector in his arms like a mother carrying her baby and trotted briskly away from the field.

Drenching wet, we gathered up our blanket, now soaked from the rain, and with our soggy Twinkies still in the paper bag, fought our way against the heavy torrent all the way back to Dick's house, only a couple of blocks away.

Dick's mother greeted us at the door and scolded us for waiting so long to get out of the rain.

"You boys should know better. You should have known that a terrible storm was coming. What were you thinking?"

"But, Mrs. Harrison, we thought . . . well, we figured that the rain would pass over us. You see, we were looking forward to seeing Rin Tin Tin at the free show. Understand?" My comeback, while not assertive, at least attempted to absolve our actions.

"I don't want to talk about it any longer. Now get out of those wet clothes and let me feed you," she replied. It was obvious that she had made her point and besides, we knew that we would be getting better food than peanut butter sandwiches.

So, there was no free show that Saturday evening, no Rin Tin Tin and with heavy regrets from both Dick and me, the *Lightning Warrior* never returned to Benton.

But, all was not lost. Soon afterwards, Ches Frobase built Benton's first movie theater, right across the highway from the courthouse. And you know we never got soaked trying to watch a movie ever again.

◣ ◣ ◣ ◣ ◣

Taps

Life in Scott County went on despite the war and its heavy effects on my father. As a boy, I found the war very exciting. My friends and I could play war. We could kill Japs and Nazis. We'd go out on patrols in the nearby woods pretending that the hiding enemy was ready to show itself and bring death and destruction to our town. We dug foxholes, threw hedge apples like they were hand grenades, made real-like sounds for machine guns and M-I rifles, and always ended the day convinced that we were contributing mightily to the war effort.

About the closest we ever came to the war, however, was when a Greyhound bus stopped weekly in Benton to pick up a load of draftees and take them up to Jefferson Barracks to join the Army. It was always an exciting and inspiring place to be there those evenings when the bus finally came rolling in. You would see the men, some barely starting to shave, fathers with small children, all huddled around their loving families, sweethearts, sharing the last free moments of civilian life and wondering what the future would bring. For many, their future was limited; they would never return alive.

In the next few months, my mother went to work in the local rationing office, the Office of Price Administration. Working at the OPA, she soon became a woman of power. She was one of the special few who controlled and decided who received rationing stamps for gasoline, meat and sugar, and importantly, how much for each. She never knew how many friends she had. The eager and solicitous would shower her with candy, flowers and tickets to Cardinal baseball games, even the 1944 World Series when the

Cardinals and the Browns played. Whether she ever succumbed to those efforts to bribe her for surplus rationing stamps, I don't know, but I sure enjoyed seeing my beloved Cardinals play.

By late 1942, my father had settled down into his law practice. He was a constant, almost obsessive follower of the war news. His ear was constantly tuned to a radio, early morning to late at night. When he was contacted to help form an American Legion Post for the county, he leaped to the challenge with great vitality.

Not surprisingly, he was elected as the Post Commander of the Scott County Memorial American Legion Post 75. His organizational and leadership skills, along with his total dedication to excellence, soon brought the Post into prominence as a positive and revered county and community symbol. Its members marched at the head of all area parades, sold war bonds and provided a meaningful patriotic outlet for those not able or too old to serve in the armed forces. Of all the Post's activities, the creation of a burial team for those county military men killed in action was his proudest accomplishment.

Dad was delighted with his American Legion uniform. He wore it at every opportunity, at parades, at Memorial Day and July Fourth celebrations, and even once to church after President Roosevelt died. He would have the uniform cleaned and pressed before every wearing. Despite the uniform's blue gabardine material, he never complained when the sweltering sun of summer bore down on him unmercifully, and sweat poured endlessly down his face. He never flinched or even tried to brush away the running stream. He was serving his country. That was very important to him.

Three years into the war, I began to play the trumpet. A nun from Oran, Sister Agneta, came over to Benton just after the New Year to start a grade and high school band. My folks encouraged me to join, and I asked them to buy me a trumpet. They did. It was a used silver-plated Conn and in a short time, I learned the fingering and started blowing notes that actually sounded like I knew what I was doing. At least, Sister Agneta thought so and encouraged me to take lessons.

My parents agreed and by late spring, I had progressed enough for her to suggest that I play a solo at her annual spring recital.

Harry James I was not, but Dad heard enough to suggest that I might be good enough to join the American Legion Burial Team and play the echo. After taps was played at the graveside, it was repeated at a distance in the form of an echo. I had seen the team perform at the funeral of one of my classmate's fathers, a sailor who had gone down with his ship when struck by a torpedo in the Coral Sea. The team's military preciseness and class were one thing, but hearing Charlie Wade, the best trumpet player in town play taps, and for me to be his echo . . . now that was really something!

Gene and his mother, Ruth Humphreys Munger, on their porch in Benton with his new Conn trumpet in 1945.

Public burials of the county's war dead were always a solemn occasion. As the war wore on, the number of troops killed in action was increasing. Consequently, Dad's team of six, all hand-picked by him, was averaging at least two funerals a month. To my father, burying the war dead was a special honor bestowed on the Post. Only a flawless performance would satisfy his uncompromising principles.

It was a late Tuesday afternoon in July the day I was asked to become the echo. The dog days of Missouri's summers had once again descended on all of us. Our attic fan ran continuously and the heat converted the town's usual good mood to an attitude of complaining and impatience with everything. Dad had come home early from his office and Mother was still at work. I had been playing baseball with my friends all afternoon, and I was tired and hungry.

My father greeted me in the kitchen and said, "Son, I want you to join us tomorrow. We've got a funeral over at St. Denis' Catholic Church, and I want you to play." I knew what he expected me to say.

"Play the echo?" I asked.

"Yes, play the echo." His deep, rich voice sounded like battalion commander who had just ordered his troops to attack at dawn. With his ever present military bearing, he looked like one.

"What do I wear? Do I have to wear a suit?" I could tell my father did not appreciate my somewhat disrespectful manner.

Dad's piercing dark brown eyes drilled right through me as he answered through his fastidiously groomed mustache, "Yes, you will wear a suit, and you'll meet us over at the church cemetery at two o'clock." I never knew my father to ever raise his voice to me. He didn't need to as I was always keenly aware of what was expected.

"I'll be there," I said as I went straight to my room where the presence of war planes' pictures mounted on the high walls were much more pleasant than thinking about playing taps at somebody's funeral in the unbearable summer heat.

The next day was a typical July scorcher for southeast Missouri . . . hot, humid and uncomfortable. My navy blue Palm Beach suit, while of summer weight, was no match for the unrelenting oppressiveness of the weather.

Placing my trumpet and its case into my bicycle's large wire basket, I headed toward St. Denis' cemetery which was about a half-mile away. Boys my age always went around town on bicycles. There were no public buses in a town of only 408 people. For that matter, there were few cars.

The cemetery was directly in back of the Catholic Church. The grounds were flat and interspersed with a wide, uneven array of small gravestones pointing upwards toward the cloudless blue sky. It was a cheerless sight as I pedaled quietly to the burial team gathered around the freshly dug grave.

The team, smartly dressed in their newly pressed Legion uniforms, was chatting quietly and preparing to go inside the church to commence with their part of the ceremony, to bring the body to its final resting place. My immediate presence was unnoticed; even my father failed to see me.

"Hi, Daddy. Where do I go? When do you bury him?" My high, squeaky questioning voice caused the team to all look up at once.

The Post Commander's officious voice stirred me into action. "First, get off that bicycle and push it outta here. Then, come back and I'll tell you what to do." There was certainly no question as to who was in charge.

Nodding, I quickly pushed my trusty Western Flyer bicycle across the upper quarter of the cemetery, through some knee-high weeds, and behind a run-down maintenance shed out of sight from everybody. I removed my trumpet case from the basket, took out the horn and walked back to the team. My dad was waiting for me.

"Now, Son, what I want you to do is to go way over there by that tree, stay out of sight, and when Charlie finishes playing taps, turn away from where we are and start playing the echo. Okay?" I listened completely to his explicit instructions. My mind was on nothing else.

With trumpet in hand, I walked briskly over to my spot, weaving myself in and around some of the gravestones blocking my path. I slithered down behind a huge maple tree, its far-reaching branches protecting me from the unyielding July sun. I waited for the team to bring the fallen warrior to his ultimate destination.

I sat still for what seemed to be about 20 minutes and listened intently for some sound, some sign that my part would begin. The quiet, summer afternoon's stillness changed dramatically at the sound of rifle shots crackling through the sky. Wade's plaintive sounds of taps from his sweet horn followed. It was now my time.

I stood up, braced myself behind the tree and pointed my trumpet toward the sky and away from the gravesite. My whole body stiffened as I placed my quivering lips toward the mouthpiece. The first sound wavered only a bit, slightly off key, but I recovered instantly and took control of the task.

"TA TA TAHHHH . . . TA TA TAHHHHHHH . . . TA TA TAH . . . TA TA TAH . . . TA TA TAHHHH . . . TA TA TAHHHH . . . TA TA TAHHHHHHH . . . TA TA TAHHHHHHHHHHHHHHHHHH."

Finishing the last note, I froze in place as if I was being stalked by some vengeful enemy. I knew that I had played well. At least, I had not screwed things up. Very carefully, I again took my place behind the tree's trunk and waited. After awhile, I peeked around the tree to see that it was safe to return. The coast was clear, as the family had gone and I walked slowly back to where the team was about to leave.

"That was really nice, Son. Really nice. You played well." Dad's positive words of praise lifted my spirits mightily. "We're going over to Andy's for a beer. How about joining us for a little while?"

Dad was referring to Andy LeGrand's tavern, Benton's major social outlet where all classes, of all professions, would gather to visit, drink a little beer, or play pool. Andy's operation was housed in an undistinguished white frame, one-story building which contained a package liquor store, a fairly large bar area where beer was sold, and a smaller space where a lone pool table stood. Highway 61 motorists passing Andy's would probably ignore his place since the only identification on the building was a small, faded Falstaff beer sign hanging off center between the entrance to the tavern and the liquor store.

I retrieved my bike and sped over to Andy's to join my dad and the team. I had been to this place many times to watch my father shoot pool. Having a young boy in Andy's tavern was no strange sight for those who went there. No one ever seemed to question it.

I parked at the side of Andy's and carried my trumpet in its case inside for fear that someone might take it. I spotted my father sitting with the team at the bar. He didn't see me, but I could hear him telling one of his favorite stories to his attentive listeners, their ample butts spreading over the wooden stools that shared many a story and beer over the years. As a raconteur, he had no peer. Surprisingly, there appeared to be no sorrow or grieving by the team. The solemnity of the past hour had vanished. These men were settling in for a long afternoon of beer drinking and story telling.

Finally, one of the team members noticed me standing there just inside the bar's door. His puffy, florid face showed the effects of too much afternoon sun and two quick beers.

"What'd you think, Little Boy?" He asked. All of Dad's friends referred to me as Little Boy.

I blushed at his question and didn't know what to say. "Well, I hope I played good enough."

"You sure did. Your dad was mighty proud of you, Little Boy and he should be. You'll be able to play as good as Charlie Wade someday, I bet. Would you like that?" He asked.

"Yes Sir, I sure would, Charlie's the best. He's my hero." I replied. "He plays in a dance band, all over, even at the Cotton Club down at Sikeston." I knew exactly where the Cotton Club was, since it was where my mother and dad sometimes went to dance on Saturday nights.

The friendly man then ordered me a strawberry soda, my favorite, and asked to see my trumpet. As I removed it from my case, I said proudly, "It's a Conn. My dad bought it for me. It's the best trumpet you can buy."

He looked it over carefully and then, to my surprise, raised the horn to his swollen lips and started to play and play poorly. The man was definitely not a trumpet player, not even a good impersonation of one. Hearing the unlikely sounds of a trumpet blowing in Andy's place, those at the bar, including my father, suddenly became quiet and spun around in unison toward the discordant sound.

Hearing the terrible sounds of my trumpet, I snatched the instrument from the man and with case in hand started out the door. The crowd roared with laughter as he raised his hands above his head as if feigning surrender at the point of an automatic rifle and bellowed back, "Achtung! Achtung! I surrender! I surrender!"

Dad leaped quickly from his stool and closed in on me just as I was passing out of the building. With a gentle shove, he helped me complete my exit outside into the late afternoon sun.

"Daddy, I didn't know the man was going to do that," I explained. "I really didn't." Trying to apologize to my father was difficult. I was nearly in tears.

"Son, that wasn't your fault. You have nothing to apologize for. The man was just trying to have some fun, that's all. Why don't you come on back and stay awhile?" My dad's pleasant, reassuring voice was making an impression, but not enough for me to return to the bar.

"No, Dad, I don't think so. I better get on home," I said. As I was about to put my left leg over my bike's seat and head out, I looked up into my father's caring face and asked, "Daddy, do you think someday that I'll be able to take Charlie Wade's place at the funerals?"

My father reached down and placed his two hands gently on my slight shoulders and said, with a twinkle of great pride in his eyes, "I'm sure you can, Son. I'm sure you can."

"Thanks, Daddy. I hope I can, and by the way, when's the next funeral? Can I be the echo again?"

My question appeared to take my father by surprise as he answered, "You want to be the echo again? Of course, you can. But, Son, I don't know when we'll have another funeral. You really can't plan on those things, you know. But when we do, you can be there."

My father hugged me firmly, then took the horn, placed it gingerly in its case and into the bicycle's basket. Turning quickly, he retreated two steps backwards and said, "Well done, Son. Well done. I am very proud of you."

Spinning around on the chatted driveway, he then moved quickly across the uneven surface and through the door where his Legion comrades were now well back into their beer and memories.

I pedaled my trumpet-laden bicycle slowly back along a quiet Highway 61 toward home. While it had been a very fulfilling and memorable day for me, I had completely forgotten that Chester Frobase was opening his new picture show that night, the first indoor one in town. I sure didn't want to miss that and besides, Charlie Wade might be there.

Election

Dick's shrill voice carried upwards to our second floor apartment like a soprano's closing aria, "Hey, Genius, 'ya wanna play caaaatch?"

I knew that voice well. Dick was my best friend. He knew that when he yelled, I'd be down in a flash with a baseball tucked tightly in my well-oiled Billy Bancroft fielder's glove and be ready to go. Dick always wove a magic spell over me.

It was late May and we were finally out of school. For a 10 year old boy, living in Benton, Missouri, life couldn't be any better. There would be lots of baseball, maybe even a trip on the train to St. Louis to watch my beloved Cardinals play.

Dick's wide-faced smile greeted me as I bounded down the steep stairs two at a time. In contrast to Dick's mature look of being much older, I was tall for my age, a skinny kid with long gangling arms. My complexion was fair with light brown hair crudely sculpted in a burr haircut that kept me cool in the summertime, but made me look like some emaciated refugee from a foreign land. Folks told me that I'd fill out one day, but anyone looking at me then would have doubted such an optimistic forecast.

"Hey, I saw your dad's picture on a telephone pole . . . he's runnin' for prosecuting attorney. What's that?" Dick's direct question stumped me completely. How did I know what a prosecuting attorney was?

"Whaddaya mean, you don't know what a prosecuting attorney is? I can't believe you don't know. Everybody knows that." I was bluffing, but I knew Dick was too savvy to stand for it.

"Okay, Genius, if you're so smart, then tell me what one is . . . what does he do? Go ahead, tell me." I blushed mightily, turned my head away and attempted to muster up some sort of credible answer.

"Well, Dick, first of all, he's in an election. To be in an election, you've got to be a lawyer, like my dad. Then you can get your picture up on a telephone pole. After that, if the picture's real good, you win. And when you win, and my dad's gonna win, you become the prosecuting attorney and you start prosecutin'. Understand?"

Dick gave me a querulous look. I knew he didn't understand, much less believe what I had said. But my response, while crafted altogether in ignorance, did carry a certain ring of truth to it, or at least, it sounded like it did.

"Prosecutes? What does that mean?" Dick wouldn't let me off the hook. My youthful attempt to define the job was not working at all.

Trying to derail him from the subject, I said, "Oh, come on, Dick, I'll explain it to you later. Let's just play some catch, okay?"

I was confident that mentioning baseball would divert his mind from trying to expose my obvious ignorance. With a quick twist of his head, Dick started running down the asphalt street and hollered for the ball.

"There's a long fly ball . . . back . . . back . . . it might be . . . it could be." Harry Carey, the Cardinal's great announcer would have been proud.

I knew the routine. We had played out this baseball fantasy many times. Leading him perfectly, I heaved the ball in the direction of his long, galloping stride. Gracefully, emulating the Cardinal's great center fielder, Terry Moore, Dick easily caught up with the drifting ball and guided it competently into his outstretched glove.

"Yahoooo! What a catch! Terry Moore has done it again! He's saved a home run! Cardinal's win! Cardinals win!" Dick's pseudo announcer's voice filled the air with enthusiasm. The Boys of Summer had nothing on us.

Later that day about supper time, my father came in from his law office. He was in a particularly good mood. His campaign appeared to be going well.

I couldn't wait to ask my father what a prosecuting attorney does. He had probably explained it to me before, but I had forgotten. Besides, I knew that Dick would come back and assault me with the question, and I had to know the answer.

Patiently, my father explained once again what I didn't know. I had been a little right. "He's the lawyer who prosecutes," but Dad further clarified the definition as he explained to me the whys and wherefores of the office, like what kind of cases he would be prosecuting, where he would work and so on.

"A prosecuting attorney is the lawyer for our county, Son. He goes to court and tries lawsuits against people who commit crimes, like stealing, robberies, and even murder. He sees to it that those people who do bad things are punished. Understand?"

"Yes, Sir, I understand. But does he always win every case he tries?" I asked.

"No. Not always. But if he's good, he does most of the time."

"Are you good, Daddy?"

"I think so. That's why I'm running for the office."

"Who are you running against? Are you faster than he is?"

"No, it's not that kind of race. You see, my opponent and I will be working hard all this summer, until August, to get people to vote for us. Then the people will vote in the Democratic Primary Election, and the person with the most votes will then run against another man, a Republican, in a General Election. That election will be in November."

I was totally confused at this point. Dad's explanation was puzzling. He's not running *in* a race, but he *is* running a race, and if he wins, he'll have to run another race against a Republican. Primary? General? I sure wasn't smart enough to figure any of this out, but I supposed that if my father was involved, everything would be all right. At least it sounded right.

"Who are you running against, Daddy?"

"My opponent is Monty Montgomery. He's from Sikeston, and he's a lawyer, too."

"Is he smart? Is he as good a lawyer as you are?"

"Yes, he's smart, but I think I can beat him. Don't you?"

"Sure, I do," I said. "But, how can I help you win the election, Daddy?" Naturally, I really wanted to help him, but I didn't quite know how I could do it. For sure, I couldn't drive a car. Maybe, I could put his signs up on telephone poles and in store windows.

"Son, I want you to go with me around the county campaignin'. I want the folks to see and meet you. And you'll meet a lot of nice people. Would you like to do that?"

"Yes, Sir, I guess. But why would they want to meet *me*? I thought it was *you* they wanted to be Prosecuting Attorney."

My father laughed heartily at that particular question and my entire line of questioning. Youthful ignorance and naiveté were in full bloom. I found out in later years that he told the story of our election conversation with great pride to anyone who would listen.

He was a political junky, a devout Democrat who literally hated all Republicans. I suppose having gone through the Depression years before and after, President Hoover soured him on the GOP forever. Consequently, I never knew there was any other party but Democrats.

My dad had a somewhat checkered political career at this time. He was elected to the Missouri State House of Representatives in 1933-34. After that freshman term in the legislature, he became ambitious and despite the advice of his friends, launched a campaign in the 1936 Democratic Primary against incumbent U.S. Representative, Paul Jones. Ambition has felled many a man, and my father became its latest victim as he went down to a painful and devastating defeat. He never had a chance; he had tried to come too far too fast.

After that devastating defeat, he retired from politics to practice law full time, but the political itch returned in 1942 when he moved to Benton from Sikeston and ran unsuccessfully for Prosecuting Attorney against Sikeston's David Blanton. Blanton's machine was too powerful in the south of the county, particularly Sikeston, to overcome my father's power base in the north.

But 1944 would be different. Blanton was not seeking re-election, and Montgomery's campaign pictures made him look something like a nerd. Monty was not well known in the county and was purported to have minimal skills as an attorney. Daddy felt that this was his year.

As the 1944 campaign heated up later that summer, I became my father's constant traveling companion. We motored about from town to town in his 1939 4-door Plymouth, campaign posters pasted on its doors. He was very careful not to use up all of his precious rationed gasoline. We were still in a war, you know.

Shaking hands with anyone in sight, handing out matchbooks with his picture, making speeches, we worked the county like a couple of ole time politicians. I was sure that my dad was going to win!

Dad's campaign poster showed a handsome, but serious man. Bedecked in coat and tie, with his black mustache smartly trimmed, he wore wire-rim glasses and presented to the voters that he, at least, looked like a prosecuting attorney.

On the poster, tightly outlined with a thin, black border was this message:

My Pledge

If elected as your Prosecuting Attorney, I pledge that I will devote
all of my skills and energies to represent
the citizens in this county to the best of my ability.

EUGENE M. MUNGER

If not the classiest campaign sign in the campaign, it was certainly the most intellectual. Whether the picture or the pledge was successful or not successful in the outcome, no one will ever know. I suspect that like in a lot of elections, local or otherwise, "class" had nothing to do with it.

The campaign appearance at Oran Missouri's Annual Fourth of July Picnic was my first experience with big crowds. Dad held my hand tightly as he led us in and out among the heavy throngs of people, townsfolk, farmers, and even visitors from out of town, shaking hands, asking for their votes, and introducing me as "my boy."

My father was a born campaigner. He had an affable manner, a glib tongue and was comfortable in all situations. He was sincere and conversed with everyone who crossed his path, be they a wealthy landowner or a sharecropper.

Eugene M. Munger, Sr.—1896-1964
This picture of Gene's father was taken
in 1941 and resembles the image that
appeared on his campaign posters.

Although well under 6', my father had the swagger and confidence of a Prussian general as he waded fearlessly into swelling crowds, the courtroom, or wherever. A raconteur without peer, his stories were legendary. He was tireless that summer in his quest to be elected, leaving early in the morning, returning exhausted late at night. Naturally, I didn't go with him every day, but when I did, I always knew that the day would be very, very long.

Later in the summer, we campaigned at Morley's Annual Fish Fry. Although Oran had at least a thousand people, Morley had barely 500. Nevertheless, the fish fry was always an anxiously anticipated happening. The city park, located in the center of this small, rural town, extended itself to the limits to accommodate the huge crowds of people.

It was at the fish fry that Dad introduced me to Monty Montgomery. I already hated him, of course. Seeing this slight, short bald man wearing horned rim glasses only reinforced my feelings.

My dad's opponent couldn't have been more gracious. After shaking my hand, he rubbed his small, almost tiny hand across my burr cut, noted that I was going to be a big boy when I grew up and affirmed what everybody thought would be the case, that I would be a lawyer like my daddy. Maybe, he wasn't so bad after all, but still.

Dad continued to be optimistic about winning the election. Of course, I knew that those living in Benton *all* vote for him. I just knew that. However, Sikeston, the biggest town in the county, was the real key to victory. While Sikeston had been my dad's Waterloo in the 1942 election, Dad had developed an active group of volunteers to go door-to-door with campaign material. He had set up headquarters in a second floor building in the downtown and things were looking up. He believed he was making progress in Monty's town.

On Election Day, Dad left early by himself and traveled down to Sikeston in one last effort to get votes. I stayed close to home, anxiously awaiting the election results that evening and telling everyone, "My daddy's gonna win!"

Since Benton was the county seat, voting returns were transmitted to election headquarters there mostly by phone, a few by personal messengers. The results were hand-posted on butcher paper spread across a huge wooden frame, billboard size, measuring at least 10'x 20', and located in the cavernous court room in front of the presiding judge's bench.

As the results were received, "Buzzy" Watkins, the County Clerk, would shimmy his slender body up a tall ladder where, with a heavy black crayon, he would tally the reporting town or precinct's votes for each candidate.

Just as I was about to go over to the court house to watch the election results, I heard my father's heavy, deliberate footsteps coming up the stairs. He usually flew up those steps . . . something was wrong.

"Hi, Daddy, how are you?" I greeted him at the door giving him a big hug.

His seersucker suit's jacket was thrown loosely over his shoulder, and his usual well-combed hair was in nearly total disarray. He was without tie, his crumpled white shirt showed the effects of the hot, humid August day.

He quickly brushed by me and headed into the kitchen where Mother was fixing dinner. I followed closely behind to hear what he had to say.

"Well, they did it to us again. Sikeston beat us!" His voice was flat and unemotional. He appeared to be a beaten man. He said nothing more as he stood there quietly with his head bowed and hands clasped as if he were praying.

After what seemed to be a dreadfully long time, my mother finally spoke, "I'm sorry, honey. I'm really sorry." That was all she said as small tears eased slowly down her tired, strained face. She had been through this before; she knew what it was to lose an election.

I was rocked by the bad news. My heart pounded fiercely and tearful words came out in short, staccato bursts.

"That can't be, Daddy. It can't be. How do you know? How do you know?"

"We just do, Son. We just do."

"Well, I don't believe it. I'm goin' over to the courthouse now and just see who won. You'll see. You'll be the winner . . . just you wait." Without another word, I dashed down the long steps and headed for the courthouse.

Dick was already in the courtroom when I came in. He had saved me a seat right in the front row under the election board. It was about 7:30 pm and there was a bundle of activity in the big room. Everyone was talking at once, some out loud, others in whispers. Who would win? Who would lose?

Benton's results were posted first. Daddy had carried Benton by nearly 6-1. Despite what he told me earlier, I was still convinced that he was wrong.

The other northern county towns and precincts reported in, and my father continued to hold a substantial lead . . . about 2-1. I just knew he was wrong. He was going to win.

As the votes were marked up on the board, I kept a running count for "our" race. But, then, about 8:30 pm, the tide turned. The southern half of the county's towns began to report in, and the news was not encouraging.

As the votes added up in Monty's favor, my math suffered correspondingly. If my dad received 40 votes from Sikeston's Precinct #1 and Monty received 240, I'd add

Monty's count to Dad's. Some of my friends, once excited about his early lead were now shaking their heads. He was losing. I ignored reality. I could not accept the truth. I could not accept the fact that my father was losing the election.

As the rest of the evening wore on, the results were plain to see. I was now totally resigned to the fact that Monty Montgomery was the Democratic winner for the race for Scott County Prosecuting Attorney. I didn't stick around until the end. I couldn't bear to watch what once appeared to be a landslide for Dad turn into an old fashioned slaughter. He eventually lost nearly 2:1.

Walking back home together from the courthouse, Dick tried to cheer me up, laughing, joking and putting the best spin on the situation that he could. It was too painful. I was mortified with the loss. I just knew that I would never recover.

Dick tried to brighten my spirits with one last time. "'Ya know, Genius, you never did tell me what a prosecuting attorney does. The way I figure it, it's not much of a job anyway since 'ole Monty lives in Sikeston. If he lived here in Benton, it would be a good job, but he don't, so, it ain't. If I was you, I'd forget about it and start worrying about whether the Cardinals are going to win the pennant."

As usual, Dick's logic and good counsel made sense. I eventually recovered from Dad's loss, although it was a painful recovery. As someone once said, defeat has few heroes. They were right, but my father, despite his loss, was one of my biggest heroes.

The summer of 1944 ended quietly for me and my parents. Dad returned to his law practice with renewed energy and dedication, although, his political ambitions vanished, never to return. Mother continued her daily 12 mile commute to Oran for work with the local rationing board. And yes, I got to go to St. Louis on the train to see my Cardinals whip the hometown American League Browns in the World Series.

At least, I had one victory to cheer about that year!

Cotton

Excitement was running at a feverish pitch that early October day in 1944 among Benton Grade School's students. It was that glorious time of year in the fall when school would be dismissed for a whole two weeks for the kids to help their parents and neighbors pick cotton in the fields around town.

All around school, ringing voices were joining in to sing song the familiar limerick of the season:

> "School's out, school's out. Teachers let the mules out. Mustn't whine, gonna shine 'cause it's cotton pickin' time!"

Joe Marks nearly ran over me as I scooted out of Miss Jackson's third and fourth grade room to have my lunch. Big for his age, his shuffling gait along with his stooped shoulders gave him a simian appearance, but he was an affable sort, kind and friendly to everyone and popular at the school.

Eight-year-old Gene Munger's fourth grade school picture, taken in 1943.

He lived on a farm about five miles east of the small southeast Missouri hamlet and rode the school bus into school everyday. He always carried homemade biscuit sandwiches filled with fresh, cured ham in his lunch sack.

"Whoa, Joe Marks! You nearly knocked me over!" I said.

Joe quickly balanced himself, grinned ear-to-ear with his infectious smile and responded, "Sorry 'bout that, Genius, I didn't see you. Wanna have some lunch?"

"Yeah, sure. Did your mother pack you with some more of those ham biscuits, Joe Marks? Mine fixed me some roast beef "samisches" with lettuce and tomato. Wanna trade? My lunch for yours?"

"Deal!" Joe Marks loved to do that. He knew my Mother packed my sack lunches daily with a wide variety of sandwiches, fruits, and raw vegetables as well as some kind of delectable dessert like a cake, pie, cup cake, or whatever sweetness she had recently created.

Joe Marks never seemed to have that luxury, his lunch was always the same . . . ham and biscuits. Occasionally, an orange or some persimmons would make an appearance, but almost never cake or pie, not even a Twinkie.

Now, he wasn't poor, not by any stretch of the imagination, but his lunches were mostly plain, although, I could have eaten those ham biscuits for every meal. They were simply delicious.

I was a city boy, the son of a lawyer and a teacher mother. To the town's people, I guess, we were rich, although, I'm sure my mother never packed a lunch for me with the idea that rich kids had to uphold some high standard at the Benton School. To her, it was standard fare, usually left-overs from dinner. She never gave it a thought, I bet. It was just good, nutritious food for her fourth grade son.

Joe Marks and I walked together to our favorite eating place, the stairs, a sort-of private eating place. The school had no formal lunch room, therefore lunch took place wherever it was convenient—the school yard, on swings, see saws, around the ball diamond. When it rained or was too cold, we all had to eat inside at our desks or, for a lucky few, on the stairs.

Apparently, the stairs were once the school's north-end path to upstairs where the fifth and sixth grade room was located. Sometime in the past, for whatever reason, somebody completely closed in the steps about half way up, giving the students only one way upstairs, via the stairs at the school's east end.

The weather outside stubbornly held the last days of summer at heel. Therefore, kids flocked to the playground to soak up the sun and talk about the two-week vacation ahead. Joe Marks and I didn't care. We were heading for the stairs.

We slithered up the steps and out of sight. Anxiously, we swapped lunches and tore into our lunch bags like preying eagles devouring shore-locked salmon.

"You gonna pick cotton this year, Genius?" Joe Marks asked with a mouth half full of a roast beef sandwich.

"I've never picked cotton, Joe Marks. Besides, I don't know if I'm old enough yet," I said as my long fingers seized a ham biscuit and jammed it ravenously into my open mouth.

"Whaddaya mean, not old enough? You're old enough. Don't you know some kids are pickin' cotton before they even can walk?"

Joe Marks' authoritative manner was most reassuring. Perhaps, I was old enough and my mother and dad would let me pick cotton this vacation. I didn't have a cotton sack, but I was sure my mother would make me one. Maybe I could even go down to Joe Marks' farm and pick cotton with him.

"Do you really think I could do it, Joe Marks? Really?" I asked. "If I did, could I go out to your farm and pick with you?"

"Yeah, you could, but we ain't growin' any cotton this year. Dad's growin' soy beans 'stead, and you sure cain't pick beans, Genius." Joe Marks again dug his hand deep into the paper bag and drew out a bunch of grapes. "Ooooooo, I bet these green grapes are good! Want one?"

"No thanks, I'll just stick with these ham biscuits. Your mother sure knows how to do it. I wish my mother would put ham biscuits in my lunch like this." Despite eating Joe Mark's lunch, I was still hungry, but I wasn't about to share *his* grapes with him. I just wouldn't do it.

Finishing our lunches, we went out to the playground to enjoy the rest of the lunch hour. In a few minutes, the bell rang noisily above our heads announcing that classes would resume in five minutes. Like bees returning to the hive, swarms of students, grades one through eight, flew back to their respective home rooms.

Watching the school busses arrive from my fourth grade room's seat, I knew it wouldn't be long before school would be out. The "yellow birds" would take the little ones to their farm homes outside of town, some as far as 30 miles away. We city slickers had no busses to take us home. We'd walk.

After all, the town was less than a mile across in either direction.

As I ambled home that late afternoon, I could barely contain myself with the future prospect of picking cotton and making at least a dollar for my labor. The word around town was that they were paying two cents a pound, and if you worked real hard, you could make as much as two dollars a day!

The Missouri autumn had shown its kaleidoscope of colors early that year, but the trees' leaves refused to fall that October day despite a persistent south wind blowing from the flat plains below Benton's elevated terrain.

I glided easily up the quiet neighborhood street, with its small, unpretentious houses sheltered by the turning soft maple trees and crossed a quiet Highway 61. I passed the sprawling county courthouse and headed home on the last block to our apartment, a duplex on the second floor of what looked to be a former bank building.

Bounding up the steep wooden steps at two, sometimes three steps at a time, I couldn't wait to see my mother. I was on a mission. "Mother! Mother, I'm home! Mother, are you here?" My high pitched ten year-old voice echoed through the apartment's high-walled, spacious rooms, but to my disappointment, there appeared to be no one there.

Mother's familiar voice broke the silence. "I'm in the kitchen, Honey. How was school today?" The fragrant, tempting aroma of a freshly baked cherry pie broke my concentration, but only for a moment.

"School's out, Mother. We've got two weeks for pickin' cotton . . . two weeks! And I wanna pick. Can I?" I asked as I moved quickly in to see her.

She greeted me with her customary warm hug, her long, thin arms wrapping themselves tightly around my skinny frame. She smiled approvingly at her ambitious young son and replied, "Why, of course, you can. Where do you want to go? Do you have a sack?"

She relaxed her hug, stepped back, and with her twinkling pale blue eyes asked, "Would you like a piece of pie?"

"Yes, please, I'd love a piece. It's my favorite. It's cherry!" I exclaimed as I hovered over the warm delicacy.

"But, Mother, can you make me a sack? It doesn't have to be a big sack, but I need a sack. You can't pick cotton without a sack. Can you, Mother?" I had never been so excited.

"I can't make you a sack now, but I'll go over to Miller's tomorrow morning and get some material. Then I'll make you one. What field are you going to pick?" She then asked.

"I can go down below the hill to Herman Schwartz's field, Mother. It's so close I can even walk down there. I'll ask Buddy Frobase if he wants to pick with me. Buddy told me at school that he wanted to pick. Think he'll want to?"

"You'll have to ask him, Gene. I'm sure he will." Mother then shooed me out of the kitchen and started getting dinner ready. Dad had been in court all that day, but he had called from his law office and announced that he would be home around 5 pm.

I could hardly contain myself during dinner. Sounding like some babbling magpie, I went on endlessly to my parents about my anticipated entry to the lush cotton fields of southeast Missouri and an opportunity to make a least a dollar for my toils. One would have thought that I was on the verge of completing some mega-million buck merger. One dollar or a million, it didn't matter a scintilla to a ten year-old boy whose mind had become completely filled with a vivid imagination and longing anticipation of getting rich.

True to her word, Mother left our place early that Saturday morning and walked the one block over to Miller's to hold up her end of the bargain, to make me a cotton sack. Miller's, a one story, but expansive dry goods and grocery store essentially served Benton and the surrounding countryside residents. It was an early hybrid of a modern day supermarket, less the price scanners, check-out conveyer belts, and trendy delicatessens.

Those were the days back then when your mother would give you a quarter and ask that you go to the store and bring back a bottle of milk and a loaf of bread . . . and have enough change left over for some stick licorice or a jawbreaker.

While my mother was a talented and dexterous seamstress, she never really intended to make me a cotton sack from scratch. She would buy one. She did, paying, I suppose, at least two dollars, and promptly returned to the apartment and a sleeping ten-year-old. I never knew the difference, because when I awakened, the sack was already there, folded neatly and ready to try on to see if it would fit. Oh, yes, it did. It was the finest cotton sack in the whole world!

I was simply ecstatic. My wonderful mother had gotten up early, gone to Miller's, bought material, returned home, and had already made me a cotton sack. It was mine, all mine! Nothing she could have done could have been more pleasing to me.

I walked over to Buddy's house that Saturday and asked if he wanted to go pick with me down at Schwartz's field. Buddy was smaller than I, almost frail. He wore wire-framed glasses, and had a full head of thick, red hair with countless freckles spread over his face.

Yes, he would go, and he even had a cotton sack. I didn't tell him that mine was better than his because my mother had made it from scratch, and I just knew that he had bought his at a store, probably Miller's.

On Monday, there was a clear, cloudless blue sky, but the temperature had dropped down to below 50 degrees. It was a bit chilly. Mother saw to it that I had plenty of clothes to keep me warm. I was a bit overdressed with a heavy wool shirt over a sweatshirt, an extra sweater, even a windbreaker. She gave me my father's woolen ski cap that would have been better suited for the Alps. She was not going to let her little boy get cold.

The lunch she prepared for me would have sufficed for a three day hike to anywhere: two chicken breast sandwiches, spread generously with mayonnaise and lettuce, an orange, an apple, two bananas, a choice piece of Friday's cherry pie, and a thermos jug filled with Kool Aid.

Buddy's mother volunteered to take us down to the field, only about a mile from town. They picked me up around 7 am. As I stumbled down the apartment's long steps to her car, the sight of me and all my belongings must have made her think that I had left home for all time.

There I was, with eyes beaming out from under my stocking hat, bundled up in two layers of clothing, carrying a white, canvas cotton sack, neatly folded, and a huge brown paper bag crammed full of food along with a thermos bottle balanced precariously on top of everything.

"Hello, Mrs. Frobase. How are you?" I said peaking out from under by burden.

"My, Gene, do you think it will snow?" Her light brown sweater hanging over her sloping shoulders was a stark contrast to my preparations for a seemingly arctic winter. "Do you think you'll be warm enough?" Her sarcasm escaped me completely. I thought she was totally serious.

"Yes ma'am, I think so, but I don't really know. I've never picked cotton before," I said as I crawled into the tiny backseat of the two-door Dodge coupe where Buddy was sitting, huddled tightly against the seat, arms firmly crossed against his body. He looked cold, but said nothing.

The trip down to Schwartz's field was short. Our place of employment was just at the bottom of the hill going south from Benton on Highway 61. The field, about 10 acres, lay adjacent to the highway with an entrance through a wooden gate about a quarter-mile from the base of the hill. From the gate, we drove on a sandy loam road through the field for about 200 yards until we came headlong into a two-story barn.

We could see a group of men already heading out to the field, walking together, all stooped over as if they were carrying some heavy load. Their long cotton sacks trailed behind them on the ground like the extended tails of prehistoric animals.

Buddy and I pried ourselves from the car's tight back seat, thanked our smiling, but understanding driver, and advanced boldly towards the barn where we hoped to line ourselves up with some work.

We didn't know my Dad knew Herman Schwartz well, and he had already told Herman what we kids wanted to do. That was fine with Herman. He would have his field boss waiting for us. Mrs. Frobase had been told of the arrangements which, I'm sure, she appreciated. Only Buddy and I didn't know.

"Hi, boys. How can I help you?" said a tall, skinny man wearing a pair of faded blue overalls and an olive-colored baseball hat turned up at the bill. He had the grin of an anxious suitor accentuated by a wide gap between his two, tobacco-stained front teeth.

"We'd like to pick cotton, Sir," I said. "Can we pick some in your field?"

"Have you ever picked before, boys?" I could tell that he was seriously questioning our credentials.

"No, Sir, but we'll work hard . . . honest we will. Will 'ya let us try, mister?" Our anguished look must have convinced the man we were serious, or, perhaps, he was a caring soul who remembered that once upon a time he had been in the same position as a kid and had been seeking an opportunity to make some money.

"Shore, you can, Fellas. You can start over on those two rows next to the highway. We're payin' two cents a pound. Go to it . . . go to it!" He said as he turned abruptly and swaggered toward the barn.

"Mister, can we put our lunches in the barn?"

Not even looking back and in a barely audible whisper, the man replied, "Reckon you can, but I cain't guarantee that they'll be there when you get around to eatin' it. There's mice in there, 'ya know."

We carefully placed our lunches in one of the barn's corners, covered them with loose straw in the hope that no one would steal our precious food. The barn, itself, was practically empty. Only a few bales of hay remained, serving as silent reminders of earlier days when the barn was filled with alfalfa for feeding grazing cattle in the winter.

With our cotton sacks slung over our slight shoulders, Buddy and I walked briskly to the beginning of the cotton row especially designated for us. Looking down the row, it appeared that there was no end, only a thin bare line of sand flanked by an infinite number of cotton bolls hanging over like great clumps of snow bonding to pine trees in a northern winter forest.

The morning's chill began to diminish as the bright sun moved higher into the sky. We slowly picked our way down the long endless row, painstakingly removing each piece of cotton like a skilled surgeon removing some nasty tumor from a long suffering patient.

We were becoming quite proud, even heady, about our progress and new found skill when we heard a coughing sound. One of the men pickers that had started out early was coming up fast behind us. Instead of staying in the row and picking around each plant like we did, he was straddling the cotton and removing it in machine-like fashion.

The man smiled briefly and said nothing as he pulled away from Buddy and me, great puffs of cotton falling rapidly into his half-filled bag.

"How many pounds have you picked today, Sir?" Buddy asked.

The fast moving picker didn't stop to answer as he muttered, "I'm going on my second bag."

"How many pounds is that?" I asked.

"The scales said 87 pounds. Guess I misfigured. I thought I had at least a hundred." His flashing, productive hands didn't miss a beat.

"A hundred?" Wow, mister, that's really somethin'. How many pounds do you think you'll pick today?" Buddy's admiring voice seemed to stop the man in his tracks.

"Hell, I don't know. Yesterday, I picked nearly 300, but I had to quit early 'cause I had a toothache. I'd like to hit at least 400 before I quit today." The man then proceeded with his work.

"Golly, Buddy," I said. "Do you think we can pick 100 pounds today if we tried hard?"

"I dunno," replied Buddy, "I'm getting hungry and tired, too. What time is it?"

"Buddy, I don't have a watch, but I imagine it's getting close to noon. I'm hungry, too, let's quit for a while and go eat."

Dragging our cotton behind us, we backtracked to the barn, found our lunches intact, went outside, and ate our food on top of our sacks. We were both very hungry, and before we knew it, our sack lunches had disappeared. Only banana peels, apple cores, and orange rinds remained.

"You know, we must have at least 50 pounds. I know I have that much," I said. "How much do you have?"

"At least 50," Buddy replied, "I think I can make a 100."

"Let's weigh our sacks now and find out how much we have," I suggested.

Agreeing, Buddy led the way over to the weigh-in scale where the cotton boss picked up my sack and placed it on the hook to wait for the results.

"37 pounds for you, Boy. You got 37 pounds." There was somewhat of a derisive tone to the boss' voice. Needless to say, I was not at all encouraged by what I had picked. After all, we'd been at it before 8 am, and now, it must at least be noon, or close to it.

"And 33 pounds for you, Bub. That's all you got . . . 33 pounds." The man's voice appeared to be a lot more cynical in response to Buddy's meager production.

"Come on, Buddy, we gotta do better than that. Let's at least try to get 50 pounds."

Buddy grunted his approval to my challenge and dragging the light loads in our sacks, we again took the walk to our unfinished rows of unpicked cotton; cotton that didn't appear to be too threatened by the slow fingers of two 10-year-old town boys.

After an hour or so, our bags began to feel a little heavier. We thought we were near our goal, but we were really tired now.

"Do you think we got enough, Buddy?" I inquired. "Do you?"

"I think so, Gene, but if we don't, I'm gonna quit anyway. Let's go weigh in." I could tell from Buddy's voice that he had definitely retired from picking cotton that October day.

Once again, we dragged our sacks to the barn for the final accounting of our day's effort. The boss man was waiting to take our bounty from us, weigh it, pay us off and add it to the day's pickings. It wasn't much, but he seemed pleased to see us. Most likely, he was pleased to be getting rid of us.

"Let's see what you got there, Boy?" he said as took my bag.

"Hummmmm, let's see. The scales say . . . let's say . . . 50 pounds. I owe you a dollar." He reached into his overall pocket, pulled out a wad of green bills, plucked out a dollar bill and with his rough, red hands, smoothed it out and gave it to me.

"Thank you," I said. "Thank you very much." It was the first dollar that I had ever made. I carefully stuffed it into my pocket and watched Buddy's bag weighed.

"You got 48 pounds, Bubby, 48 pounds. Since I gave your buddy here a dollar, that's what I'll give you. You both done good . . . really good. You're good workers," the man said as he repeated his ceremony with the passing of the green.

"Oh, thank you, Sir. Thank you very much." Buddy's round face seemed to stretch twice in size. He was clearly satisfied with every pound that he had picked, more than satisfied with the largess the cotton boss had bestowed upon him.

"Can I count on you fellas tomorrow?" The boss man asked.

"Uh, well, I don't know, my mother may have something else for me to do." My reluctant voice was fooling no one.

"Yeah, me, too," snapped Buddy.

"Well, okay, you're more than welcome to come back anytime." The man smiled, shook our hands, and waved us goodbye.

With our newly earned riches secured safely in our pants, we skipped jauntily up the hill and home carrying our abandoned excess of clothes and our money making friend of the past six hours, the cotton sack. We were rightfully proud of our work, although, it hadn't been nearly as exciting as we thought it would be. It actually was pretty hard work, particularly the way we took it on, but we had each made a dollar and that was really special.

I could hardly wait to show my mother my dollar. Again, I flew up the steep stairs to our second floor apartment at break-neck speed.

"Mother, I'm home!" I yelled. "I'm home. I made a dollar. Come see!"

Mother came out of the kitchen and met me with her usual warm hug and bright smile. "Let's see?"

I smiled coyly, spread my thin, lanky arms up towards the ceiling and said, "Well, let's see what I have here?" I then reached slowly into my left pants pocket to retrieve my fortune to show my mother.

Alas, there was nothing there. I quickly reached into my right pocket . . . nothing there either. Panicky, I searched my two hip pockets, then my windbreaker, now tied around my waist. Nothing. I repeated the process. Still nothing. I had lost my dollar.

"Mother, I've lost it! I've lost my dollar. I've lost it!" Tears quickly filled my eyes and I felt totally empty inside. I was devastated. "I put it in my pocket, Mother, when the man gave it to me. I made a dollar for picking 50 pounds of cotton. He gave it to me. I put it in my pocket, and now I've lost it. It's not here!"

Mother reached down and gave me another warm hug. "It's all right, Gene, it's all right. It's not your fault. We all lose things now and then. It's all right." Her soft, consoling voice helped relieve the pain and despair that had come over me.

"But, Mother, what am I going to do? I don't wanna go back. It wasn't much fun. I don't wanna go back," I said as I wiped away the tears away with my grubby hand.

"Well, I hear that they're making sorghum out at Diebold's farm, and they need kids like you to strip cane. How does that sound?"

"Strip cane? Do they pay you for that? Do they use kids like us to do it? How much could I make? Can we go out there tomorrow?"

Before I came up with any other questions, Mother explained the process of stripping cane and making sorghum molasses to me. She explained about removing the cane's leaves with a paddle before it is cut and how sorghum molasses tasted good on hot biscuits with butter. I liked the sound of that!

"'Ya know, Mother, if they paid me in sorghum, I bet I wouldn't lose it on the way home. You think?"

■■■■■
Rinky-Dinks

Baseball was my complete passion as a 10-year-old in the summer of 1944. It consumed all of my play time, all of my friends' play time. Baseball was the thing to do for kids in the rural southeast Missouri town of Benton.

Most of this passion generated from the National League's Cardinals and the American League's Browns, both playing in St. Louis' Sportsman's Park, about 130 miles north. Cardinal fans were fairly limited and Browns' fans were in much greater numbers since the Browns trained that spring at Cape Girardeau's Capaha Park, only 16 miles north of Benton. The Cardinals trained in Cairo, Illinois, only 20 miles or so from Cape. The country was at war and traveling to sunny Florida was out of the question.

My parents were both Cardinals' fans, having been hooked as they enjoyed the 1931 team winning the World Series and watched Pepper Martin dominate the Philadelphia Athletics with his hitting and base running. Since they were fans, so was I.

My first major league game was in 1942, watching the Cardinals play the New York Giants. Cardinals won 7-2, and one of my heroes, lefthander Max Lanier, was the winning pitcher. He broke my heart a few years later when he jumped to the Mexican League. I just couldn't understand why anyone would ever leave the Cardinals. My dad explained that he "did it for more money." I always thought that major league baseball players were already the richest people in the world.

From that time on, I became a devout Cardinal fan and followed them in every game, listening to the honeyed voice of the venerable France Laux and then Harry Carey on the radio and hoping that some day I could play well enough to go to the majors and become a Cardinal. Television didn't exist, and none of us kids even dreamed about it. We had no idea what it was.

In those days, Little League was unknown, at least to us. We played on a high school softball diamond that could hardly be described as groomed. Benton had no Parks and Recreation Department—it didn't even have a Police Department. Scott County's Sheriff's Department was our law enforcement body. We really didn't care nor did we feel deprived, since we were growing up in a small town, a long way from a big city. Life was good.

Getting my friends and me to play down at the diamond was never a problem. When any of us wanted to get up a game, the ongoing mantra was "Let's round 'em up!" Quick phone calls reached most of them, and in a short time, we always had enough to play Indian Ball. As to its genesis, no one knew. If it was politically incorrect, we hadn't learned about that, either.

Indian Ball was a game composed of either four players, two on each side, or more. The idea was to have the batting team's player hit the ball between the other team's players— that was a single. Four singles counted as a run. A ball hit over the outfielder's head cleared the bases, counted as a home run. A batting team's player lobbed the ball to the hitter, since there was no such thing as a strikeout. However, an out was made when the infielder or outfielder caught a fly ball or a grounder. Three outs meant the teams changed sides.

This was the best we could do since it would have been impossible to have 18 players available to have an actual game. At best, the round up process usually accounted for no more than 6-8 players. It was doubtful there were even many more youngsters than that living in Benton at the time.

For my first six years, I lived in Chaffee, a railroad town of roughly 2,500 people and about 15 miles southwest of Benton. My hero was Joe Perry Rice. He and his parents lived right across the street from our house. He was at least five to six years older than I, but he became my "big brother." I worshiped him, talked about him all the time, and trailed proudly behind him every chance I had. He was a king in my young eyes! When my parents would go over to

Chaffee, my question when they returned was always, "Did you see Joe Perry? Did 'ya?"

One of our visits back to Chaffee, I ran into Joe Perry and started talking about playing baseball in Benton, wanting to become a major league player. Listening to a ten-year-old kid babble about such a lofty ambition most likely didn't make his day, but he clearly must have enjoyed listening.

After hearing all about my baseball playing, Joe Perry asked, a bit of a tongue in his cheek, "'Ya know, Gene, why don't you guys get a team up and come over and play us here in Chaffee?"

I was dumbstruck with such an idea and responded, "But, Joe Perry, we've never played a real game, only Indian Ball. We don't even have a team."

"So, get your guys together and make a team. It only takes nine guys. We'd love to play you."

With such an idea and a challenge from my champion, I told my parents about what had been said, and enthusiastically made my case. "We can make up a team, practice, and come to Chaffee and play Joe Perry's team, the Red Devils. We can do it, and I bet we can beat 'em. Our guys are that good. And please buy me a uniform, and I can be the first baseman."

Their response was most encouraging. "Okay, let's do it, but you'll have to get your friends together to make it happen. And yes, we'll buy you a uniform. You already have a glove, and that'll do for now."

Back in Benton, I started telling my friends what I had found out. They, too, were excited and started planning to put together a team. We asked Bob Harrison to be our coach. He was my best friend Dick's older brother. He agreed and in a short time, we had put together nine players to form a team with boys ranging from 10-13.

In a week or so, Bob asked me, "Whaddaya want to call the team? Do you have a name?"

"Hellcats!"

Bob smiled, even grimaced slightly, and said, "Uh, Gene, maybe, uh, we ought to think about another name."

"Another name? What's wrong with Hellcats?"

"Well, I believe that name wouldn't be one that would fit your team. It's just a too grownup name for you guys."

"Okay. What do you suggest?"

Bob thought a second or two, smiled and called out, "Rinky-Dinks!"

"Rinky-Dinks?   What kind of name is that?" I questioned. "What's a Rinky-Dink?"

"Oh, it's just a team name to call a bunch of kids. You know, Rinky-Dinks."

"Okay. We'll call our team that, but I still like Hellcats."

*Gene warming up for his team, the
Rinky-Dinks, in the summer of 1944.*

And so Rinky-Dinks became the team's name. Practice started with only eight players, but we finally persuaded Billy Gene Wilhelm to play right fielder for us to make it nine. He was smaller than the rest of us but we felt that the right fielder would never get any balls hit to him anyway.

The strength of the team rested with older players like Dick Harrison, our pitcher, and John Bradford, the shortstop. Charlie Benson played centerfield, probably our best fielder. I played first base, and while only ten, I could catch the ball pretty good, was tall for my age, and weighed a hefty 100 pounds. Besides all of that, I had a uniform, and no one else had one. I felt pretty special.

Our practices went well. While we weren't exactly strong at each position, our confidence ran high. We Rinky-Dinks were going over to Chaffee to show Joe Perry and his team, the Red Devils, just how good we were.

The *Scott County Democrat,* Benton's weekly paper, became aware of our team and its challenge. With its continuing articles featuring the near future game, town interest grew, and folks started stopping us on the street and talking about the game. Many even said they would be going over to Chaffee to watch us play.

We played the game on a Sunday afternoon. Many of our parents' cars formed a caravan over to Chaffee. It was really a happening.

When we arrived at Chaffee's field at the local grade school, there was already a huge crowd waiting to see the game. Benton's fans lined the third-base side; Chaffee's the first-base side. Some were sitting on their blankets, others standing tall, all enduring the stifling hot, humid August day.

Since we were the visiting team, we batted first with Jack Arnold leading off. As the second hitter, I knelt major league-like just off home plate. Looking at the older Chaffee players, I had a gnawing pain in my stomach and for the first time, began to get a feeling, just a little tiny feeling of "I'm not sure we're gonna beat these guys. They're older and really look like good ballplayers."

Jack's initial effort was futile. He did hit the ball, but right at the pitcher. He ran hard to first base, but was out by at least 15 feet. I was the next batter.

The Chaffee pitcher threw hard, at least by our standards and experience. I knew I wasn't going to even get my bat around against him, so I thought I'd try a bunt. At the count of two balls and one strike, I swung around in position and laid down a beauty right off the left side of the plate. The pitcher came swiftly off the mound, set himself squarely, and threw accurately to Joe Perry, their first baseman.

I had a good jump off the plate and ran as fast as I could to first base. About 10 feet from getting there, the ball had already arrived. I was going to be out. Instead of running past the base, I decided to slide and unfortunately, the slide never even got me to the bag.

Joe Perry looked down at me sympathetically with the ball in his glove and said, "Good try, Gene. Good try." At least, that was some consolation with my becoming an out. He was my champion, and he knew I had given my best.

The more experienced Chaffee team scored at will, although they mercifully held the score down to only 18-2. We finally scored in the seventh inning as our opponent's pitcher eased up on our batters, its infielders made a couple of purposely errant throws to let our hitters get on base and score. Being down by 18 runs and at least scoring a couple left us leaving the field feeling not so bad. But, it wasn't pretty!

The trip back to Benton seemed to last forever. My parents were consoling, but I wasn't in much of a mood to care. The Rinky-Dinks just weren't very good. I guess if we had been named Hellcats we could have done a lot better. We'd never know, as the team folded soon after, left only with a memory of what could have been.

As school started that fall, the whole town and I became totally engrossed in the World Series. The Cardinals won the National League pennant easily, and the Browns won in the last week of their season. St. Louis would be the site of the Series, and I was sure my beloved Cardinals would win. And they did in six games!

I got to thinking that maybe in a few years, I'd be playing first base with the Cardinals. The good thing would be that I wouldn't be playing against Joe Perry and his Chaffee team, the Red Devils. They were just too good for the Rinky-Dinks.

Smokin'

In the summer of 1944, my parents and I enjoyed our supper one afternoon with watermelon that Daddy had brought home from Blodgett's sandy fields. Mother and Daddy both sat contentedly as they watched me dig my fork aggressively into the juicy delight, my favorite dessert. Their cigarette smoke curled lazily across the table into my young face.

I gingerly wiped my eyes, waved my hand back and forth to clear the foul air, and asked, "Daddy, when will I be old enough to smoke?"

Both parents laughed at their son's bold question and my father replied, "When you're old enough, Son. You're too young now."

"When will I be old enough? How old were you when your dad let you? How 'bout you, Mother? When?"

Both parents looked uneasily at each other and I could see that they were searching for words. After a long pause, Mother answered, "Well, Gene, I never smoked when I was your age. Your grandfather would never have allowed it. But, when I went away to college at Cape, I guess I started. He never knew that I did, and being a preacher's daughter, he would have never allowed it. But, really, you should never even start. It's a bad habit."

Daddy quickly ground his half-finished Camel cigarette into the ashtray and continued, "I started, I guess, when I was a little older than you. All of us children, your Uncle Martel, Aunt Mary, and I smoked. Your grandfather and grandmother never seemed to mind as everybody our age smoked. When I went into the Army, well, everybody smoked . . . everybody. Your mother's right. Don't ever start it!"

"I won't. I really won't! I promise, but, I see you all smoking and I just wondered what it would be like," I replied. "I guess I'll never know."

Reaching my tenth birthday on June 29 and continuing throughout the rest of that summer, my best friend who was just two years older, Dick Harrison, and I took long hikes into the woods just outside of Benton. We'd see a multitude of rabbits and squirrels, but despite the reported sightings of bears, we never saw one, but we were always looking. Bears in southeast Missouri? What did we know?

One day while we were trudging around among the trees and leaf-covered ravines, Dick stopped suddenly, walked over to a dangling grape vine, pulled out his pocket knife and slowly cut about three inches off the end. He sat down on the soft, mossy ground, reached into his pocket, brought out a book of matches, placed the brown, crooked vine in his mouth, and with a swift strike of the match against the cover, lighted the vine. A swirling gray puff of smoke blew quickly from Dick's mouth.

"What are 'ya doin', Dick?" I yelled. "What are 'ya doin'?"

"Well, Genius, I'm smokin' a grape vine. Wanna try it?"

"Oh, no, Dick. I promised my mother and daddy that I would never smoke. Okay?"

"Well, this ain't smokin'. Well, it ain't exactly smokin'. It's not a cigarette, it's a grapevine. Come on, try it."

Dick's explanation seemed plausible. It wasn't a cigarette. It was only a grapevine. So, I sat down next to my friend, carefully took the vine from him, placed it into my mouth, struck the match and attempted to light the vine. The ensuing flame was too close to my face and it immediately singed my eyebrows. After all, I had never lighted a cigarette before. How was I to know?

"Easy, Genius, you don't have to burn your face off. Just light it, but easy does it." Dick's sarcastic voice echoed loudly through the overhanging oak and maple trees.

I tried once more. The vine glowed from my steady match. I puffed heartily and blew a great cloud of smoke into the blue sky above me. Puff after puff, I began to feel really important. I was feeling real good about myself. Maybe, just maybe when I got old enough, I could start smokin'.

So, with every hike into the woods after that, Dick and I would smoke a grapevine. I never told my parents, because, after all, it really wasn't smokin'. It was only a grapevine.

With the fall upon us, we returned to school, me in the fifth grade, Dick in the seventh. Our regular hikes and smokin' in the woods trailed off as we busied ourselves playing softball on Benton School's team. But, I did miss my grapevine.

One Saturday afternoon in early October, Dick called and asked me to come down to his house, only a short block away. I figured he wanted to play Monopoly or some other game, so I told my mother where I was going, scampered down the long, narrow steps of our second floor apartment, and skipped away to see him.

I knocked, he called, "Come on in, Genius."

I let myself in and yelled to an empty living room, "Whaddaya want to play, Dick? Monopoly?"

Dick answered from another part of the house. I didn't know where. "Naw, I want to show you something. I'm in the bathroom."

Why in the world would he be in there? Dick's surveyor father sometimes used the tub to process some of his drawings which left brown chemical stains on the bottom and sides. The sight of those stains always portrayed a menacing picture to me, but Dick shrugged it off saying they wouldn't hurt anybody. Nevertheless, I never even thought about taking a bath in there.

Poking my head inside, I saw Dick proudly holding a cigarette, not a grapevine, but a real cigarette and said, "Whaddaya have there? It looks like a cigarette."

"Of course, it is. Let's you and I smoke it."

"No, Dick, I promised my folks that I would never smoke. I know I've done grapevines, but that's different, they weren't cigarettes."

"They won't know, Genius, you don't have to tell 'em. Come on, let's light up. My folks have gone to Sikeston this afternoon. They won't know, either."

Before I could say anything else, Dick lighted the cigarette with great confidence and did a long, deep drag blowing smoke toward me. He looked somewhat disdainfully at me and said, "Come on, take a puff. No one will know."

I reached for the burning cigarette as if it were some rare plant, its smoke slowly rising toward the small bathroom's ceiling.

"Well, if you won't tell, I'll do it." I said. "Promise?"

"Sure, I won't tell," Dick replied. "Go ahead."

I placed the cigarette in my mouth, a Chesterfield, I believe, and cautiously puffed a meager drag. One would have thought that I had just kissed the Hope Diamond. "There. I did it. But I won't do it again."

"No, no, no. You've got to inhale. That's the way you smoke. You've got to inhale." Dick's voice turned sinister.

"Inhale? Whaddaya mean, inhale?" I asked still holding the cigarette tightly in my hand.

"Inhalin' means you have to take a drag and then take a deep breath sucking the smoke in. I've seen my folks do that. It's the way they do it."

"Well, okay. Lemme try," I said. "If that's the way you're supposed to do it, I'll try it."

Once again, I placed the cigarette into my mouth, took a deep drag, and inhaled the smoke deeply into my lungs. A crisis unfurled . . . I thought I was going to die. I coughed, turned green, and my eyes watered like a flowing fountain. I coughed again and again. It had to get better to die. What had I done?

Dick laughed loud and long at my first attempt at inhaling. "You'll do better next time, try it again," he said as he started pointing his long forefinger at me.

"No thanks, Dick," I said as I pushed him aside and rushed out of the bathroom, through the living room, and out the door. Crying uncontrollably, I ran home as fast as I could. Bounding up the stairs and into the kitchen where my mother was cooking dinner, I rushed over to her, sobbing and holding her tightly with my long, skinny arms.

"What's the matter, Gene? What have you done?"

"Oh, Mother, I smoked. I'll never do it again. I'm so sorry."

"It's okay. It's okay." She responded in her sweet caring voice.

"Please don't tell Daddy. Please don't."

"I won't. I promise," she replied as she slowly pushed me away, smiling lightly with her pale blue eyes sparkling. "We won't tell Daddy."

"And Mother, one thing else, I have smoked grapevines. But, that wasn't smoking, was it?"

"No, I don't think so, but . . . ." She quickly left the room trying desperately to keep from laughing. Her son had learned a valuable lesson . . . never again.

Gene and his Benton friend, Dick Harrison, in Benton in 1949 visiting after Gene moved away to Cape Girardeau with his mother.

� ▲ ▲ ▲ ▲ ▲

War

It was the summer of 1945 in Benton. America was heavily involved in its fourth year of World War II. I was ten years old, and totally ignorant about the ravages of war and the price our country's men and women were paying to support it. Families grew victory gardens, and collected paper and tin cans to help. My friends and I played war endlessly with our toy guns and universal hatred for the sinister Nazis, "Japs" and "Eyetalions."

Baseball entered my life that summer in a big way. We kids played ball almost every day on the softball field across from the high school, a few blocks east of downtown. New baseballs and bats were few and far between, but with the aid of friction tape for first aid to a coverless baseball and tiny nails to mend a cracked bat, we never missed a chance to play.

Mitch, the curmudgeon owner of a filling station located at the southwest corner of Highway 61 and the county court house, would let us kids take motor oil from a 30 gallon dispenser located in his back room and lubricate our gloves, anytime and without asking. He operated out of a concrete block building with an overhanging canopy sheltering a single, extended pump island containing two pumps, gravity fed, from glass cylinders each containing about 12 gallons of gasoline.

Mitch was a short, portly man whose khaki pants and shirt seemed to hang from him like heavy wash from an overcrowded clothesline. He was always attentive to his customers, at least when they were not interfering with his omnipresent game of Pitch going on a cluttered desk just inside the front door. He was recognized as the best Pitch player around those parts and many a customer, both local and transient, would have to wait for service while Mitch and his cronies finished a hand. Mitch had his priorities and playing pitch was at the top of the list.

My pals and I had just finished playing a pick-up game of baseball on this hot, humid July Tuesday. On the way home, I stopped at Mitch's to treat my mitt to the sacred ritual of preserving the fine leather for another day. Doing this, of course, was essential to my development as a baseball player.

As I walked into the station, Mitch and one of his friends were deeply immersed in a card game of Pitch. I nodded quietly to both and walked straight back to the dispenser. Placing my glove directly under the spout, I eased the pump handle ever so lightly. The light golden stream of oil oozed softly from the pump and into the soft pocket of my fielder's glove. I quickly reversed the handle to halt the flow and started kneading the oil vigorously into the smooth leather.

Mitch turned away from his precious game and asked, "You gettin' any better, Boy?" His ruddy, round face beamed as his squinty, blue eyes gazed up at me from his sitting position on his desk.

"Yes, Mitch, I think I am. I got two hits today. Really, I should have gotten three, but Jimmy Wilhelm made a good catch on a ball I hit to him at third base. Jimmy's 14 years old, 'ya know, and he's better than I am."

"Where's your buddy Dick? I haven't seen him around today. Was he playin' with you boys down at the diamond?" Mitch asked.

Suddenly, his head snapped back at the sound of a car, a big, long Cadillac, driving up to the pump island. Uncharacteristically, he threw his hand down hard on the desk and headed smartly out to the waiting car. He liked to fill up Cadillacs because they'd almost always take a full tank of gasoline.

Leaving the station right behind him and caressing my beloved Billy Bancroft glove with the thin leather thong connected to the thumb and forefinger, I said, "Mitch, I haven't seen Dick today. He's got a paper route now, you know. He doesn't play with us as much as he used to."

Without looking at me, Mitch only grunted as he continued to fuel the hi-test gasoline into the Cadillac's rear gas tank. He figured that a 12 gallon fill-up would be worth at least a quarter of profit, maybe more.

Having a paper route, to me, was a big thing. Dick really had two paper routes, the *St. Louis Globe Democrat* delivered every morning, including Sunday and the *St. Louis*

Star Times every evening but Sunday. Through the courtesy of a rapidly deteriorating fleet of Greyhound buses, he received his papers seven days a week at the World War I Memorial Fountain located right across from Mitch's place.

As the bus would arrive at the curb, the driver opened the door and threw the bundle of papers into Dick's waiting arms. Then, Dick rescued the tightly rolled pieces, bound by light, piano-like wire, stuffed them in his large, canvas bag, jumped on his fender-less (no chain guard, either) bicycle and pedaled off on his route with the heavy bag hanging awkwardly off his shoulder.

There were about 20 customers on his morning route, a few less in the evenings. A month's subscription ran a reader around $4.50, maybe less. Dick collected once a month. His take, based on collecting from all his customers, came to around $15 a month, which for a 12-year-old boy was pretty good money. Unfortunately, paying in full didn't always come easy in those days, and when Dick didn't collect, his ultimate remuneration was sliced accordingly, which was more the rule than the exception. Dick would hear many excuses for non-payment, but mostly "Sorry, Dick, there's a war on."

To me, being able to ride alongside Dick on his evening paper route was special. He got up too early in the mornings for me to help him deliver the *Globe,* at least, too early for me. I didn't always join him in the evening, but when my homework was done, I knew that I could call and he'd let me go. I'd then pedal down to the bus stop on my bicycle, complete with chain guard, white walled tires and mud flaps, and wait with Dick for the bus to come in.

It was about 5 pm when I got home that afternoon. I was tired and hungry, as usual and no one seemed to be home. But as I was inclined to do, I poured several bowls of cold cereal and devoured them as I read the latest issue of my favorite comic book, *Captain Marvel*. With no sign of my parents, I called Dick. Perhaps, I could help him deliver the *Star*.

Picking up the telephone receiver, I heard the familiar sound of Francis Anderson's raspy, always tired voice, "Number please."

"Hi, Miss Anderson, would you please ring me Dick Harrison's number? Thanks."

Two long rings later Dick answered, "Hello?"

"Hi, Dick, this is Genius. You gonna deliver papers this evening?"

"Hi, Genius. Yeah, the bus'll be in around 6:00. You wanna help me?"

"Yeah, I'll see you down at the fountain." I was elated I could be with Dick. Bolting down the long steps from our second floor apartment, I retrieved my bike from under the steps and headed for the bus.

Dick came along a few minutes later. "Hey, Genius, guess what? They're goin' to take a bunch of folks up to St. Louis this evenin' to join the Army. Did you ever see 'em leave from here?"

"Whadda 'ya mean . . . join the Army?" I answered in an uncertain voice.

"Well, you see, a Greyhound bus comes by, stops in front of Frobase's Cafe and a bunch of men get on the bus and go up to St. Louis, a place called Jefferson Barracks. They get off the bus and then some sergeant lines 'em up and swears them into the Army. They get on a train and go off to war to fight the Nazis and the Japs."

"Have you ever gone with them?" I asked. My curiosity was piqued. The closest I had ever come to war was playing soldiers out behind John Bradford's house. We would set up our fortress camp among the weeds and brush to defend ourselves against the Japanese snipers and invaders. We never fought against the Nazis . . . always the Japs. The movies in those days, like *Wake Island, Purple Heart* and so on, made us against them in a violent way, at least violent by our standards.

We'd gather up limbs and make lean-to shelters tied with sumac bark ripped assiduously with Dick's pocket knife. I was always the sentry to warn the troops against anybody who would dare to surprise us, always repelled with loud sounds of rat-a-tat tatt . . . rat-a-tat tatt from our carbines and machine guns. We'd play this game nearly every Saturday and Sunday, even some days after school.

"Naw, Genius, I've never had to go with 'em. I'm too young. But I've watched them get on that bus and go up there many times. There's lots of people who show up, but only the men go to St. Louis . . . it's a pretty big deal. By the time we finish deliverin' papers, the bus'll be here. Let's go!"

Dick was a master at his new profession. Following along closely behind him, I tailed his speeding bicycle up and down streets, through alleys, across yards, never slowing down for a minute as he artfully tossed his papers to the front porches of his customers, each landing squarely in the middle of a porch or a front step, always followed by Dick's gleeful cry, "Banzai! Banzai!" I didn't know what Banzai meant, but we yelled it all the time when we played war. Besides, hearing Dick yell "Banzai!" sure sounded like the right thing to say.

Gene and his friends playing war in Benton in 1945. Pictured from left to right are Gene, Larry Bradford, Tom Miller, Baby Bradley Lisle, and John Brussman.

Our wild ride ended where it started, back at memorial fountain. We parked our bicycles at the rear of the limestone structure and waited for the bus to arrive to take the men off to war.

It was about 7 pm and being summer, there was nearly two hours of light left in the day. Huge crowds of people were gathered in and around Frobase's. Everybody seemed to be talking all at once. It sounded like a hive of busy bees. Cars and trucks crowded one after another on the highway and along the streets around the town. There must have been more than 200 people waiting for the bus to come in.

We positioned ourselves on top of the fountain, all alone and able to see everything that was happening. We didn't want to miss a thing. Men were going to war!

As excited as Dick and I were, not everybody was sharing that enjoyment with us. Couples clung closely together and sons and daughters tugged tightly to their father's legs like giant centipedes wrapping themselves around some defenseless insect. Mothers, fathers, and grandparents huddled around their sons chatting animatedly, all embracing . . . some crying softly.

Why were they crying? These men were going to war to fight the Japs and the Nazis. They should be singing, laughing, but it wasn't happening like that. This was more like being in church. Only a few nervous laughs here and there broke the seriousness of the moment. Dick and I sat very still at our strategic post, taking it all in.

Just then, a diesel-powered bus belching heavy clouds of black acrid smoke came into sight as its noisy engine was heard from the top of the hill leading northward into town. Coming closer, the letters S-P-E-C-I-A-L stood out on the front of the bus' marquee.

"Here's the 'pup'!" a voice cried out from the gathered throng. A few cheers erupted, as the small close circles came toward the bus to form a horde of massed humanity around the foul-smelling engine.

The driver bounded out of his charge and quickly opened the baggage compartments at the bus' side. Strangely, only a few large bags were loaded on board. The men, now climbing up the steps into the bus single file, mostly carried small duffel bags in their hands. Windows were opened as anxious heads peered longingly outside and yelled final words to those special people gathered closely around them.

"Bye, honey . . . don't 'ya forget to write, hear?!"

"I'll write ya soons I get stationed Darlin'. I promise."

"Billy, you take good care of yer mama. She'll need you to help more with the chores."

"Gramps, now stay off that tractor. You're too damned old to be doin' that." And so on.

The driver called out to the remaining crowd, "All 'board! This bus' is goin' to Saint Louis. All 'board!" The bus' doors closed quickly, the crowd parted like the Red Sea being commanded by Moses' strong voice. And the bus' red tail lights disappeared into the warm summer's night as it now rolled northward toward the big city carrying its precious cargo of America's future fighting men.

Gene was only ten years old and almost in the fifth grade when he watched the men go off to war. This is his school picture, taken in 1945.

A few sobs and some questioning voices from small children were faintly heard among the rapidly dissipating crowd. Soon, there was no one left around the café as most of the cars and trucks had left. Only an occasional car broke the dusk's silence as it sped unknowingly through the small country town that had just released its young to far away places of peril.

"Gee, Dick, I gotta get on home," I said as we climbed down from our vantage point atop the fountain. A steady stream of water spewed steadily from the fountain's lion head flanked by those names of World War I's war dead honored by the town.

"Thanks, Genius, for helping me. You gonna play ball tomorrow? I'll have Jimmy round 'em up for us. Let's play about 1 pm. Okay?"

"Yeah, I'll play. See ya down at the diamond."

I pedaled my bicycle the short block back to the apartment. Climbing the steep steps, I could smell the familiar scent of fish frying. My dad had been fishing. He always caught something.

"Hi, Dad, Mother," I cried as I strolled into the apartment's main foyer leading into the kitchen. "We're goin' to have fish tonight, huh?"

"Yes," Mother answered. "Where have you been? It's almost dark. We were a little worried."

"Oh, I was down at the corner with Dick watching the men going off to war. It was kind of fun."

Just then, my father came into the kitchen. The unmistakable scent of my father's fishing togs and the after effects of his cleaning fish for our dinner nearly over-whelmed me. "Hi, Son, where have you been?"

"Watchin' the bus come in to take the men to St. Louis. Dad, they're going to war. They're going to fight the Japs, the Nazis. It was a lot of fun. Dick and I sat up on the monument and watched it all."

Before responding, I saw my father's face blanch a bit. He glared at me sternly in the eye and said, "A lot of those men will never come back home, Son. Did you know that?"

"They won't come back? Why not?" I couldn't believe what my father said. I had never thought about that.

"Because, they're going to war, far away from here. Some will get killed fighting. They won't be coming back home. Some'll come back seriously wounded. A lot of these men could be gone for a long, long time before they come back home."

"They won't? Is that why everybody seemed so sad when the bus finally left? Was that the reason?"

"That was the reason, Gene. That was the reason."

Author's Note:

Needless to say, I was clearly shaken by what my father told me, yet I still had only a vague idea of what the reality of war meant. I was entirely too young. True, many did not come back to their beloved families. Some of those that did wished they had never gone in the first place. They returned with disabling injuries, mental cripples. But they all went as their country called them. And for young boys like Dick and me, we never really appreciated the extent of their sacrifice at that time. We were too young. They were America's finest.

Cape Girardeau, Missouri

1946 -1956

🐾🐾🐾🐾🐾

Strap

The late summer of 1946 was a very traumatic time for me. My mother and father separated after more than 25 years of marriage. Mother and I then moved to Cape Girardeau, Missouri, about 16 miles north and nearly 50 times larger than the small country town of 408 friends I was used to in Benton. Even worse, the only friend I knew in Cape was Johnny Brussman, my best Benton friend. He had moved to Cape with his Aunt Nona and Uncle John Hobbs a year earlier and had settled on South Middle Street.

Gene and Johnny Brussman resting on the porch in Cape Girardeau in 1946.

Wanting to be close to the Hobbs, my mother selected the same street and a duplex apartment, affordable quarters at $35 a month. Although small, it was fairly comfortable and was heated by a coal-fired stove, which was located in my room between Mother's bedroom and the kitchen.

Privacy was the only shortcoming that I could remember. The walls were paper thin, and the domestic conversations, some not so pleasant, could be heard. How well I remember.

Had I stayed in Benton, I would have started the seventh grade there. Our new home in Cape would place me in the May Greene School, but my mother had a friend, Doris Mabry, who was the principal at the Lorimier School. Miss Mabry insisted to Mother that I enroll at Lorimier so she "fixed" it. Since Johnny lived only a few houses down from our duplex, Miss Mabry agreed that he could enroll there, too. I was happy with that, as we could walk to school together, and be in the same class and on the same softball and basketball team.

The Lorimier School was a sharp contrast to Benton's old, brick two-story building with only four classrooms. Lorimier was new and modern in every way. Its sixth, seventh and eighth grade students rotated their classes in separate rooms, while the lower grades each had a separate classroom. This was unlike Benton where two grades, first and second, etc., would study and learn in the same room. Further, we had a music teacher and a well-equipped woodworking and metal shop with an industrial arts teacher. For the first time in my life, I had a coach—a softball and basketball coach. I felt like I had arrived from a third-world country.

Both Johnny and I were good athletes, or at least, we thought we were. We both made the softball team. I pitched, and Johnny played in left field. Our team didn't do too well against other grade schools in Cape, but we figured that since we were the smallest, the other teams had more to choose from. When the basketball season started, we knew that we would be much better. No reason. We just felt like we would be.

Coach Steck was our softball and basketball coach. He was a tall, thin man with dark brown eyes that would bulge wildly out of his head when his team's actions resembled nothing similar to a game called Softball. He would point his long, skinny forefinger at either one or all of us and scream in short, emphatic words: "No! Stop! Don't! No!" Unfortunately, his words never helped us much as runs would be scored at will and our wild throws ended up either in the woods behind the diamond or down on the Missouri Pacific railroad tracks.

As basketball season neared, Coach Steck held tryouts. Before one ball had been dribbled, Coach met with his minions. Dressed in gray sweats, he laid out the rules for future practices and the season. His strict, authoritarian voice more than demanded our rapt attention.

"Practice will start sharply at 3:45. Since school is out at 3:30, that'll give you 15 minutes to get to the gym, dress and be on the court. Now, as for dress. You will wear tennis shoes, shorts, and t-shirts at all times when you're on the court. When my whistle blows, all play stops on the court. Hear me? All play stops. And during games, you will never question the referee's call. If you commit a foul, you will raise your right hand and let the scorer know that you have committed a foul. Understand?"

All our heads nodded at once as Coach Steck spoke. "And after the game, win or lose, you will shake hands with the other team. And oh, yes, each player here will always wear an athletic supporter while on the court. Are there any questions?"

Johnny raised his hand very slowly and in a soft, almost whispering voice said, "Coach, what's an athletic supporter and where do we get one?"

Coach's full dark eyebrows raised dramatically on his long narrow face. "Err, you don't know what an athletic supporter is? Or where you get one? Can anyone here help John?"

No one raised a hand; all our heads bowed down as if in silent prayer. Coach asked again. "Anyone? Can anyone tell him?" Heads looking at the coach from the wooden bleachers bowed even further against their skinny chests.

"Well, since no one knows, I'm going to tell you. All athletes wear supporters. Supporters help protect them below the belt."

Johnny asked in a sheepish voice, "Is it kinda like an ankle wrap?"

Coach's face reddened as he pointed his finger at Johnny. "No, it's not like an ankle wrap. Not at all. You wear it like you wear your shorts. Understand?"

Without raising his hand, Johnny blurted out in a loud voice, "I still don't understand. What does it support, I mean protect?"

Arching his back and peering directly at his young men sitting there waiting for more explanation, Coach Steck pulled his sweat pants down below his spindly knees and displayed his athletic supporter to the wide-eyed and curious players. "See? See what I've been telling you. This is an athletic supporter. You wear it just like shorts. And it supports, protects your genitalia. See?" He then pointed downward in the direction of the supporter. "And as I told you before, each player must go out and buy one. You need one if you want to play basketball on this team."

"Where do you buy one?" asked Johnny in a puzzling manner. He and the rest of us had never heard the word "genitalia" but we got the idea. I thought about my genitalia and wondered why in the world I would ever need a supporter to protect it. But, he was the coach, and if he said I needed to have one, I guess I needed one.

"Any drug store will have them." Coach added.

"How much does it cost?" asked one of the boys. "Is it expensive?"

"No, it isn't expensive. I'd say about two bucks. Now let's get on with the tryouts."

We were all confused about the merits of having and wearing an athletic supporter, but since Coach had ordered us to go out and buy one, we would obey. After all, if that were what it took to play basketball for him, we'd do it. But, I still didn't understand how this thing could protect or support anything.

I was too embarrassed to talk to my mother about buying an athletic supporter, but I had to have the money to buy one. Without telling her, I reached into my hidden stash of coins I had saved from receiving nickels and dimes from my grandfather. I had about three dollars I had saved, and if the Coach were correct, it would be more than enough to buy my first athletic supporter.

On a late Friday afternoon, I walked over to the Cape Cut Rate drug store where I guessed I'd be able to buy a supporter. The store was loaded with all kinds of drugs and health stuff, including wines, liquors and beer. I walked slowly through the aisles looking to find what I needed and I couldn't find it. I suppose I should have asked the clerk who, to my chagrin, was a lady who looked to be about the same age as my mother. There was no way that I was going to ask her where to find an athletic supporter!

Now frustrated, I approached the saleslady and asked, "Ma'am, I'm, err, I need, ahhhh, a, uh, uh, an athletic supporter?"

"Fine," she answered. "What size?"

Size? Coach didn't talk about size. "Err, Ma'am, I don't really know what size. Whatever you think I need."

The lady was barely able to keep from smiling. "Well, looking at you, I'd say you need a small. Don't you think?"

"Yes, I think so. Small would be just about right. Just about right." I began to relax now as the lady walked over to one of aisles that I had patrolled so carefully only a few minutes ago and brought it back, my own athletic supporter.

The supporter came in a small rectangular-shaped box. A large red S stood out. Of course, I was getting a small supporter. The S confirmed it. "How much is it?" I confidently asked.

"That'll be two dollars, with tax, two dollars and four cents. Would you like a sack?"

"Yes ma'am, please," I said as I handed her most of my entire life savings.

With the brown paper sack hiding my treasure, I walked home as if I had just purchased some rare Van Gogh painting. I was so proud. I had done it!

Now that I had it, how would I wear it? Was small the right size? Wonder what size Johnny bought?

My mother must never know what I had done. I wondered whether she had ever had to wear one of those things. Someday, I'd get enough nerve to ask her.

Caddy

Doots Garner and I shuffled home slowly from Capaha Park savoring our baseball victory against the league leading Cardinals. Despite a summer temperature and humidity both edging toward the century level, we were excited about what we had done. It was the Cardinal's first loss of the season. We, the Reds, were now tied for first place.

Doots and I became good friends while teammates on the Reds, one of Cape Girardeau's summer playground league teams in the summer of 1947. He played third base. I pitched.

Both of our mothers worked, and neither of us had fathers living with us. As such, we never talked about our dads. Perhaps it was too painful to discuss their absence especially since most of our other friends seemed to have parents active in their daily lives. Baseball was our sole interest, nothing much else mattered.

"'Ya know, Eugene," Doots said, "My two hits today put my batting average up to nearly .400." His gloveless right hand wiped away tiny beads of sweat dripping from under the red wool baseball cap fitted snugly over his round head. Doots was about two or three inches shorter than I and a few pounds heavier, most of which was centered around his soft belly.

"Whadda 'ya mean, two hits? You wouldn't call that pop fly to left field a hit, would 'ya?" I loved to tease Doots about his obsession with a batting average. He was clearly a good hitter, exceedingly better than I, but I was a pitcher. I didn't have to hit, all I needed to do was to get batters out.

"It certainly was! No question about it! The left fielder didn't touch it, did he? Hey, what do you know about hittin'? You swing a bat like an ole washerwoman. It's a good thing that you can pitch 'cause no one would ever want you on their team."

"Oh well, it doesn't matter, Doots. We're now tied for first place with the Cardinals, and we play them again next Thursday. If I pitch as well as I did today, we'll beat 'em again . . . then we'll win the league."

We decided to stop by Faust's, a dingy storefront candy store on Independence Street just west of the police station. We could spend our nickel on a popsicle instead of taking the Ellis Street bus and spending it there. It was an easy decision for us to make.

We strolled innocently the rest of the way home savoring our frozen delights, the sides of our faces sticky with the cherry sugar water. We were oblivious to the world around us and feeling quite upbeat about our conquest earlier that morning.

"Doots, I'd like to find a job, but 'ya know, nobody wants to hire a 12-year-old kid," I said.

"Yeah, but you could go out to the country club and caddy. You can make pretty good money out there," he answered.

"Caddy?" I asked. "What's a caddy?"

"You don't know what a caddy is? You got to be kidding! Everybody knows what a caddy is."

"Well, I don't. I really don't. What is it?"

"Euuugene," Doots drawled in his soft southern Missouri twang, "A caddy carries a golfer's golf clubs on a golf course. For that, you get paid. You get fifty cents a round. Some golfers will even tip you. I once got tipped a dollar!"

"What's a round?"

Doots stopped suddenly and turned to me with a look of complete surprise. "You really don't know, do you? I thought you were just putting me on."

"I told you, Doots. I've never even seen a golf course. I don't even know what a country club is, much less where it is."

My 13-year-old friend shook his head over and over again in disbelief and motioned for me to join him on the front porch swing of his duplex as he laid out the basics of caddying. Doots had caddied at the club the past summer. He seemed to know everything, but I wondered why he wasn't back there this summer.

"How come you're not caddying this summer?" I asked.

"I guess I got tired of it, Gene," he replied.

"Well, I'm not that lucky, Doots. I need to make some money. I'm just gonna go out there and try it. If I can make as much as you say I can, that'll help me a lot." I leaped down from the shady porch, picked up the pace down Merriwether, turned right on South Middle and continued up the sidewalk to our duplex.

My mother, who had separated from my dad, worked in a small loan finance office as a receptionist, secretary, or whatever job her demanding boss decided he wanted her to do. It was the first job that she had been able to land since we moved to the Cape in the fall of 1946. Her salary was about $75 dollars a month for Monday through Friday and a half-day on Saturday. From that, she paid rent, $25 a month, maintained a 1942 Plymouth coupe, bought food and clothing, and tried to keep a 12 year-old boy focused and active, but off the streets and out of trouble.

When I told her what I wanted to do, my mother seemed pleased. She knew the country club well from happier times with my dad. She sat down and drew a simple map to show me how to get there.

Since there was no direct bus line out to the club, my bicycle was the only option. I could save a dime, and I could pedal fast. The four mile journey north of town would take less than 30 minutes. With a few shortcuts and turns here and there, I could avoid most of the heavier traveled roads. Big Bend Road was the worst.

Doots told me that caddies were hired on a "first-come, first-to-work" basis. In other words, if I was at the club first, and a golfer needed a caddy, they'd pick me. So the next morning, I got an early start and left the neighborhood around 8:30 am. My route took me down to the river, across Water Street, north on Main, and then through the pot-holed and run-down streets of the Red Star Addition, a blue collar area supported by the International Shoe Company factory. At the intersection of Country Club and Cape Rock Drives, I pedaled furiously the remaining one-half mile over the rolling and winding asphalt road to the club.

As I passed through the stone-walled entrance of the country club and onto a huge parking lot, the clubhouse, a massive white wooden structure with a wide screened-in second story porch, loomed ahead of me like some antebellum southern mansion. I had entered another world, where I figured only the very rich could afford to be.

Climbing off my bicycle, I ushered it gingerly in between a large swimming pool on my right and the clubhouse on my left. Proud and tall maple trees formed a shady cover over my head.

No one seemed to be around. It was about 9 am.

Coming out again into the open, I got my first real glimpse of the golf course, a magnificent view of seemingly endless green stretching to lush woods that formed a natural boundary for the course. A nearby large island, flat and filled with sand, rested almost obscurely beneath a sloping hill to the east of the clubhouse. The large, circular stand of brown-like, oil sand amidst the green presence of grass seemed totally out of place.

Just then, I noticed a wizened man dressed completely in khaki walking slowly toward me pushing a lawnmower. "What do you want, boy?" He yelled in a snarling, unpleasant voice.

"I'm here to caddy, Sir. Are you a golfer?" I responded. The man's face broke into a broad grin. The few teeth left in his tiny mouth stood out like rusted iron stakes deeply embedded in rich, chestnut soil.

"Naww, I ain't no golfer. I work here. I work for Coach Muegge." I'd heard about Coach Muegge. He was the long-time Central High School football, basketball, and baseball coach. I didn't know he worked at the club. I thought all he ever did was coach.

"Say, Sir, do you mow this course with that lawnmower? I bet it takes you a long time, doesn't it?"

"Gawd no! Boy, this here course is mowed by big mowers pulled by Coach Muegge's jeep. Coach is already out mowin' this morning. He's down around number five and six. I'll do one, two, and three tomorrow."

"Five and six? What's that?"

"The course's five and six holes, Boy. Don't you know nothin' 'bout golf?"

"Oh, I know a little bit. I know I want to caddy."

"Well, boy, golfers don't start playin' 'til later, at least most of them don't. You're too early. But, tell 'ya what, go on down to the caddy shack. Maybe some of the caddies are already there." My new friend pointed beyond the first tee to a small white-framed hut nestled about 100 yards or so down the hill right off the first fairway.

Still chauffeuring my bicycle, I edged down the hill to the shack. As I approached the small shelter, a brown, curly head of hair poked itself out of the shack's open door. A soft, high voice said, "Who are you?"

"Hi, I'm Gene Munger. I'm here to caddy. Who are you?"

"I'm Sonny. I'm the caddy master here at the club. Did 'ya ever caddy before?" Sonny was only a few inches taller than I, but his sinewy arms hanging down from his faded green tee shirt reflected a picture of strength far greater than my pencil-like limbs.

"No, but I know a little bit about golf. Besides, I know I can pick it up pretty quick."

"Well, here's the way it works around here. It's strictly a "first-come, first-serve" thing. Except for me, I always go first whenever I'm here and I'm here everyday. If you get down here first, there's a pretty good chance that you'll get work. Oh, yeah, some of the golfers like their own caddy. Like Mr. McDonald, he always asks for me. If he asks for me, I go. If someone asks for you, you go, regardless of when you got here. Understand?"

"Yeah, right. I understand." Doots had been right on the mark about the way things were for a caddy. Now, all I needed was to have a golfer appear and need one.

From the direction of the first tee, I heard what seemed to be the loud cry of a person in distress.

"Caaaaddddddyyy! We need two caddies!" My heart jumped. Doots was right and Sonny was, too. I got here early and I already had a job!

The caddymaster and I walked briskly up the hill to the two waiting golfers. One of the golfers recognized Sonny immediately and seemed obviously pleased to have him with them.

"Hi, Sonny. How've you been?" The golfer was Mr. Brady, a lawyer in town whose pear-shaped body caused me to wonder what exactly he was doing on a golf course. I thought that all golfers had to be in good shape, lean and mean. How else would you be able to walk around a golf course and swing a club hard enough to hit the ball?

"Fine, Mr. Brady. Just fine," answered Sonny. "You're certainly out early this morning."

"Yeah. Earlier than usual, for sure. Meet Mr. Sneed, he's a friend of mine. He lives in Memphis," Sneed offered his outstretched hand and shook Sonny's hand firmly.

"Who's your other caddy, Sonny? I don't believe I know him." Brady asked.

"Oh, that's Gene Munger. This is his first time out here, Mr. Brady."

"Gene Munger? I know your dad, Son. I'm a lawyer, too." The fact that Brady recognized my father boosted my spirits a bit, but I was afraid that he would ask awkward questions about my father's whereabouts and so on. Fortunately for me, he didn't. His mind seemed to be on the golf game ahead.

Brady's first drive off the tee went slicing and curving straight into the woods. He hit his second shot weakly in the fairway, only about 125 yards out. Sneed followed suit with a drive into the woods and then a puny second drive a few yards behind Brady.

As the golfers headed for their second shot, Sonny easily lifted Brady's golf bag by its leather strap, placed it over his broad shoulders and motioned for me to follow. Aping my mentor's lead, I lifted Sneed's bag over my right shoulder and boldly trailed Sonny into the woods to try to retrieve the errant and misguided missiles from the opening drives.

I had visually marked where Sneed's ball had gone out-of-bounds. Following my instincts, I marched right to the spot where I thought the ball would be and there it was, resting in a dry creek bed at the bottom of a shallow gully. Although I was elated at my good fortune, I had no idea, none whatsoever, of what golf balls cost or even where you bought them. Turning to help Sonny find Brady's ball which seemed totally lost, I found a U.S. Royal Special that appeared to have been hit only once, out of bounds deep into the thick woods.

Sonny seemed impressed with my newly discovered forte. "You can keep that beauty, Gene," he said. "That'll be worth some money if you try to sell it."

"How much would I get?"

Looking carefully at the ball to see if there were any cuts or noticeable scuff marks, Sonny paused briefly, sighed and said, "Oh, I'd say at least fifty cents."

"Wow! Fifty cents! You're kidding. That much?"

"Oh, sure, at least that much, maybe even a little bit more."

Our twosome's next two shots from the fairway were equally as poor as their first. While I had never seen a golf game played, I could immediately tell that these two gentlemen were certainly not going to break any course records that day. As their game continued, however, they did improve.

After their third shot, Sonny pointed at me and barked out some strange commands. "Gene, get up to the green and hold the flag." The flag I understood. There it was flying limply and held by a pole inserted into a hole. But a "green?" It looked more like a giant sandbox for a roomful of young toddlers.

What I saw before me was definitely not a green. It was the same kind of flat, level sand island that I had noticed earlier that morning. The lonely island, surrounded by lush, green grass was about 100 feet in diameter and filled with thick, coarse sand. Why did they call it a green?

Heeding Sonny's call, I sprinted up to the green, bag over shoulder, approached the flag and stood there holding the pole while the golfers prepared to make their final approach shot.

Sneed's ball, hit from about 70 yards out, came off his club like a rocket and it headed straight for the flag in a low line trajectory. It hit about 10 yards in front of me, skipped twice and came to rest deep into a thick bunker filled with sand about 20 yards to my rear.

Brady's ball took on an entirely different course. He was about 50 yards from the green when he carefully stroked his ball with a full, easy swing: The ball seemed to have wings as it went high into the sky and came down on the sand only two feet from where I held the flag. I watched paralyzed. The ball seemed to have eyes and rolled straight to the hole as if drawn by some strong, unseen magnet.

"Take it out . . . take it out! Damn it! Take it out!" Both Sneed and Brady screeched at me like eagles about to snatch unsuspecting spawning salmon. Brady's ball continued to roll toward the flag and finally wedged itself between the pole and the outer rim of the cup. Frightened by their woeful cries, I jerked the flag from the hole. The ball dropped straight down into the bottom of the cup.

"Son, you've got to remove the flag from the cup when a shot gets that close. You could have cost me a stroke!" shouted Brady.

"Don't ever do that again!" I was mortified at my ignorance, but, I didn't know. I just didn't know.

Since the greens were filled with sand, not grass, it was necessary to make a smooth path for golfers to putt. With a three foot long pipe, four inches or so in diameter and connected in the middle with a five foot heavy steel handle, Sonny began to rake a smooth path from the hole to the outer limits of the green for Sneed to putt from about 15 feet from the hole. Two putts later, his ball finally found the bottom of the cup.

Despite his almost being deprived of "holing out" from off the green by my irresponsible action, Brady waxed ebulliently over his good shot as he pranced toward the second tee moving his driver up and down like a drum major leading his band. The weather had turned considerably cooler, and the golfers walked with good energy and enthusiasm over the next four holes. Sonny and I walked obediently behind our men carrying their bags. Sneed's bag was light. Only two woods, five irons and a putter supported him. Silently, I wondered why he would even want a caddy. It seemed to me that he would have been able to carry his own bag. Besides that, he could have saved fifty cents!

On the fifth hole tee, Brady again sliced his drive deep into the woods on the right. I felt sorry for the man and attempted to console him with some words of encouragement. "Oh, no . . . too bad, Mr. Brady. Bad shot, bad shot. But, don't worry, I can find your ball!"

Brady turned quickly like a striking rattler and glowered at me. Mauve colored veins spread across his forehead like a string of faded neon tubes. "I do wish you would keep quiet, Son. As for finding that ball, forget it! I'm trying to play golf, and you're not helping me."

Undaunted, I replied, "I'm sorry, Mr. Brady, but I can find your ball. Let me try. I'm sure I can!" Sonny moved quickly toward me, pointed a forefinger to his lips and signaled that his neophyte, bumbling associate should keep quiet. I understood.

Brady hit another ball, a terrible, topping shot that bounced twice on the hard, almost grassless surface in front of the tee and ended up about 30 yards forward. Cursing quietly under his breath, he came over to his bag, thrust his driver deep inside like a buccaneer plunging his sword into some hapless seaman's belly, drew out another wooden club (it said #3 on its head) and stomped off to hit his second shot. Mr. Brady was a little tense.

From there until the ninth hole, my mouth stayed shut. In the interim, I began to pick up some of the terminology applicable to golf. Terms like par, bogey, eagle and so on. The ninth hole, a par five challenge of more than 400 yards, had the golfers hitting from a long, gradual hill ending just north of the clubhouse.

I was feeling fairly good about my first round of golf. I figured that I would at least collect fifty cents, and if the twosome decided to play another nine holes, I'd be a dollar richer and a lot smarter. They had not declared their intentions to do so at that time. After my initial nine hole's dismal performance, I could see why they might wish to rid themselves of me forever.

As the golfers prepared to make their final approach shots, Sonny motioned for me to go to the green and hold the flag. This time would be different; I knew what to do. Unfortunately, instead of placing Sneed's bag some distance away from the golfer's line of fire, I foolishly laid the bag just off the green.

Brady's approach shot, towering high against the partly cloudy sky, hit well past the flag, falling on Sneed's misplaced bag and caroming wildly into the bunker below.

Again, Brady went ballistic. He started jumping up and down like a man deranged, cursing loudly and profanely. Had there been another hole big and near enough, I would have climbed inside, gotten into the fetal position and stayed for the rest of the day.

Without a word, I ran from my flag position across the sandy green and down to the ominous bunker. I plucked Brady's ball which was almost hidden from view and returned it to where his bag lay. "There, Mr. Brady, that's where your ball would have been had Mr. Sneed's bag not been there. Okay?"

The two golfers glanced at each other in complete silence. They were simply awe-struck at what they were seeing. By then, Brady had composed himself and walked slowly over to his ball.

"Son, it was not, not, not, not necessary to return my ball from the sand trap." His lower jaw trembled as he spoke. "Please, put it back. Please!" I obeyed quickly without a word.

As the twosome finally finished play, I stood stoically at the side of the green wondering whether I would even get paid for my morning's labor. Mr. Sneed had every reason not to. Sonny and I followed a few paces behind the golfers as they made their way slowly up the hill to the clubhouse.

"Sonny, I don't think we'll play another round this morning," Brady said as he turned in the direction of the club's bar. "Thank you. You did a good job." He then reached into his leather, well-worn wallet and pulled out a dollar. "Here! Thanks a lot. I believe I need a beer."

Looking like a cowed dog that had just been punished by his master, I tramped forward to Sneed in deep remorse. "I'm sorry, Mr. Sneed, for everything I did. I promise to do better next time."

Sneed grinned slightly as he reached into his light brown linen slacks pocket and pulled out a half dollar. "Thanks, young man," he said in a paternal tone of voice. "Thanks."

Turning away from my charge, I suddenly remembered the ball that I had found at the first hole, pulled it out of my jeans pocket and held it out proudly to the retiring golfer.

"Mr. Sneed, I found this ball in the woods. Would you like to buy it?"

Sneed carefully examined the ball from my hand and said, "Ummm, it's almost like new. What do 'ya want for it?"

"Oh, I don't know. Whatever you think is fair."

"Well, how 'bout a quarter?" he said as he proceeded to throw the ball up in the air over and over again, first with the right hand, then the left.

I immediately countered Sneed's offer. "Sir, I don't think that's enough. Sonny told me that a U.S. Royal . . . it's only been hit once and it's worth at least fifty cents and I believe it is."

Sneed was taken aback by my response, so much so that he held the ball in his hands and peered straight down into my anxious eyes and smiled. "So, you don't think that a quarter is enough, eh? Well, what if I told you that a quarter is all I'm going to give you?"

"No, I'd like for you to have it, but I have to have fifty cents for the ball, Mr. Sneed. That's what it's worth. It's practically brand new." My adrenalin was flowing fiercely now as I found myself in an earnest haggle with a man at least the age of my father.

Sneed paused, took a deep breath and conceded, "Okay, fifty cents it is, Son. You drive a hard bargain. If you could caddy as well as you can bargain, I believe you'd do all right around here," he said as he reached down again into his slacks and pulled out another fifty cent piece. "Here, now we're even!"

Sonny observed this heavy transaction by standing quietly at my side. As he and I walked back to the caddy shack, he turned to me and said, "Wow, Gene, I never seen any caddy do that with a member. And he gave you your price. You made a buck this morning . . . the same thing that I made. You're goin' to do all right around here."

Author's Note:

I continued to caddy for the rest of the summer of 1946, riding my bicycle from South Middle almost every day. In a good week, I could make up to $10, sometimes even carrying "double" bags. In time, certain club members would ask for me to caddy personally for them. Sometimes, they'd even call me at home, pick me up, and take me to the club. That was a very heady thing to happen to a 12-year-old kid.

As to my negotiations with Mr. Sneed over the price of a used golf ball, my actions at that time were highly uncommon, especially for a youth of my age growing up in southeast Missouri in the mid-late 40s. But at the moment of my success, I began to become my own man, and to stand up for what I believed, an experience that served me well in my later adult life.

Awakening

Catcher Gene Munger in 1948 in Cape Girardeau, when baseball was his passion.

It was the late summer of 1946. I had turned twelve in late June. Life was good.

I was mowing lawns, making up to $2 a yard and caddying at the country club, $1 a round. With tips, $5 a day wasn't that unusual. Pitching for the Reds at Capaha Park gave me visions of someday taking the mound at Sportsman's Park with my beloved St. Louis Cardinals.

Centenary Methodist Church, a magnificent Gothic-style limestone structure, was also a big part of my life. My Grand-father Humphreys, a retired Methodist minister, had been a positive influence on me. His death in 1944 was devastating for all of us, and shortly after-ward, I decided that perhaps I should try to follow in his footsteps and become a minister.

Sunday school was a must and I'd even go to church afterwards. Although I wouldn't always understand Reverend Robert Holliday's sermons, I'd always join in with the choir bolstered by the fine tenor voice of Steve Limbaugh, his big brother Rush Limbaugh II's booming baritone, Alene Sadler's excellent organ playing and the spirited congregation singing with great gusto those good Methodist hymns.

Just to the east of the church stood my favorite house, and a yard that would more than challenge my meager mowing abilities. It was an impressive Tudor-style residence that must have had at least six bedrooms. Facing Bellevue Street was a wide-sweeping, lush, verdant, and impeccably groomed lawn that blended majestically into a series of carefully manicured bushes fronting the house. I probably would never be able to afford such a fine place, but maybe, just maybe, some day, I could.

Successful Main Street merchants, the Hechts, owned and operated the most fashionable women's store in town, at least in my mother's view. She shopped there now and then, always finding the latest in fashions. I would occasionally go with her, careful that none of my friends saw me gawking into their spotless, glistening window showing lifeless mannequins dressed appealingly in the latest in women's finery. I really never went inside, but instead would walk down the block to the Montgomery-Ward store and browse through its sporting goods department never buying anything but wishing I could afford a better glove.

Late one afternoon, one of my Red's teammates and I left Houck Stadium where we found the heat and humidity too uncomfortable for running the quarter mile cinder track. Leaving, we walked down Bellevue over to Sprigg planning to stop, cool off, and buy a soda at the Cape Cut Rate store.

Crossing Ellis Street, I pointed proudly at Centenary Church there on the corner, and said, "That's my church, that's where I go to Sunday school and church. Isn't it beautiful?"

He grunted somewhat disgustingly and replied, "Naww, I wouldn't go to church there, only rich people go there."

"Whaddaya mean, rich people? My mother and I go there and we sure aren't rich."

With a wave of his skinny hand and a look of sheer haughtiness, he responded, "Well anyway, I don't go to Sunday School much and I never go to church. I guess you do."

Not answering, I moved ahead and quickly pointed to the lovely, graceful house with the green, sweeping lawn. "Look, there's my favorite house in Cape. The Hechts live there."

Not missing a beat, my friend replied, "Hechts? They're kikes, 'ya know."

"Kikes? What's a kike?"

"You know, they're Jews. Jews are no good. They're kikes. They cheat people. They're no good."

"Wait a minute," I said. "The Hechts are really good people. Mr. Hecht is always nice to me. My mother buys dresses at their store. They don't cheat anybody. How can you say that?"

"You just don't know, Gene. Those people are no good. And you better watch out for 'em."

"Where do you get this stuff?"

"My daddy tells me all about it. And he knows."

"Well, I just don't believe it, no matter what you or your daddy says. I just don't believe it."

We continued walking, neither of us saying much. I was confused at my friend's inflamed outburst against the Hechts, against Jews. I didn't understand. I had to talk to my mother about what he had said.

Saying goodbye to my friend at the drug store, I walked home, south on Sprigg, east on Frederick and south again on South Middle to our duplex. Mother wouldn't be home until after 5 pm, and it was almost that time.

Around 5:30, Mother arrived through the front door carrying a small sack of groceries. "Why, Gene, you're here. I suspected that you'd be out playing ball. Johnny and Lawrence Matney were playing catch up the street."

"Mother, what's a kike?"

Nearly dropping her groceries, she stared unbelievingly at me, her soft blue eyes turning hard, her tall thin body stiffening at the sound of my question. "What did you say? Did I hear you correctly?"

I asked again, "What's a kike?"

"I never want you to ever say that word again! Do you hear me? Never again!" Mother turned quickly toward the kitchen and left me standing completely bewildered that I had said something so very wrong.

I followed her and attempted to apologize, "I'm sorry, Mother, but one of my buddies called the Hechts that name. He also said they were Jews and Jews are no good, and they'll cheat you. Is that true?"

"You heard me, Gene, you are never to use that word . . . never again. And whoever told you that Jews were no good is simply wrong. They don't know what they're talking about. Don't listen to that kind of talk. It's disgusting, despicable and I'm sorry that you had to hear it."

"Then, it's not true, is it?"

"No, it isn't. Not a single word of it."

This was Mother's way, never going into a long lecture attempting to justify her position or philosophy on some secular or moral issue. When she announced, "It isn't true," that was all it took. I got it! And it stuck!

At the tender age of 12, I made a positive first step over and beyond the contaminated world of anti-Semitism, ignorance and prejudice . . . a step that thankfully I never had to retrace.

■ ■ ■ ■ ■

Smelterville

It was July 1946. My best friend, Johnny Brussman, both of us approaching 12-years-young, and I bicycled ourselves over to May Greene Elementary School, about a half-mile from our houses on South Middle Street, to join our friends in a continuing and fun game of Indian Ball.

True to form, the weather was beastly hot and humid. We were used to that. It didn't bother us since we had both gone to Boy Scout Camp Lewallen for the first time in June experiencing the same weather, and besides, it was summer and we didn't have to go to school.

While we went to Lorimier School and not May Greene, we had lots of friends who did attend there, and in those days, there was really no great rivalry between the schools. It didn't matter. We weren't sophisticated enough to know it was any pressing issue or important to our young lives.

Playing on May Greene's diamond wasn't exactly like playing on a smooth, well-groomed field, and neither was Lorimier's. It didn't make any difference to us as we avoided the uneven choppy dirt surface and the fast-growing weeds making ground and fly balls somewhat difficult to catch since the school year's wrap up for the summer vacation. We just didn't care. It was summer and playing baseball and softball was our priority regardless of where we played.

At nearly 6 pm, we all decided we had had enough of the game, and our stomachs told us we'd better go home for supper. One of our friends, Ranny Young, clearly the most athletic of us all, a sure-handed fielder and good hitter, suggested we cycle on down to Smelterville and watch their softball game.

Smelterville was located on the south end of Sprigg Street, Cape Girardeau's primary north-south route through the city. Why it was called Smelterville, we didn't know. We did know however, it was where most of the town's African-Americans lived, and there was sub-standard housing, a lack of city services, no plumbing, minimal electricity, and of the Mississippi River's annual flooding of this low-lying area. Other than what we knew, we never gave it a serious thought. It was just the way it was, and we knew we didn't want to live there.

Our parents would drive through the area on our way to the Marquette Cement's Natatorium, an indoor pool where Marquette's employees and our scout troop was allowed to swim. We didn't know what the word natatorium meant, but we sure enjoyed the opportunity to swim there during Cape's cold winters.

"Hey Ranny, I don't think Johnny and I have ever even been to Smelterville to watch a softball game. Where do they play? Where do they go to school? They sure don't go to Lorimier, and I bet they don't go to your school either." I asked knowing that both of us were totally ignorant of where most anything was located there. Maybe we could find a grocery store, a school, a church, but nothing else. To us, it was also the way to the cement plant, passing the "blue hole." This was a huge, gigantic hole in the ground previously mined and evacuated by the plant and the *Blue Hole* drive-in restaurant, home of about the best barbeque this side of Memphis.

Ranny replied, "I don't know where they go to school, at least not at May Greene. Their diamond is right at the foot of the hill as you drive down. They play most every day late in the afternoon, and the games are good. The pitchers especially are really good. There are a lot of strike outs. You wanna go down and watch them?"

"Yeah, I guess we could, but I'm afraid we're going to have to get home for supper. Maybe next time." Johnny and I left, and during supper, I asked Mother about Smelterville, and asked if we could go down there to watch a softball game.

Her response was so typical, aware, but not concerned about the racial differences between us and its residents. She and Johnny's parents permitted us to refer to African Americans only as "colored."

"Why not, Gene. But be careful riding your bikes down Sprigg Street. There's a lot of traffic. I wasn't aware they played softball down there. Who told you?"

"Oh Ranny Young did. He says they really play good, that there's lots of people who watch 'em. Johnny and I wanna go there one of these days to see 'em play."

She nodded in her quiet, pleasing way. Neither Johnny nor I were particularly aware of the prejudices toward African Americans. We only knew we didn't go to school or church with them at our young age, and we never questioned it. It was just the way it was in those days.

The next week, he and I decided to go to Smelterville to watch the softball game. Ranny had told us when the game usually started, so we hopped on our bikes and pedaled down Sprigg, catching the first inning already underway. To our surprise, there was a huge overflowing crowd of people lined up and squeezed between each other on both sides of the diamond. One would have thought we were about to watch the first game of the World Series.

We parked our bikes in back of first base, sans locks. We didn't have any nor did we ever think we needed them in those days. The thought never even entered our minds.

Neither team had uniforms. Most wore no shirts with a heavy sheen of perspiration glistening off of their svelte bodies. None had spiked shoes on their feet. Some wore tennis shoes, many wore regular street shoes, and some were even barefoot. It didn't seem to make any difference, as their attention to the game was in total focus. They were there to play softball, not to be on parade or to be viewed and idolized as well-dressed athletes.

A strong westerly wind continued to blow unobstructed across the diamond with loose sand from the bare field whipping fiercely into the eyes and bodies of the players. None seemed to notice as they concentrated completely on the game at hand.

As we watched, looks of disdain appeared from those around us, especially those of our age, some a little older. We couldn't help but notice this attitude, but we were certainly aware we were the only white boys in the crowd of cheering and enthusiastic colored onlookers. We looked at each other with puzzling looks as to why they appeared to be such an unfriendly group of people. After all, we hadn't talked to or insulted anyone as we continued to watch the game attentively in front of us.

As the game wore on, the day's dying sun slowly disappeared in the west. There were no lights, but it didn't seem to bother them, although by around 8 pm, it became harder and harder to even see the game as each pitcher's fast ball became only a blur past the anxious hitters. Finally, in a spirit of complete agreement, the game suddenly came to an end. The score didn't seem to matter. They players laughed, shook hands, and left the field joyously and in a spirit of total camaraderie. The final score didn't appear to be of over-riding importance. They looked forward to another day and another game.

As we walked back to our bicycles, a group of young men, some of the same group that had continued to give us such nasty contemptible looks, stood dauntingly in front of our bikes, menacing and stern in their postures. For the first time, both Johnny and I began to feel a bit uneasy with fear slowly edging up our bodies. After all, as 12-year-olds, neither weighing more than 110 pounds, painfully skinny and totally white, facing boys larger and threatening, acting "cool" was out of the question. Indeed, we were scared.

"Hey, white boys, what y'all doin' down here?" Their apparent leader, a stocky, well-muscled boy who looked much older than us, by at least 10 years, moved headlong into our faces, his brown eyes peering down on us like laser beams.

Johnny answered quickly. "Oh, Hi. I'm Johnny Brussman, and this is my friend Gene Munger. We just came down to watch the game. That's all." Johnny's high-pitched young voice was hardly the voice of control. Knowing his as I did, I knew he was less than comfortable with the gathering. I stood by quietly with hands dug deep into my blue jeans and my face looking downward at the wind-swept sandy soil.

"Well, you guys don't belong down here. You hear? This is our place, so don't think about comin' back. Hear?" The leader's voice, booming as if coming from cannon, had to be heard by others leaving the field. Many stopped, came over and surrounded us. They obviously sensed a rumble brewing.

Suddenly, Johnny stood up straight from his somewhat cowering stance and responded loudly and defiantly, "Whaddaya mean, we don't belong down here? We just came down here to watch the game, that's all. What's the matter with that?" I shuddered at what would come next from the leader and his band of friends. Indeed, we were tottering on the brink of a fight neither of us were capable of winning.

To our surprise, the leader backed off a bit. His voice lowered and he replied, "Well we don't want you to come back. You're not welcome here. This is our place, not yours. You white boys go on and play up yonder. That's where you belong, hear?"

By this time, Johnny, now bolstered by his earlier bold and assertive voice, answered, "Okay, we hear ya, but why don't you guys bring your team up to May Greene and play us? We're pretty good too, and we think we could give you guys a good game. Do ya think ya could?"

"Hey, Buck, did ya hear what the boy said? They wanna play us up there at their place. Whaddaya think?" Buck's friend seemed to like the idea and sought their man's opinion. Others around him nodded positively, as they seemed to really like the idea.

"Well I don't know 'bout that. Maybe we could, but I don't know. I'd have to think about it. For sure, they ain't ever gonna be good enough to beat us. That's for damned sure! White boys ain't ever gonna beat us colored. Never!"

I chimed in to reinforce Johnny's offer. "We sure would like for you to come on up. Anytime would be fine. If you can and want to, gimme a call at 335-7898, my name's Munger, and my mother is in the phone book. We really would like you to play us."

The group looked at each other anxiously waiting for Buck's response. "Well, we'll see. We'll see." The group then turned away from us and walked slowly back across Sprigg mumbling to themselves, out of our hearing as to what they said.

"Johnny, I can't believe you talked back to that guy. What got into you anyhow? I was scared to death they were goin' to start beatin' us up."

"Well, Gene, my Uncle John told me never to be afraid of anyone, and I just figured I had to make a stand with those guys. That's all! I think it worked 'cause I think they will take us up on our offer to play us. Why, with players like Ranny Young, Ronnie Seitz, Jack Fowler, and Doots Garner, we could get up a good team and...."

"Maybe you're right, but you sure made a believer out of me, Johnny. I don't think I would ever have been able to talk to that guy like you did. Never. And did you notice we were the only white guys there, the only ones?"

"Yeah, but that was all right by me. It didn't matter. We went down there to see them play softball, and they played really good. I'm not sure we could beat 'em, but I bet they're not really sure about whether they can beat us, either. I think they will call you and come on up. I hope so."

Peddling back to South Middle in near darkness, we talked about watching the game, being confronted by those guys and at the end challenging them to a game with us at May Greene. We felt pretty good about the day.

We stopped at Johnny's house, and sitting on the porch with a cold glass of iced tea, I said, "'Ya know, wonder why those guys don't go to May Greene, even Lorimier or Central? What I saw was that they were pretty good players, and I bet they would be good in football and basketball. Wonder why the colored kids don't go to school with us? I'll ask Mother. She'll tell me. She'll know."

Editor's Note:

Cape Girardeau is made up of a number of distinctive neighborhoods. In the middle of the twentieth century when Gene Munger was coming of age, "Smelterville" was the most widely recognized of the ten or so neighborhoods in town. In modern times the region is simply referred to as "South Cape." In the 1940's and 50's the area was identified as the region along Sprigg Street south of Highway 74, and down to the quarry.

Although viewed as a single place, there were actually three separate entities that made up Smelterville: the Village of Girardeau, Leadville, and Smelterville. The entire neighborhood took its name from the failed attempt early in the century to establish a lead smelter between the railroad tracks and the Mississippi River. The combined population of the area varied widely, but in the 1950's ranged between 500 and 700 residents, in approximately 165 households.

Many of the houses in Smelterville had been constructed for the employees of the Hely Stone Company early in the century. Residents employed at the quarry paid a nominal rent to live in the houses, in the 1950's generally around $5.00 per month. The area had no sewers or water system, thus the community hand pump and outdoor toilets were accepted fixtures. To a large degree Smelterville was a community to itself. Many residents worked at the quarry, and walked to work. There were four churches, a ball field and nine stores to serve their needs. This was also the location of perhaps the most famous restaurant in Cape's history, the Blue Hole Barbeque. For a period of time the Holy Family Catholic church served not only the religious needs of the African-American population, but also sponsored an elementary school and a lunch program.

But, the most distinguishing characteristic of the region was its vulnerability to flooding from the Mississippi. Without a protective wall or levee residents frequently had to flee the rising waters, some returning to their former homes, others moving to new locations. Every flood changed the area, and there were many. Severe and long-lasting floods in 1951, 1973 and 1993 did significant damage to the area and eventually brought an end to the unique neighborhood.

Swimmin'

It was late August, another hot and sweltering day during Cape's summer of 1946. Johnny Brussman and I had returned from our first trip to Scout Camp Lewallen, survived our ordeal as Papooses during the camp's traditional Indian Day, and more importantly made Swimmer, swimming 50 yards in the St. Francis River during the waterfront's swim test.

John Brussman and Gene Munger swimming in the St. Francis River while spending part of the summer at Boy Scout Camp Lewallen in 1946.

Before we moved to Cape from Benton, we used to pedal our bicycles on the road running east, down the very steep hill leaving Benton on the way to First Ditch, a narrow, grassy-filled stream about two miles away. You couldn't swim since there was no open stretch of water. But as young boys, that never deterred us. We would strip off, naked for the world to see, run along the straight, sandy bottom stream and in a wild and uncontrolled leap, plop down butt-first in a clear stretch of shallow water. We affectionately called ourselves, the Bare-Ass Beach Commandos!

Every now and then when I was younger, my parents would take us over to the pool at Chaffee, about 15 miles from Benton. This was always a real treat. The pool, built during WPA days, was circular in shape, with the dressing room below the pool's deck. I guess it was there that we learned to swim. To our way of thinking, this was the ultimate in swimming pools.

But to Johnny's and my chagrin, Cape's swimming pool was a huge disappointment. We thought that all pools would be like the one in Chaffee. It wasn't. The price to swim was right, only 10 cents a swim, but the pool's bottom was always slimy, from the shallow to the deep end. After the experience of swimming in the St. Francis River, we were always begging my mother or Johnny's Uncle John and Aunt Nona to take us either "to the river" or even Chaffee where we could go swimming and escape Cape's slimy bottom pool.

Although we now lived on South Middle and so near the Mississippi River, neither of us had much of a desire to swim there. Neither of our parents would allow it, as it was strictly off-limits. While we would play along the river and watch the tugs towing their heavy barges northward, laboring mightily against the swift current, the thought of swimming in its turbulent, treacherous waters was never taken seriously. Maybe later, when we were older, we could brave its currents, but not now as 12-year-olds.

Three-Mile Creek soon attracted our interest. It was about three miles west of town along Route 61. We would bicycle out there and pedal northward for another mile or two where there was some clear, open water, not a whole lot, but enough for us to swim. Our folks weren't too happy about our pedaling along a busy highway, but we were always careful, staying well off the road and avoiding the fast moving traffic.

My phone rang that summer afternoon. It was Johnny's voice that cut through the humid air. There was sheer excitement in his words. "Gene, I've just found out about a new place to swim."

"Where?" I replied.

"Over by Ozark Packing. There's a creek over there that has a really good swimmin' hole. Ronnie Seitz was over there yesterday. He says it's really good."

Somehow, the idea of swimming near a packing house where cattle and hogs were slaughtered didn't sound too appealing. "Are you sure we want to swim there?"

My hesitant voice caused Johnny to counter quickly. "Naww, Gene, Ronnie says it's really good. There's a rope tied to a tree where you can swing out over the creek and dive into the water. It's deep enough, too. Wanna go over there today?"

"Oh, Johnny, I just don't know. But, if Ronnie says it's okay, I guess I'll go. We can take our bikes?"

"Sure. Come on down and we'll ride over there."

I didn't call my mother and let her know what our plans were. I was sure she wouldn't be too keen about our swimming in a creek down from and near a packing plant, but we could at least go over there and see what it was all about.

In a hurry, I gobbled down a peanut butter and jelly sandwich, downed a Fresca, slipped on my trunks over my jeans and pedaled down the street to pick up Johnny. He was ready to go.

Moving west along William Street, we crossed Highway 61, hoisted our bikes over a barbed wire fence, and pushed them through a weed-filled field to where Ronnie described the new swimmin' hole.

Cutting through the weeds, we saw a small clearing where we saw a bunch of other kids, none that we knew, playing and frolicking on the creek's dirt-packed bank. The water, looking almost stagnant, was muddy, deep dark chocolate in color, and a far cry from the clear waters of Three- Mile Creek, even the St. Francis River. Actually, absent the Mississippi's brisk current, this creek's water color looked the same.

Just then, one of the boys let out a Tarzan-like yell as he swung himself over the creek from a rope secured by a hanging limb from a huge cottonwood tree. His entry into the water was awkward and clumsy, but it received loud cries of approval from his friends. Johnny and I just gaped unbelieving at the sight before us.

"I don't know, Johnny. I don't know if I want to go swimmin' here."

"Oh, it'll be all right, Gene. Let's go in. It looks like a lot of fun."

We quickly pulled out of our jeans, walked warily toward the creek and inched ourselves slowly down the steep bank to the muddy water below. With a hearty lunge, I spread-eagled into the creek and swam swiftly to its center. Johnny followed quickly. We paddled around the creek, fairly wide and deep, too, for a spell before we got out and crawled our way up the slippery bank.

"Wanna try the rope now, Gene?" Johnny asked in a positive way. He was really excited about swinging over the creek like Tarzan.

"No, why don't you go first. I'll just watch."

Johnny retrieved the rope and with a determined push from his thin, skinny legs, propelled himself over the creek and with both arms reaching for the sky, yelling loudly, as he dropped into the muddy water below. He came up with a broad grin and shouted, "This is really great, Gene! Go try it!"

Heartened by Johnny's enthusiasm for his daring feat, I retrieved the dangling rope and made a cautious approach to the bank's edge. Frankly, I was somewhat scared, but Johnny had made it look so easy. I must follow.

With a firm push from the bank, I soared over the creek, dropped my strong grip from the rope and fell straight down into the water below. My fall didn't have the verve of my best friend, but it was all right. I knew I would do better the next time.

Throughout the afternoon, we improved our skill with the swinging rope, sometimes even actually diving head first into the water. Even those watching us appeared to be impressed with our courage and fearlessness.

We had had a great time at our newly found swimmin' hole. We would go back, for sure. But, it was not to be.

Over supper, I quietly informed my mother that Johnny and I had gone swimming over near the packing plant. Her response shocked me. It was completely out of character for her.

"You did what? You went swimming in that creek over by the plant? Is that what you said?"

"Yes we did. And both of us swung on a rope into the creek. It was really a lotta fun." I tried to be upbeat and confident, but I knew that what I had done wasn't to her liking.

"Gene, I've never been too happy with your taking your bike out to Three-Mile Creek, but I don't want you ever to go swimming at that creek near the plant. You have no idea as to what might be in there. You do know that they butcher cattle and pigs there, don't you?"

Suddenly, I understood. Johnny and I had a lot to learn.

Pin Boy

Johnny Brussman, my best friend, knocked lightly on the front screen door of our duplex on South Middle Street. Our neighbor Max Cumbie's petulant, mixed breed terrier yipped at him from behind the safety of his screen door. His staccato bark disturbed the solitude of the early fall Saturday afternoon.

The leaves from the street's regular line of maple and elm trees were just showing their fall dress of soft gold and brown. School had started. Johnny and I were classmates in the eighth grade at Cape Girardeau Missouri's Lorimier School. It was September 1947.

"Geeeene . . . Geeeene," Johnny shouted into the dark front room as he cupped his small hands around his mouth to increase the timbre of his call. "Are you theeeere?" he drawled in a slow, measured voice.

Johnny and I had grown up together in Benton. His Uncle John Hobbs, the sheriff of Scott County, and Aunt Nona had raised him. When Johnny's father died unexpectedly in the early 1940s, and his mother could not support both Johnny and his younger sister, the Hobbs took Johnny to live with them. Re-election didn't go Uncle John's way in August 1945, and they moved to the Cape and settled on South Middle. It was a middle class neighborhood bordered on the east by river bottom shanties with a scattering of low to middle income families living all around us. My mother and I moved there from Benton the next year when she and my father separated.

I was down in the basement when I heard Johnny calling. I yelled back as loudly as I could, but he didn't hear me. Hot water, when needed, had to be heated by a fire from the small, efficient stove in the basement, fueled by kindling and coal. One of my main chores was to build that fire and I was pretty good at it, too.

After a few more minutes, the fire was well on its way. I rushed up the basement stairs, ran around the house, and snuck up on my friend standing at the door. "Gotcha!" I yelled, as I threw my arms around his skinny waist. Johnny wheeled around quickly and started to pound his tiny clenched fists against my shoulder.

"Don't ever do that again, Gene," he screamed. "The next time you do, I'll really hit you." Johnny was about five and one-half feet tall, at least four inches shorter than I, and he weighed just over 100 pounds . . . 25 pounds lighter than me.

"I'm sorry, Johnny, I didn't mean to scare you. I was down in the basement. I yelled, but I guess you didn't hear me."

"No, I didn't, but, I mean it. Don't do it again. Let's go inside, I've got something to tell you." Johnny's demeanor had cooled considerably, but the way that he looked at me with his intense brown eyes convinced me he was no person to tangle with in a fight.

We went inside the house, through the first room, Mother's bedroom, past the stove that heated our place, my bed, and back to the kitchen, which was barely larger than the tiny bathroom. No one was home.

Mother was at the A & P buying groceries. Since she worked on Saturday mornings at the St. Clair Loan Company, she usually did her week's shopping before coming home. It was about 1:30 pm.

"Gene, the reason I came down is I've found a place I think we can get a job," Johnny said. Cumbie's dog continued its annoying bark. Maybe somebody else was at the door. Perhaps, Mother was coming home.

"Where?" I asked.

"At the Lutheran Bowling Alley. We can set pins. They pay ten cents a game. First, the bowler bowls his ball down a long lane, an alley. You sit up on a ledge while he does, and he knocks pins down. You put his ball on a kind of slide which returns his ball. Then, you pick up the pins and then put 'em in this steel rack right above the pins. When he finishes, you pull down the rack. It's mechanical, and it sets the pins perfectly for the next bowler. It's easy." Johnny's pin-setting description was accompanied by a series of animated motions which enhanced each step as he described it. While it was a bit confusing, the thought of making ten cents a game got my attention.

"I've never even been to a bowling alley, Johnny. When did you learn so much about bowling?"

"My Aunt Rosalie took me. She and her boyfriend, Bud, went there last night." The front screen door opened and Mother came through the three-room apartment carrying two small bags of groceries.

"Well, hello, Johnny. How's Uncle John and Aunt Nona?" Mother looked tired. Shadowy gray circles under her pale blue eyes stood out from under her eye glasses and offered a sharp contrast to her milky white skin. Nevertheless, she seemed glad to see me and Johnny there waiting for her.

"Oh, they're fine, Miss Munger, just fine. I was telling Gene that we can get a job setting pins at the Lutheran Bowling Alley. I've talked to Mr. Brunke, the owner, and he'll be glad to talk to us. We could work on Friday and Saturday nights."

"Would you like to do that, Gene?" She asked. "You know you can't work on school nights, only on the weekends." Mother had never compromised her rule that I stayed home during school weeks and that included going to movies.

Before I could answer, she started to unload her groceries and place them in the small wooden cupboards above the plain, one faucet-sink. We had no refrigerator, so any perishables had to be kept in a battered ice chest, a castoff from Uncle John's quail hunting days, on the screened-in back porch.

"Yes ma'am, I would. Johnny says that we can make a dime a game." Turning toward my buddy, I then asked, "How much could we make in a night, Johnny?"

"Oh, I don't know, but I bet at least a dollar. They were busy last night. Aunt Rosalie and Bud bowled three games and the pin boy made 60 cents. When they finished, two more bowlers came on and started bowling. I'd say that the pin boy made at least two bucks before the night ended . . . maybe even more!"

"Didn't you bowl with them, Johnny?" Mother asked.

"Oh, no, I just watched. It costs thirty five cents a game. Aunt Rosalie didn't have enough money for me to bowl; at least she didn't ask me to. But I enjoyed it anyway."

"When can we go down and talk to Mr. Brunke, Johnny? Can we go this afternoon?" I asked. The thought of getting a job and making money energized me completely. I wanted to get started as soon as possible.

"I guess so, but Uncle John's not home so he can't take us."

"Mother, can you take us? Can you?"

"Sure, I can," she replied, "But I need to get a bath. Did you remember to heat the water, Gene?"

"Yes ma'am, I did. The water should be hot by now. I'll take my bath later when we get back from seeing Mr. Brunke."

About an hour later, Johnny and I squeezed into the front seat of Mother's two-door Plymouth coupe. The fragrance of her sweet smelling hair and skin was a pleasing change from the car's worn and somewhat stale interior. My mother always smelled good to me.

The trip to the bowling alley was less than two miles through middle-class neighborhoods. The south side of Cape Girardeau where we lived was not considered to be the best place to live in town. Around the state college was much better. That kind of thing was not that important to me or my friends. Playing baseball and basketball and talking on the phone held a much higher priority.

The bowling alley was in the basement of the Lutheran Grade School, a huge red two-story brick building shaded by an abundance of well-spaced trees at the top of a long sloping hill coming up from Pacific Street. It was only one block south of Cape's main street, Broadway. I had never been inside the school, and when Johnny pointed out that there were bowling alleys in this massive building, I began to doubt him.

We parked behind the school. A softball diamond lay at the far northwest corner of the spacious lot. As we approached the building, we could hear the loud and exciting sound of wooden pins crashing against each other. I figured I could learn to set pins in a snap especially after watching Johnny's dizzying histrionics.

The three of us with Mother leading the way, entered the school through a side door, and walked down some wide steps into the basement. At the end of a broad, tiled passageway, the alley's entrance displayed a small neon sign that read BOWLING in bright, shiny red letters.

Entering, we saw Mr. Brunke standing behind a long, glass counter. Through the glass front we could see various bowlers' accessories, gloves, even a new bowling ball. To the right of the counter and against the dull, concrete block wall were four wooden shelves holding bowling shoes, their sizes shown by crudely marked black numbers on each shoe's heel.

Looking directly out from the counter were six bowling lanes with straight-backed oak benches available for seating behind each lane. Bowling balls, also to be rented, rested quietly on the return racks, top and bottom, like black cannon balls ready to be fired from a mighty cannon. Two bowlers continued their game on Lane #6. The rumble of toppling pins reverberating against the walls of the compact room sounded like thunderclaps echoing loudly across a nearby field.

Johnny stepped forward toward the manager and said with great confidence, "Mr. Brunke, my Aunt Rosalie and her boyfriend, Bud, were here last night. You and I talked a little. You said that you might be able to use some pin boys on the weekend. Remember?" My mother stood quietly by

in the background. She seemed to enjoy watching two 13-
year-old boys trying to get themselves a job.

"Why, yes, I do remember you. Your name's Johnny,
right?"

"Right, and this is my friend, Gene Munger. He's my
best friend, and we'd like to set pins here."

"Have you ever set pins before, boys?" he asked. Brunke
was small, barely taller than Johnny and weighing less than
I. He wore small wire-rimmed glasses perched precariously
on a narrow nose. His green eyes twinkled in Mother's
direction. He, too, was enjoying himself.

"No, but it looks easy. We're good learners, Mr. Brunke.
Just give us a chance. Please." Johnny, the experienced one,
was taking charge of this job interview. He seemed to like
being in control. I was confident that if anybody could get
us a job, Johnny could.

"Well, I think I can use you boys," Brunke said as he
leaned his bony elbows against the counter. "Now, follow
me and I'll show you the pits where you'll be working." The
manager led us down the right side of Lane #1 to our future
workplace. There, he showed us how the steel mechanical
rack that set the pins worked, and how you needed to avoid
being hit by fast moving bowling balls and so on. It was
essentially the way that Johnny had described. I felt a lot
better.

"Now, you boys don't need to know how to keep score,
but there's a few things about bowling you do need to know.
A game consists of 10 frames. Each bowler has two chances
to knock all the pins down in a frame. If he knocks them all
down with his first ball, that's a strike. If he takes two balls
to knock 'em down, that's a spare. The more strikes he gets,
the higher his score. Spares will help a bowler, too, but not
as much as a strike. If any pins are left after his second ball,
then you pull the rack down which sets up the ten pins all
over again. The rack works good, and you don't have to be
too strong to operate it. Got it?"

"Yeah, I think so," Johnny answered. "It looks easy. Is
that all there is to it?"

"That's right. That's all there is to it. Now, in the 10th
frame, it can get a little tricky. Listen closely. In the tenth

frame, a bowler can bowl two more times if he can keep striking. If he spares, he has one, and only one more chance. After he bowls that last time, then you pull the rack down. He's finished his game. He's all done."

"But, how do you know when the 10th frame comes around?" I asked. "Does the bowler tell you?"

"No," Brunke replied, "But you'll know. Just watch the bowler. If he keeps bowling after a strike or a spare, then you'll know it's the 10th frame."

"Sounds easy, Mr. Brunke, when can we start?" Again, Johnny assumed the lead and pushed to get an answer from our new boss. "How 'bout this evening?"

Brunke seemed to be stunned by Johnny's bold assertiveness. Such a presence must have been foreign to him, especially from a 13-year-old kid who weighed just a little bit more than 100 pounds. He paused a beat or two before responding. Pushing his slender fingers through his thinning hair, he answered, "Well, why don't you come down here about 6:30 this evenin'. We'll give you two a try at it. Let's go up front. I've got some more customers wantin' to bowl."

Walking quickly up the side of the alley, Johnny exclaimed, "We'll be here, Mr. Brunke. We'll be here." We couldn't have been more excited. We were being hired for a job, a job that paid money! To us, it seemed like a lot of money.

I spotted Mother sitting on one of the benches behind the empty Lane #1. "Mother, Mother, we gotta job! We gotta job! Mr. Brunke wants us back here by 6:30. We need to get goin'." Anybody looking at the grins on our faces would have thought that we had just won the lottery.

"That's wonderful. Sure, let's go," she replied nodding approvingly to the smiling Brunke. "You both need to eat. Johnny, why don't you eat at our house? I'll fix some hamburgers. Okay?"

"Great, Miss Munger, and I'll ask Aunt Nona if she can drive us back." I liked having him over for supper. He was my best friend. We returned to the car and Johnny and I crunched up beside my mother. She drove and we babbled all the way back home. The front seat's tight quarters didn't matter to us at all.

After a quick dinner of hamburgers and fries, Aunt Nona drove us to the alleys. We sat in the back seat of her four-door Chevrolet and felt like royalty being chauffeured to the Queen's Ball. Mother confirmed that she would pick us up around closing time at 10 pm.

Pinboys Gene Munger and Johnny Brussman strolling along Cape Girardeau's South Middle Street in 1946.

As we walked back into the alleys, there were already customers trying on shoes and getting ready to bowl. Brunke assigned Alley #3 to Johnny, Alley #4 to me. We took our places quickly like sleek jets catapulting off a rolling carrier's flight deck.

A man and his wife strolled over to my alley and started to bowl. Unfortunately, my charges were not very good. In her case, more balls found the gutter than the lane. He was a bit better, but not much. Bowling was definitely not their thing. I didn't mind at all. I was going to earn twenty cents for my work. Setting pins was exactly the way I thought it was going to be, and it wasn't hard work at all.

Near the end of their second game, I heard a steady scratching coming from the screened window in back of the alley. I looked back from my perch above the heavily padded backstop to see what was making the noise.

All I could see was some object, perhaps a coin of some kind being rubbed against the screen. Turning around, I spotted a face I thought I recognized. It was Alice Jean

Porritt, one of Lorimier School's eighth grade classmates and one of the prettiest girls in the class.

"Gene? Gene? What are you doing here?" She asked in a lilting, laughing voice. Hearing her voice, I knew it was Alice.

"Alice? Is that you? What are you doing here?" I responded.

My girlfriend was Dixie Lou Bader. I suppose that Alice Jean would be all right for a girlfriend, too, but Dixie Lou had been my choice the first day I met her in the eighth grade.

"I live right across the school yard, on Benton Street. Are you working at the bowling alley?" Obviously, she could see that I was. She apparently had been watching me set pins for some time. I wondered why she asked.

"Yeah, Alice. Johnny and I started working here this evening. He's in the next alley. We make ten cents a game. 'Ya ever bowled before?"

"Oh, gosh no, but I hear bowlers over here all during the week. They have leagues, you know. The parking lot is always full. You should hear them holler and shout. They're really noisy."

Alice stayed throughout the evening and we chatted back and forth as four bowlers came over to Alley #4 and bowled until closing. Between them, they completed 24 games. My arithmetic brought me to the realization that I had earned $2.40 from them alone. This pin-setting was going to get me rich quick.

Johnny was not so lucky. After only four games, Alley #3 remained vacant. He tried to talk to Alice Jean when I was busy doing my job, but her response to his conspicuous interest was lukewarm. She pretty much stayed put behind me for the rest of the evening. Having her there made the evening go by rapidly. I liked that . . . I was beginning to like her.

The alleys closed and just as I had reckoned, I made $2.80 for my evening's work. Johnny had made only forty cents. He wasn't very happy, but I was ecstatic. At this rate, I'd be able to buy me a new chain guard for my bicycle.

As promised, Mother met us outside in the parking lot. On the drive back home, Johnny sat jammed up against me and said nothing as he peered out into the night's darkness. I knew he was disappointed that he had made so little money, but I knew that it was just the luck of the draw. Skill or knowledge of the game had nothing to do with it. My fortune came about by pure luck, that's all.

As we turned onto South Middle from Morgan Oak, Johnny finally opened up and in a snarky, but officious tone of voice, said, "'Ya know, Gene, I know why Alice Jean spent all of her time talking to you."

"Why?"

"'Cause she knew that you were making all that money, and I wasn't making any."

"Whaddaya mean by that?"

"Well, that's just the way girls are, Stupid. They always go for the guys with the most money. Next time, I'll be busier than you and I'll be making the money, and you'll see just who she talks to then, you'll see. Girls are like that, 'ya know." I had no comeback for my friend's strong notion. What did I know about girls?

Mother drove straight ahead down the narrow street toward home, an understanding and caring smile beamed on her face. She must have had a hard time trying to hold back her laughter at Johnny's worldly idea that girls know that whether you're rich or poor, rich can sometimes be better.

Johnny and I set pins throughout the eighth and ninth grade, mostly on weekends, but sometimes, rarely really, on school nights when a substitute was needed. We became so good at our craft that occasionally when we'd work league nights, we'd hold down two alleys at a time. What would we make for such a monumental effort? Three whole dollars!

Earning money, big time money, for the first time in my life was very exciting to me. Once I started making it, I wanted more. The next summer, between eighth grade and high school, gave me more opportunities to do that.

River

The summer of 1948 was not unlike any other summer in southeast Missouri—hot, humid, and barely livable. As a young boy turning 14, however, summer was a wonderful time. School was out, we were going to scout camp, playing baseball, and having rubber gun fights. Nothing could have been much better than that.

Where we lived, South Middle, was a typical Midwestern street, with fully grown maple trees shading the sidewalk and the neat, always mowed yards. Neighbors would sit out in the early evening swatting at the omnipresent mosquitoes and trying to cool down from the day's heat and humidity.

Gene, at the age of 14, in Cape in 1948.

Along with my best friend, Johnny Brussman, there were lots of kids living on the street, some a little younger, but mostly our age. We were an active bunch, doing all the things that most kids would do in summer, but as in most neighborhoods, there was always the one boy who was the leader. Now, leadership is an admirable trait, but sometimes, that leader would and could lead his impassioned followers into places where none of us needed to be.

Our leader was Sonny Rowe. Sonny was a year or so older than the rest of us, a status that he felt was akin to being a king. We feared him, I guess, but he was a benevolent king. He wasn't a bully and would never pick a fight, but we weren't inclined to challenge him. He was no taller than any of us, but he was at least twenty pounds heavier and had muscles!

Sonny wasn't that great an athlete, but he'd always take his place as the pitcher, the quarterback, or be the first in the water when we'd go swimming. That didn't make much difference to the rest of us as he would always quit playing or swimming long before we were ready to quit. Then, he'd just sit on the sidelines and make ridiculing comments about our lack of skill or finesse. No one dared to counter with any kind of a comeback response suggesting that he wasn't so hot, either.

Our neighborhood's postman would always greet the king in his loud, friendly voice, "Why, there's Sonny Rowe. Sonny Rowe, from Webb City." None of us ever heard of Webb City, but we soon picked up the mantra, "There's Sonny Rowe from Webb City!" Sonny liked that.

Cape Girardeau's Municipal Pool was not very popular with us. There were two reasons: 1) it required a nickel to ride the bus over to Capaha Park and another dime to swim there and 2) the pool wasn't very clean. In addition to the slimy bottom, a nasty lifeguard kept watch and would never let us run along the sides while playing tag.

The Mississippi River was a distant option for us to go swimming, but our parents would warn us constantly, "Stay away from the river and don't even think about going swimming down there." We heeded their warning, but we'd sneak away sometimes and walk about a quarter-mile down to the river to watch the slow moving tug boats towing their flat barges up and down the river.

Occasionally, we'd wave to deck hands and yell out in loud voices, "Hey, how 'bout givin' us a ride?" They'd wave, yell something ugly back at us and then go on about their work.

The usual spring flooding period had ended, and the river had settled down to its normal course as July came in with an unusual burst of high temperatures. There was absolutely no breeze and insufferable humidity. Even the baseball diamonds became empty, as no one wanted to play. Swimming was the only way we could cool off since none of our houses had air conditioning, and the open window and fans gave almost no relief.

Sonny presented us with an idea to beat the heat. "Why don't we go down to the river and go swimming?"

Such a suggestion seemed like a great idea, but our parents' continuing admonition, "Stay away from the river and don't even think about going swimming down there," had been pounded into our heads over and over. But, it was really hot and we would be careful. Besides, we were both strong swimmers!

So, right after lunch, Sonny, Johnny, and I met behind Max Cumbie's house, which was actually the other part of our duplex where Max and his family lived. Then we slipped away to the river.

We figured that a good spot to go in would be just below the toll bridge connecting with the Illinois side. Our place was fairly secluded and since we had no suits, no one would see us. As Sonny started undressing, he stopped suddenly and announced, "No, I don't think this is such a good idea. I can't do it."

Johnny and I were taken aback by Sonny's abrupt change of heart. After all, he was our leader, the king. What was he afraid of?

"Well, I'm going in anyway," said Johnny as he quickly removed his T-shirt and started disrobing. "It's too hot. I'm going in." I undressed and with both of us in the Full Monty, we cautiously entered the water, slowly at first, and then dove together into the current. We were both good swimmers, at least we thought we were, and who would ever know or care what we had done? My mother would for one. She would have skinned me alive had she known!

Despite the river's flow appearing to be fairly benign, we soon found out that it was just a mite faster than it looked. We'd swim out directly perpendicular to the shore and before we knew it, we were at least 50 yards downstream from where we started. By the time we swam back to shore, we were 100 yards away from where Sonny was sitting quietly on the bank.

Fearlessly, we walked back to Sonny and chided him for not going in the water. "Aw, come on, Sonny. You're a good swimmer. Come on!"

"Naww, I think I'll just watch. Maybe next time."

We then spotted a log floating upstream from us. Actually, it appeared to be a telephone pole, and the river's force made it appear more like a torpedo launched from some lurking submarine.

"Hey, Gene, let's catch it as it goes by!" shouted Johnny. "We can ride it down the river."

Neither of us thinking, dove again into the brown swirling water, and swam boldly to head off the log making its way toward us. I reached our target first and after a few tries, mounted it successfully. Johnny then swam alongside and in one easy motion, hoisted his skinny leg over the log about six feet in front of me. Surprisingly, we both maintained our balance as the log twisted and turned continuously as if it were some wild, unbroken stallion trying to throw its rider.

And there we went, floating down the Mighty Mississippi, yelling loudly at a tug and its crew struggling upstream to tow a barge laden with sulfur, and waving to Sonny who by now was walking along with our progress and gaping at us. We ignored his "Get off it! Get off it!" as we were now merrily on our way, in the buff, to New Orleans, or at least we were heading in that direction!

Reality overcame our euphoria as the tug and barge's heavy wake caused our log to veer wildly up, down, and under the surging water. I yelled to Johnny, "I think we better get off this horse before we get thrown off! We need to swim back to shore. Don't you think?"

"Yeah, that's a good idea. Let's get off." We dismounted together in one rolling motion, both of our bodies going deep into the muddy water. The current was now much stronger. We were at least 100 yards from shore and it looked like a mile as we both came to the surface. We patiently, but steadfastly, swam toward shore at a 45 degree angle, sometimes resting by simply floating along with the current, but always heading to shore. Thoroughly exhausted, with red welts all over our bodies caused by the log's rough bark, we finally reached safety absent the vehicle that was to take us further south. Tramping upriver over a rock and brush-strewn shore, we met Sonny, standing red-faced with anger and pointing his stubby finger directly at us.

"You guys could have drowned! Did you know that?"

Johnny responded in a very condescending, but assertive voice, "Naww, Sonny, we weren't going to drown. We were just havin' fun. You gotta try it next time. We'll let you go with us."

We both knew there would be no next time. Those future logs would have to get to New Orleans without us.

■ ■ ■ ■ ■

Rope

The month of August 1948 was showing its familiar face in Cape Girardeau—traditionally hot, humid, and uncomfortable. Further adding to my suffering during the annual "dog days" period was the extreme fear of starting my freshman year at Central High School.

I don't suppose my fear was any less imagined than any normal 14-year-old adolescent boy, but to admit that to anybody, particularly my friends, was simply out of the question.

My experience at Lorimier School's seventh and eighth grades had been very positive. Starting in the fall of 1946, I had easily made the academic transition from Benton's rural school, a two classes per room environment, to the more sophisticated city school with its classes rotating among six teachers, a cafeteria, and an indoor gymnasium.

While Benton was only 16 miles south of the Cape, I was more or less a city boy anyway, since most of my classmates lived out in the country and were bussed into school. I may have been considered a city slicker to the farm boys and girls, but to my new buddies in the Cape, I was viewed as the "new kid who moved into town from the country."

My ego had been boosted tremendously in the spring of 1948 when Central's football coach, Robert Beard, gave me permission to participate in spring drills even though I was just finishing my eighth grade year. What a coach could see in a 125 pound, 6'1" gangling, clumsy, left-handed aspiring quarterback was of no interest to me. The important thing was that he let me try out and show what I could do. Frankly, I was overwhelmed by the experience and never really felt comfortable with the cultural and athletic change brought on by competition with boys three and four years older.

The competitive experience, however, was relatively uneventful. The squad never put on pads, scrimmaged only once or twice, and hardly broke a sweat before Coach Beard announced that spring practice would be terminated. There weren't enough players.

My mother was less than thrilled with my desire to play football. She never really said that I couldn't, only that she wished that I wouldn't. My father, who had separated from us two years previously, probably had the same concerns, but he never expressed himself one way or the other during the occasional times he would come to visit.

Of course, I believed wholeheartedly that all freshman boys went out for football at Central and to not do so would, in the eyes of my peers, be an unconscionable sin. I had no idea that high school freshman boys would ever seek other options. What else would there be? The band? The orchestra? The glee club? After all, if you weren't going out for football, you just weren't going to be "one of the boys."

Despite my tiny taste of what high school football was all about, I struggled with the decision to play or not to play all that summer. I was not that convinced I wanted to spend my next four years knocking heads in the fall with men in pads and helmets who were dedicated to hurting me and grinding my face in the dirt.

When the late August day came to report for fall practice, I didn't have the courage to walk those two short blocks from my house to the back side of the school to announce to

Coach Beard that his prayers had been answered. Rather than strut mightily in front of the other players and show them a freshman who was one tough guy, I started thinking seriously about playing the trumpet in the high school band.

My spirits and confidence rose and fell like a leaf caught by a restless wind. I would start out from my back yard full of hope and enthusiasm, but I wouldn't get very far before I would turn back and decide that it wasn't such a good idea after all. I repeated that indecisive action at least three times before I finally came to the conclusion that football was not for me. I was tall and if I were going to be a high school athlete, I would make my mark in basketball, and practice wouldn't start for at least two months.

Not reporting for football practice was one thing, but much worse was the awful vision of facing and hearing my friends' put-downs about what I had done. Would they call me a chicken? Would they tease me? I could not bear to think of the ill consequences of what they would surely perceive as cowardice on my part.

Starting to high school that fall brought none of the anxieties or the imagined rebukes I expected from my peers or classmates. They didn't seem to care. The fact I didn't go out for football was no big news to anybody, but my grateful mother was certainly relieved.

Making the adjustment from junior high to high school went fairly well. I joined the orchestra, even the marching band. After a few workouts I wondered if football was an easier alternative. Instead of studying right after school, I started playing a lot of basketball on the well-worn asphalt courts of St. Mary's High School or any place where a hoop could be fastened—to the back of a garage, a telephone pole, or even the trunk of an aging maple tree located at the rear of an abandoned warehouse.

I suppose that freshman year in high school had to be the most difficult time of my life. While I was able to mask my insecurity and attempted to present an appearance of calm and assurance to my peers and parents, my hormones were galloping at breakneck speed out of control through my rapidly growing body. My gangliness, accentuated by my size 15 shoes, was always a focus for ridicule among my friends. But despite all of those perceived inadequacies, my mind became haunted with the thought of my physical education class and Coach Louis Muegge.

Cape Central High School freshman Gene Munger standing by his mother's 1942 Plymouth in 1948.
Freshman year Gene and his friend, Johnny, faced the rope and Coach Muegge.

Coach Muegge was a legend at Central. A graduate of the University of Illinois, Coach had played as a starting right guard on the Fighting Illini team that saw the immortal Harold "Red" Grange achieve All-American recognition. From college, he came to Central in the early 30s where he coached football, basketball, and baseball with no assistants. This was all preceded by teaching five physical education classes and driver's education on alternate days. I suppose in those days such a schedule was customary. It would be considered completely unacceptable by today's teaching and coaching criteria. Coach Beard had been added to the faculty a few years earlier as his assistant, and 1948 was Beard's first season as the head football coach. Muegge, however, continued to coach basketball and baseball along with his classes.

Coach Muegge had banged up his knee playing football which left him with a disfigured left leg and a very pronounced limp. Despite his physical limitations, his students and players were forever enthralled by this under-six-foot man whose upper body strength was accentuated by bulging biceps on his blacksmith-like arms.

His bark, like the roar of a whirring turbine engine, could be heard from every corner of the practice field, the gym, or the locker room. His language, not altogether unfamiliar even to a high school freshman, was

Cape Central High School's Coach Lou Muegge.

liberally sprinkled with well-chosen expletives as he bellowed forth his exhortations and threats to those who would dare try to run around or disobey him.

Notorious, too, was the Muegge brand of punishment brought on by either freshman or senior who failed to follow his rules. That punishment manifested itself in the form of a canvas paddle. About 18 inches long and four fingers wide, its handle was wrapped tightly with white athletic tape. We boys never had a name for his tool of justice, but its reputation was indelibly etched in the mind of any student who had ever felt the sting and humiliation of the weapon's magnum force.

For sure, once victimized, you never again wanted to hear the words, "Okay, bend over and grab your ankles." Secretly, though, being hit by Coach's paddle was a true badge of honor to all of us students. The precious few who never experienced that moment were regarded as being "jellybeans" or wimps.

In my case, I always followed Coach's rules to the letter. If he dictated that the class was to run full laps around the barren practice field in a driving rainstorm, I would run them. If he ordered that lockers be cleaned out and replaced with clean gym clothes and towel, I did it. To say I was terrified of Coach Muegge was not accurate. Petrified was more the truth.

Even speaking to him was a painful experience. He had confronted me in gym class early that fall and asked me whether or not I intended to try out for the basketball team. "Hey, Munger," he yelled one fall day as I was finishing up my last lap, "Can I count on you to go out for basketball or are you goin' to keep playing in the band?" Hearing him call my name was scary enough, but how did he know that I was playing in the band? How could he have known that?

"Err, yes Sir, I want to," I responded meekly. I headed obliquely away from him as he watched the straggling runners dragging themselves around the track.

"Want to? Damn it, I didn't ask you if you *wanted* to, I asked you if you were *going* to? Don't you understand English?" Muegge's bronzed, wrinkled face took on a slightly reddened hue. He seemed to be angry at me.

I stopped abruptly, made a sharp about face, and walked directly toward the coach. "Yes Sir, I will try out. Yes Sir."

"Have you been working out?" Muegge asked.

"Yes Sir, every day, Sir. Every day. I think I'm in good shape, Sir." A feeling of uneasiness came over me as I figured that I had said more than I should have.

"We'll see about that." He then reared up like a grizzly bear waving its arms at some renegade misfit and cried out to a runner who had been caught cutting short the southwest corner of the field, "Hey, boooooooy. I told you to run full laps, not half. Now keep running 'til I tell you to stop." I didn't glance back as I ran at mach speed to the locker room. I had had enough of the coach for one day.

As summer's fading green colors evolved into autumn's golden hues throughout the gently rolling hills around the river town, our gym class days slowly moved from the practice field to inside the school gymnasium.

The gym, which had been built in the 1920s, was pitifully small. A wooden balcony surrounded the floor with a single row of permanently anchored wooden theatre-like seats providing onlookers a chance to see what was going on down below. Central didn't play any of its games there anymore. Consequently, the only people who ever hung out there were the curious—watching the girl's intra-murals and the men's basketball practices, or those hiding while cutting class.

Even at Lorimier School, I had already heard about the frightening and fearsome story of what happened when Coach Muegge brought the boys inside. There, you were expected to be able to climb a rope hanging from the ceiling without using your feet! In the minds of those ever taking boy's physical education classes at Central, this was the ultimate test, the only test to prove that you had the right stuff.

Although Coach Muegge now knew me as a potential member of his basketball squad, I had no illusions he would excuse me from climbing the rope. While I was tall, the strength of my upper body was comparable to that of a broken down block and tackle. In other words, I didn't have any!

Being fairly athletic, however, I had no trouble performing the other requirements for Muegge's gym class. Push ups, chin ups, sit-ups, swinging on the rings, those I could do fairly well. Obviously, I was not a candidate for the Olympic squad, but I could certainly meet his standards for every one of the exercises, except the rope climb.

In a short time, I became totally obsessed with my failure to climb the rope without using my feet. What was at stake here was my pride, my ability to show my classmates that this freshman boy, this skinny kid, could do it with the best of them. As the semester wore on, I wondered if pride, that resolve to accomplish, wasn't on a collision course with something I was finding out a whole lot about . . . reality.

From time to time, Coach Muegge would watch his students struggle with the rope, then move over to the hanging demon and order to the class to watch. The entire group would stop what they were doing and gaze at this physical marvel in silence and awe as he prepared to do his thing.

He would approach the rope, grab it with his right hand, swing his legs straight out perpendicular to the floor and in an easy, effortless display of physical strength and coordination, he would pull himself, hand over hand, up the rope until he reached the ceiling. In a sweeping motion, as if he were swatting away some pesky gnat, he would touch the ceiling's beam where the rope was secured and reverse his path quickly down to the floor. There, he would slowly look around and hearing nothing but silence, he would limp out the gym door, and disappear into his cramped, cluttered office.

Only when the door was closed would the spell of his performance end as the students joined into small groups and started a non-stop chatter of adulation about what the coach had done. Then, like swarming bees, they circled the rope and one by one, each would try to at least emulate what they had just seen. Some did, most didn't.

Seeing my mentor accomplish this herculean feat was depressing enough, but when I saw one of my peers do the same, I'd choke up inside, attempting to recover my will and then stride quickly over to the demon, brace myself, and start the climb. Like air being released from a balloon, my strength would instantly leave me. I wouldn't even get ten feet up the rope before my arms gave out and, rather than fall painfully to the floor, my long, skinny legs would rescue me and allow me to pull myself up to the top. This was my gym class's recurring ritual, always trying, never succeeding . . . always failing.

Johnny Brussman and I would spend at least some part of every day talking about the rope and our inability to master it.

"Johnny, I just can't do it. I've tried, but I just can't do it. I don't know what I'm going to do. What are you going to do? You can't do it either," I whined.

"Yeah, but I'm doing better than I used to. I can get about half way up there now. I think I can do it. I think I can." Johnny would answer in a much more confident tone.

"But the final is coming up in a week, and I know I can't do it," I retorted with even more uncertainty.

"Sure you can, you just have to try harder." Johnny's words were heard, but not believed. My attitude was one of total defeat.

The day of our final test came on the same day as my finals in Algebra and Latin. I had stayed up past midnight cramming for those two monsters giving little thought to the physical rest I needed for the rope climb and the rest of the exercises.

Our gym class was the last before noon. Johnny and I met at my locker at the start of the fourth period and, as if we were heading off to meet our executioner, we strode in a brisk, military lock-step down the winding steps to the gym floor, past the menacing rope, and into the locker room. We dressed silently and noticed that there was almost no conversation going on, a dramatic departure from the horseplay and levity that usually preceded the coach's roll call.

We moved neatly and smoothly through the other tests, saving the rope climb for last. Like a condemned man anxiously watching the sharp, shiny blade of the guillotine, our eyes never left the hanging rope and the many students, some victorious, some vanquished, pushing their bodies to the limits.

Our scores on all the other tests—push ups, chin-ups and so on—were recorded by the honor system. Whatever you did, you reported it to Coach Muegge whereupon he would record it dutifully on his sheet. There was no honor system, however, for the rope climb. He would call your name arbitrarily to let you know that you were next up, and once called, you would go over to the rope and start with his watchful eye viewing every upward movement you made.

"Mung, you're next!" Coach yelled as he marked the grade of a student who, with hands and feet straining, had climbed less than eight feet.

I gazed forlornly at Johnny as if my death sentence had been sounded. I walked over to the rope, gave a deep breath, reached high with my outstretched right hand, gave a strong leap, and started upward toward the ceiling.

My spindly legs churned vigorously in a bicycle-like movement in complete synchronization with my rapidly moving hands. It was as if I were treading water in some deep pool, only I was moving inexorably upward with incredible alacrity toward the iron beam holding my villainous foe. I touched the beam lightly, and with what seemed to be about three touches of the rope, I dropped downward and ended firmly at the feet of Coach Muegge. I had done it!

My whole being was on fire with the excitement and satisfaction of conquering the rope. I suppose I expected my classmates to join in sustained and wild applause, but no one even seemed to notice. They didn't care. My mentor's disappointing lack of response or recognition hit me hard. Didn't anyone give a damn?

"Okay, Brussman, you're next!" were the only words spoken by Muegge. "Let's go, you're the last one."

Johnny seemed to do even better than I, completing the rope climb with seemingly ridiculous ease. His broad grin clearly echoed his achievement as he signaled to me with his clenched right fist held high over his head. A winning World Series pitcher could not have been more pleased with himself.

We skipped off the near empty gym floor together in joyous commemoration of our victory not caring that what we had done was getting no more attention than carrying our books to class. We didn't mind. We were in our own beautiful world.

Later that day as the last bell was sounding, I was about to make my way out of Central's wide, swinging front doors when I bumped headlong into Coach Muegge. His strong, muscular arms grabbed me tightly and spun me around as if I were a piece of delicate balsa.

"Whoa there, Mung! Watch out where you're going." His strong, intense blue eyes met mine firmly.

"Oh, I'm sorry, Coach. I didn't see you," I replied. Totally embarrassed, I tried to break away from his firm grasp and escape this man who intimidated me so much.

"By the way, Mung. You sure went up that rope today. That was really good!" I could have melted at the sound of his glowing words of praise.

"Err, thanks, Coach. It was pretty easy." I said in a remarkably shameless and brash manner. "I gotta go now."

He removed his strong hands from my shoulders and with a slight push, sent me once again toward the front doors. I could feel his hand pat me softly on the butt as he said, "See you later."

I walked on air all the way back home.

Putzie

By the end of my freshman year, I had pretty much settled into the routine of high school. It was May 21, 1949, and classes were winding down at Central High School with less than a week to go. I was excited, but it wasn't because school would soon be out, it was because that evening I was escorting Barbara Putz to the Beta Alpha Delta/Sigma Alpha Sigma Spring Formal.

I wasn't a member of Beta Alpha Delta. I didn't even know what a fraternity was or what it did. Someone told me earlier that spring that Bill Mabry, one of my football playing classmates, had been asked to join. Since freshmen were almost never asked to join Beta Alpha Delta, some students thought it was a big deal. The only thing that I knew was that the Betas were made up mostly of upperclassmen, and as an anxious freshman, I wanted to stay out of their way.

Soon afterwards, I learned that Sigma Alpha Sigma was the girl's sorority, and a few freshmen had been asked to join. Like the Betas, most of the Sigma members were juniors and seniors. A freshman girl's selection was also rare.

I had settled into the high school routine very well that first year. I made good grades, and took Algebra and Latin, both considered tough courses, generally reserved for those students going to college. Not going to college was never an alternative for me. I had grown up knowing no other way. After all, I was going to be a lawyer, like my father. To be a lawyer, you had to go to college. Further, I had made the basketball squad and played on the B team that had done quite well, with 13 wins, only 2 losses.

Gene as a sophomore at Cape Central High School in the fall of 1949.

As far as having a girlfriend, I didn't. Dixie Lou Bader was my secret love, going back to the eighth grade at Lorimier School, but I was too shy to even ask her to go to a movie. Besides, I was much more comfortable hanging out with my friends who didn't have girlfriends either. Oh, sure, we talked about girls, those we would have liked to date, but most of us didn't have the backbone to even ask.

So when Barbara asked me to go to the spring formal, I was really surprised. Shocked is a better word. I hardly knew Barbara. She was in my Latin class and a good student, but I don't suppose I ever talked to her alone, even once.

Known as "Putzie," Barbara was short, easily a foot shorter than my 6'2" skinny frame, but very preppie in the way she dressed. She wore black-rim eyeglasses which matched her soft, moderately long jet black hair and also served to mask a very pretty and sensitive face. Perky, always smiling and pleasant, she was immensely popular with all the girls. However, none of the guys ever talked about lusting for her. I knew of no one she had ever dated, so I was somewhat confused. Either none of the Betas had asked her to the dance, or she figured that if she didn't take action soon, she'd end up staying at home. But why me?

I was studying for a Latin test when Putzie called late in April. I surmised she wanted to ask me a question about verb conjugations, noun declensions, or something like that. She had never called me before for any reason.

"Hello, Gene. This is Barbara Putz." Her voice was clear and upbeat.

"Hi, Barbara. How are you?" I answered in a somewhat prosaic manner. My seeming lack of enthusiasm probably did little to strengthen her confidence in asking a boy to a dance. In those days, it wasn't done too often.

"Fine. Uh, Gene, uh, there's going to be a formal dance coming up on Saturday, May 21, and I, err, uh, wondered if, uh, uh, you would be interested in going with me?" Barbara must have been embarrassed to ask the question. I had never heard her voice sound so insecure, so halting.

"Weeeell, Barbara, I'm not too good a dancer, at least I don't dance fast. I can dance slow, though." I doubt if she had Fred Astaire in mind when she asked me, but she quickly reacted positively to my obvious lack of assurance.

"Oh, come on Gene, I've seen you dance before. You're a good dancer. Besides, Herb Suedekum's band will be playing, and anybody can dance to him, you know." That sounded like a put-down to me, but at least she sounded like she wanted me to go with her.

"A real live band? Where's the dance at?" My interest was piqued. I had never danced to a live band before, only to records. Listening to live bands late at night on the radio from far away places like New Orleans and New York City had always sounded so exciting and romantic. Also, I had never been to a formal dance where the girls wore formals and the boys wore suits with ties.

"At the Marquette Hotel. We have it there every year. It's the Sigma Alpha Sigmas' and the Beta Alpha Deltas' annual dance," she said assuming that I knew all about those organizations. I knew that I wasn't a Beta, and that made me feel a bit uneasy.

"I don't know, Barbara. I'm not a Beta. I just don't know." My voice must have sounded like a man who had just lost his best friend.

"Oh, that's okay. You don't have to be a member of their fraternity, there'll be girls there who're not sorority members. It'll be okay. Will you go with me?" She wasn't exactly begging, but there was a certain urgency in her plea.

"Weeell, all right, Barbara. I guess so." My passive response was not because I didn't want to go, not being a Beta Alpha Delta man was more the reason. I wasn't a member and besides, those guys could probably dance fast, and I couldn't.

"Great," she replied, "We'll be double dating with Bill Engleman and Marilyn Andrews. He drives a car, you know." Bill played varsity basketball so I knew him. Marilyn, I didn't know. But having a car was certainly better than being taken by Putzie's parents. That wouldn't have worked at all for such an occasion.

"Thanks, Gene, it'll be a lot of fun. I'm glad you said yes. See 'ya in Latin tomorrow. Bye."

Since I had never gone to a formal dance, my mother, as mothers usually do, came to the rescue. We discussed what I needed to wear and so on. It was probably a big kick for her. She knew it was not only my first formal dance but my first real date in high school.

She suggested that I go to Knaup's Florist, a half block from our apartment, to order a red carnation corsage to be delivered to Barbara the afternoon of the dance. I did, and it cost me $2.00. That was a lot of money for a high school freshman whose only money source at that time was from setting pins in the nearby Lutheran School bowling alley or caddying at the country club.

Furthermore, I had only one suit, a navy blue wool number that my growing body had all but rendered unwearable. But it was all I had, and if I were lucky, the hotel wouldn't be too warm or uncomfortable. So far, spring had been a little chilly, but the last few days were showing the early warning signs of an approaching Missouri summer.

Word traveled swiftly among my friends that Putzie had invited me to the Beta spring formal. Their response was predictable, the kidding and chiding became non-stop. I tried to ignore them, but it seemed that they had all focused on me and my willingness to go to a dance when asked by a girl. I suppose it was jealousy and insecurity on their part, but I doubted that any of them would have been overcome with joy by being asked by Barbara Putz to go anywhere. Frankly, I was pretty jazzed about the whole thing even though I would never confide that to anyone.

Bill Engleman and I had talked about the dance, when he would pick me up and where I lived. Double dating with Bill and riding in his car with a date had me feeling pretty smug about the whole thing. I knew that he and Marilyn were going steady, and they even held hands in the hall between classes. I was fearful that after the dance he'd want to go out and park. Why, I had never even danced with Putzie, much less kissed her. It would be our first date, and I couldn't imagine sitting in the back seat of Bill's car necking away. I never had done such a thing, I couldn't imagine starting, either.

As that memorable Saturday afternoon wore on, I began to get very apprehensive. My suit was pressed, and although I didn't need to, I filched my mother's razor from the bathroom's medicine cabinet, doused my face with Camay soap and warm water and ran the double-edged blade over my tender face until it was baby smooth. I doubt if the razor had any effect, my face was totally devoid of any beard, not even a trace of stubble.

I went out in the back yard to check the weather and see how hot it was. Maybe I would be able to take off my coat at the dance. I decided I would if everybody else did. The late afternoon's air was warm and muggy without the slightest breeze. Darkening cumulus clouds hovered ominously in the west. It looked like it might rain. Maybe if it rained, it would be cooler. Then, too, it could be more humid and I would probably sweat a lot. That would not be good.

Suddenly, a roar like that of a fast approaching freight train filled the afternoon's stillness. The western sky brightened as if some celestial light had shined its radiance on the horizon.

The noise continued to grow in intensity. Perhaps, it was a freight train, but the trains around the Cape all traveled along the tracks paralleling the Mississippi River, about a mile east of where my mother and I lived in our tiny duplex apartment.

I rushed back inside where Mother was fixing dinner for both of us. The familiar aroma of spaghetti and meatballs filled the cramped kitchen. "Mother, come quick, there's a bad storm, or somethin's comin'," I said in my high-pitched voice.

We hustled out the back screen door to see the cause of my concern. Mother knew exactly what it was—a tornado—or at least she suspected as much. Tornados were a way of life, especially in the spring when she grew up in the farming towns of southeast Missouri's "Bootheel." But the appearance of the murky gray sky rolling helter skelter, out of control, caused her to stand there with her mouth wide open. She was speechless as she watched the awesome sight of a tornado about to spread its fury and devastation and descend against innocent and unsuspecting people.

Recovering her composure she said quietly, "Let's get back in the house. It looks like a tornado, but I'm not quite sure. It could be a bad storm, but it sure looks bad out there in the west of town." She reached for my hand and we scurried back inside and waited for the coming onslaught of wind and rain.

Even from inside our one-story brick building, we could still hear a continuous loud blare coming from the west, which gradually diminished to an almost eerie silence. Heavy winds and driving rain followed with unrelenting vengeance.

Taking control now, Mother led me to the northeast corner of the kitchen where we huddled closely together, our hands locked tightly in a vice-like grip. The one screen-less window vibrated fiercely from the storm. The lights dimmed and then went out. Although it was only 5 pm, darkness was upon us. It might as well have been midnight.

In spite of my paralyzing fears, my fantasies took over. The storm would soon pass, and I'd be going to the dance. Bill and Marilyn would pick me up and we'd go get Barbara. She'd be wearing a white, strapless evening gown with my expensive corsage pinned neatly on her. Everything would be just fine.

Reality returned as the storm showed no sign of accommodating the evening's plans. It had to stop pretty soon. I had to get dressed. I might even shave again.

Mother turned on the small radio perched delicately on a wooden shelf above her bottles and tins holding coffee and spices. Static made it nearly impossible to hear anything, only faint sounds of music and an occasional unintelligible announcer's voice. The local station, KFVS, spewed out more static. Mother was right. It was a bad storm. Perhaps even a tornado. What else would cause our radio to not work?

We sat quietly on the cold linoleum floor in the darkness of the kitchen for another 30 minutes, saying nothing and hearing only the pounding rain, wind and the continuing deafening static from the radio. Then, a faint voice broke through it all.

"Cape Girardeau has been hit by a tornado. We do not know at this time if there have been any injuries, but it has been confirmed that a tornado has just gone through the west end of town. Please stay tuned to KFVS for more details when we have them." Soft music followed in between the radio's incessant static, but no more news, at least for what seemed to be forever.

The announcer's voice returned, this time, a little stronger, but not much. "Emergency crews, police, firemen and rescue workers have been dispatched to the residential area north of Broadway along Perryville Road. We have just heard from an eyewitness who reported that it looked like the whole neighborhood has been bombed. There's not a house standing anywhere. We still have no report of any injuries, but judging from what he said, it's likely that there have been some."

"Volunteers are now needed to help out. They are to report to the police and fire station at Main and Independence at once. That's right, at once!" Then music came on again through the unending static as if nothing were in disarray.

"Should I go over there, Mother? I can put on my scout uniform and help out." Although only 13 years old, soon to be 14, I had already had first aid training in my troop. I could talk on the telephone, I could be useful, I thought. They needed me.

"Yes, you can help," my mother answered. "Yes, you can. Go over there and see what you can do. I'll stay here and keep listening."

On hands and knees, I crawled out of the kitchen down a narrow hall and into the front room where I slept. Groping through the closet, I pulled out my uniform, complete with long pants and shirt, neckerchief, and a garrison cap. After dressing quickly, I told my mother goodbye and flew out the front door into the night.

The rain had stopped. The wind, however, was still brisk as I moved swiftly over the four blocks to the police station. The street's gutters ran heavy with storm water, and tree limbs covered with spring's new foliage lay lifeless all around me. I could see no houses blown away so I presumed that our side of town had been spared somehow by the ravaging tornado. Street lights, dark only a few minutes before, started coming back on along the way. There was some movement of cars and sirens wailed poignantly in the distance.

I really felt important. I was actually going to be part of a team, a team of men responding to an emergency in our town. This was very heady stuff for a 13-year-old lad. Strutting like a drum major leading a marching band, I covered the short distance in quick order time.

As I approached the police and fire station, there were small clusters of men standing on the sidewalk with lighted cigarettes dangling from their mouths and talking in hushed and anxious voices. Inside the police side of the building, one could see larger groups, some standing, some huddled over tables, some peering anxiously up at huge street maps stuck to dingy yellow walls. Fire trucks, normally at the ready, had already left the building to go to the disaster scene. The emptiness of the engines' vacated space was scary.

Striding briskly past the men outside, I was the object of what I perceived to be some rather sneering and doubtful glances. I guessed they were wondering what a Boy Scout thought he was going to do to help. They weren't dressed in any kind of uniform, only work clothes, blue denim overalls, khaki pants and shirts. Some wore windbreakers, while some raincoats.

I didn't exactly know who to report to, but I spotted an older policeman with an ample belly and a haggard, worried face that mirrored the gravity of the situation. He saw me standing there looking at him like some young puppy craving affection.

"Whadda 'ya want, son?" He asked. Two other policemen brushed by the two of us as they headed out the station's double doors.

"Sir, I'm Gene Munger. I'm a Boy Scout from Grace Methodist Church's Troop 2. I'm here to help, if I can," I said proudly, standing at full attention and gazing directly in the policeman's weary eyes.

The cop stepped back as if to avoid a swarm of attacking bees and glared at me in a most disgusted way.

"What? What do you think you can do? We need volunteers, not Boy Scouts. Go on home, boy, go on home to your mother. She wants you. We don't need you here. Go on home." The officer did a hasty turnaround and headed back into the room scratching his balding head. I could see that he was not too happy with the situation. My eager, but obviously youthful appearance hadn't helped, either. I stood there like a penny waiting on change not knowing what to do. I realized I was not wanted. I would take my leave immediately and go back home.

I retraced my steps in a fast trot. It was now nearly 7 pm, and the neighborhood was aglow with lights. It was if everybody was having company.

I told my mother what had happened at the police station, about my humiliation and disappointment. She empathized with me, of course, but gave me little consolation.

"At least, you offered. That's all you can do," she said in a strong, reassuring voice. "That's all you can do." Her pale, blue eyes showed heavy fatigue. It had not been a good day for her.

I then realized I had not called Barbara about the dance. Perhaps there was still going to be one. I doubted it, but at least I could call. Our phone was still working. Maybe, I could get to her.

As I dialed her number, I wondered if she had been affected by the tornado. Mother had told me that the radio had reported that there were several deaths, twelve bodies had been recovered, and the tornado had veered eastward hitting part of the Red Star Subdivision before it blew out of town across the river and over into southern Illinois.

After two short rings, Mr. Putz answered. I had never met him, but it didn't matter, I had to talk to Barbara. "Hello, Mr. Putz, I'm Gene Munger. May I please speak to Barbara?"

After a long pause he answered in a gruff voice, "Just a minute." Then I heard him yell, "Barbara, it's Gene Munger! But don't stay on the phone. I need to call your grandmother."

Barbara's spirited but caring voice gave me a rush. "Oh, Gene, isn't it awful? Are you all right? We weren't hit here, just a few tree limbs down in our back yard. Are you all right?"

"Oh, we're fine. Nothing really bad over here. I went down to the police station to try to help, but they didn't need me. At least, not now. Maybe, later." I don't know why I said that, it wasn't quite true, but then, maybe, it could be tomorrow or the next day. "I guess the dance has been called off?" I asked. "Right?"

"Yeah, it's been called off. I imagine with school nearly out they won't have it this year." Her voice sounded distressed, but it quickly elevated to a new vibrancy. "Oh, your corsage arrived this afternoon and the flowers are beautiful. They're so pretty. Thank you so much. I'm keeping them in the refrigerator."

Hearing her now on the phone, so fresh and lively, would have never led someone to believe that there had been so much death and destruction affecting our town and people's lives only a few hours before.

"I'm sorry, Barbara. I was really looking forward to going to the dance with you. I really was. But, the tornado, you know and . . . ."

"Maybe we can do it another time, okay?" Barbara replied. "There's always next year." Her hearty laugh brightened up what had been a very painful day for me.

"Right! There's always next year and maybe by then I will know how to dance fast. I'm going to work on it!"

Author's Note:

The 1949 tornado was devastating to Cape Girardeau . . . millions of dollars in damage, 22 people killed. As for Barbara Putz, we never went together to another dance. I never dated her. As I recall, she and her parents moved to St. Louis in her junior year. I shall never forget her, however, and how she gave me confidence at an age and time of my life when confidence was in somewhat short supply.

■ ■ ■ ■ ■

The Summer of the Eagle

Scouting became a major part of my life after I moved to Cape Girardeau. Actually, its influence began in those early Benton days. My first exposure to scouting was in 1944 when Benton formed its first scout troop, Troop 25. I was ten years old, two years away from being able to join.

Most of my buddies were already twelve, which meant that they became scouts and I waited patiently, almost fervently, to leap ahead in time and space to join their ranks. I didn't leap, but, oh, how I wished I was old enough to wear the uniform, go on hikes, camp out under the stars and above all, spend a week at Camp Lewallen, a sprawling acreage nestled in the Ozark Mountains along the banks of the St. Francis River about two and half hours from Benton.

I suppose one of the saddest days of my young life was when the boys of Troop 25, all ten of them, led by Scoutmaster Hess Porter, Scott County's Treasurer, left in three cars that sweltering summer Sunday morning to spend a week at scout camp.

For some reason, I held out hope that at the last minute a miracle would happen and Mr. Porter would rescue me from my travail, order me to go home quickly, pack my bags and join the troop for its impending adventure. Alas, it never happened. I prayed silently and lingered patiently at curbside as I helped my friends cram their battered trunks and duffel bags into the trunk spaces of worn out cars that bore mute testimony that World War II was still going on.

When they returned the following Sunday, they babbled for days, for weeks, about the wonderful and exciting times and fun they had sleeping in tents, eating in a mess hall bigger than the county courthouse's main courtroom, swimming in the St. Francis River, going on a fourteen mile hike, wearing a loin cloth and dressing up like an Indian, singing new songs around a campfire, and meeting new friends from such far away places as Poplar Bluff, Sikeston and even Caruthersville—all towns larger than Benton and at least 60 miles away. Wow!

The next year before I turned twelve seemed to take forever to pass. I was growing tall for my age, and seized every opportunity to do things with Troop 25. I attended every meeting, memorized the Scout oath, laws, could do all of the requirements for the Tenderfoot rank, slept outdoors under stars in the back yard of my friends and generally became a pest in my futile effort to find some way to slip in under the rules and join the scouts before the magic age of twelve.

Just after my twelfth birthday in late June 1946, my life changed enormously. My parents separated; Mother and I moved to Cape, while my dad stayed in Benton. To a 12-year-old boy, there is probably no greater trauma than living through his parents' separation. There was no peace, no happy times for me, during these two years. My parents argued constantly, my attorney father drank heavily, and he was carrying on an open affair with his secretary, or at least, it appeared to my friends that he was. They constantly taunted me with jeering accounts of her driving in his car around town with her four-year-old daughter. I, too, had seen that, but I tried to erase it from my mind and pretend that it wasn't happening. It was and it affected me greatly.

Hearing this from my peers was humiliating. There seemed to be no escape from my misery, therefore, when my mother advised that she was leaving and taking me to live in Cape Girardeau, I was secretly happy. I would be getting away from my torment, but was there a Scout Troop in the Cape? Would I be able to join when I didn't know anybody? Would I finally be able to go to Camp Lewallen?

Before we moved to the Cape in August, I went with Troop 25 to Camp Lewallen that July and did all the things that I had dreamed about doing, including dressing up like an Indian and being part of Indian Days.

First year campers at Lewallen were called Papooses, second year campers, Braves, and third year campers, Warriors. As part of Indian Day, we Papooses, with only a blanket, a loin cloth and two matches, were led in single file deep into the woods along a winding, dusty path. We were then staked out separately at some ill-defined campsite, ordered to remain silent, build a fire and keep it burning until we were picked up at the end of the afternoon.

I was terrified at the prospect that my fire wouldn't start. I had never built a fire in the woods before or, for that matter, anywhere else. One member of my troop announced that he intended to slip a can of Sterno in his blanket to help him get through the ordeal. Doing that would be too scary, as I might get caught. However, since I had never built a fire in the woods before, and there would be no paper or kerosene to help with my challenge, I became obsessed with doing it.

Fortunately, one of the troop's warriors clued me in on the how-to. All you had to do was gather up a bunch of match size sticks in the woods, and with your match, light the small sticks. It was just that simple, and it worked. I had no problem at all, although, the long day's wait in the woods, encumbered by an unrelenting July sun, was just that, a long day in the woods. As for the requirement to not talk, the heavy, humid sweltering day easily filled that void.

Braves, dressed the same way, occupied themselves by participating in camp projects such as repairing and upgrading the camp's hiking trails or building a stone wall around the chapel. It was strictly a work detail, but the workers were a bunch of 12 to 13-year-old boys wearing loin cloths and two chicken feathers held in place by binder's twine tied around their heads.

As for the Warriors, they had to demonstrate strength and stamina, both required characteristics for campers of such seniority and prestige. With a 10 pound rock—the Ozark Mountain foothills had lots of those—they were made to go on a forced hike of five miles carrying their rock over and through poorly marked trails, not stopping to rest. The rock was never to leave their side during the day, a demonstration of the human spirit's perseverance in the face of a continuing hardship.

At the end of Indian Day, all of the campers, Papooses, Braves, and Warriors were led to an evening campfire in the hallowed circle of the Indian Campfire Ring where all were extolled for their participation in the day's activities. Later, all left the ring except the Warriors and of course, the old Warriors, senior and experienced campers. At that time, the Warrior's rock was finally dealt with in an impressive secret ceremony that only those remaining would participate in. No one would ever reveal what went on. It was a sacred trust of silence, never to be broken.

To a 12-year-old country boy, the impact of Indian Day with the ceremonial Indian Campfire Ring, being at a scout camp for a week and meeting other scouts from all over southeast Missouri, was awesome! I couldn't wait to tell my folks. I couldn't wait to come back next year so I could be a brave.

And I did come back, year after year to Camp Lewallen, but from another venue, Troop 2, sponsored by Cape's Grace Methodist Church. There I settled in comfortably and continued to pursue my boyhood dream of becoming an Eagle Scout.

During the 1949 summer, I became unwittingly ambitious and tried to complete too many of those required merit badges in the one week of summer camp. I attempted the pioneering, camping, bird study, canoeing, swimming, and lifesaving merit badges. By mid-week, I was completely exhausted and was no way near nailing down any of them. Additionally, I had become the laughing stock of my troop, especially from my contemporaries who chided me unmercifully for what I was attempting to do. By Thursday, I had dropped out of all my classes with the exception of swimming and lifesaving. I did complete them successfully, but all of the others ended up in failure. I was totally crushed. While disappointing to me, it taught me a valuable lesson: stay within yourself.

After camp in 1949, I bore down and finished the remaining merit badges that could be obtained locally, becoming a Life Scout. I then set my goal to return to

Lewallen the next year and finish what I had started to do, the final step, to become an Eagle Scout.

Scout camp in those days was really a bargain for most of us. For $12, one could spend a week at Lewallen, meals, and lodging furnished, filled with swimming, camping, hiking, and everything a scout would want to do. I knew that Troop 2's week there would not be enough for me to complete the required bird study, camping and pioneering merit badges for Eagle, two weeks, maybe.

I approached Mother with my dilemma, and she agreed to send me to camp for a month. I could use the provisional scout troop option for the three weeks after Troop 2's encampment, and that should be sufficient time to wrap up all my needed merit badges and who knows, maybe even pick up canoeing and rowing merit badges.

I look back with great admiration and wonder on Mother's generous gesture. While it was only going to cost $48 for the entire time, plus a few extra dollars for spending money, her $100 a month salary as a secretary for an insurance adjustor could only be stretched so far. How did she manage to do that?

The month at Lewallen was sheer delight. I completed all my requirements easily, even getting the canoeing and rowing badges. I had made Eagle Scout! Being selected for the Golden Sun, the Council's honorary camping fraternity, further honored me. I even entertained the idea of working at Lewallen the next summer as its Assistant Waterfront Director. I was so uplifted by my success that I started thinking about making a career in scouting.

The Eagle Ceremony was scheduled for the last Tuesday in September in the Little Theatre on the campus of Southeast Missouri State College. I had attended many Eagle Ceremonies before and knew they were the last item of business at the Court of Honor. The Court recognized a scout's advancement to Second Class, First Class, Star, Life, and when appropriate, Eagle. In between, those completing merit badge requirements were also honored.

It was customary for the Eagle candidate's parents to attend the ceremony, with the candidate's mother pinning the Eagle Award on her son's chest. I looked forward to that, however, having my father there presented a serious problem to me.

My father was an alcoholic, did not live with us and visited me only sporadically since we had moved to Cape in 1946. Those few times he came on the scene to visit me in front of my peers at parades, sporting events and so on were always embarrassing to me. My uneasy feeling was caused not only from my friends knowing that he did not live with me, but also by his scruffy and unkempt appearance and the omnipresent scent of stale alcohol permeating from his body and breath. I wanted to vanish from the earth when I saw him on those occasions.

There really was never any question about asking my father to come to the ceremony. My mother made the decision that he would be invited. I imagine she made it plain to him that she expected him to be there, but to be there sober. She would not want her son humiliated by his drinking.

Dad arrived around 5 pm the afternoon of the ceremony. He had no automobile, utilizing the option of a Trailways bus from St. Louis to Cape, a distance of about 120 miles. He looked fit, dressed smartly in a blue, tropical worsted suit with a matching polka-dotted blue tie, and he was completely sober! It was the best that I had seen him look in the past several years. I was silently relieved to see his improved appearance.

Our conversation was cordial, although somewhat strained. After all, there had been few times in recent years that the three of us had engaged in any kind of family togetherness. The last time that I could remember was Dad coming to take us to dinner on Mother's birthday, an evening completely ruined when a leaking bottle of whiskey had dribbled out of the glove department on her new, voile dress. She was furious and demanded to be taken home. The night ended, sans Daddy, returning to our apartment and eating leftover macaroni and cheese.

My mother had completely surprised me earlier by presenting me with a sash containing all my merit badges, by this time twenty-six, and ranks achieved in my four scouting years. I was ecstatic as I had never had a sash. I had never expected one.

After a light dinner of chicken salad and iced tea, we squeezed ourselves in Mother's 1942 2-door Plymouth coupe. I was impressed when my father moved deftly around my mother and opened the door for her as she got ready to take her place at the wheel. He did the same for me as I slid my 6'3" slender body into the back seat.

When we arrived at the Little Theatre, the small room had already filled up with lively, well-scrubbed, uniformed scouts and proud parents. The other Eagle recipient was a classmate of mine, John Stehr, but from a different troop, Troop 8, sponsored by the Trinity Lutheran Church. We exchanged pleasantries and the introductions of both of our parents were made with kudos showered on John and me. I was anxious about the looming ceremony.

The Court of Honor moved swiftly. Scouts bounded back and forth onto the small, compact stage to receive their respective awards. There was a short break prior to the Eagle ceremony.

Representatives from the national Boy Scouts of America (BSA) fraternity, Alpha Phi Omega, now took control of the evening. Both were students at the college, both were friends of mine, Don Morgan and Sam McClanahan. Sam had been the waterfront director at Lewallen during the summer and had awarded me my canoeing and rowing merit badges. Three years later, we teamed up as instructors at the BSA's National Aquatics School at Osage Beach, Mo.

The team briefly described the significance of the Eagle Award, its requirements and what it meant to achieve the Award. The room was very quiet, lighted only by four long, tapered white candles representing Duty to God, Country, Others, and Self.

And then, Sam's strong voice resounded loudly over the hushed throng sitting stone silent below him, "If there is any person here this evening who would object to either of these two candidates receiving the Eagle Award . . . please speak."

My heart felt like erupting mightily out of control from my chest. Was there anybody here who would object? Had

I done something in my past that would disqualify me from this coveted award? The room remained silent.

"Therefore, it is our honor to award the rank of Eagle Scout to John Stehr, Troop 8, and Gene Munger, Troop 2. Will the mothers of these scouts please pin the Eagle badges on their sons?"

Morgan and McClanahan walked across the stage and presented the badges to our mothers. With one easy movement, my mother reached over and pinned the badge on my left pocket, perfectly balanced, exactly where it should have been.

"I love you, Son," she whispered softly. Tears streamed from my eyes as I reached for her and held her tightly against me.

"I love you, too, Mother. Thank you for all you've done for me."

I then started to shake my father's hand, but he surprised me with a strong, bear-like hug, not saying a word. I could feel his body quiver, almost shake. I had never experienced my father showing such emotion.

Eagle Scout Gene Munger in September of 1950 after receiving his honors at the Court of Honor.

The audience's applause broke the spell of the moment. Our parents again congratulated each other. It was a proud moment for all of us. I was totally exhausted from everything that had happened to me. I wanted to go home.

We returned to our apartment where Mother fixed coffee and served her famous coconut cake, my favorite. She wrapped up a good-sized portion for Dad to take with him. His bus was scheduled to leave for St. Louis at 10:30 pm, so there wasn't much time to visit.

He asked me to walk with him to the bus station, only two blocks from where we lived. The evening was pleasant. Fall's briskness had not appeared, but the coolness around us signaled that summer was about over. Our walk turned into a leisurely stroll, and Dad was clearly excited about the last few hours as his mood was cheerful and positive.

As we approached the station, he stopped suddenly, turned toward me and said, "Son, I have something to tell you."

"What is it, Dad?" I asked.

"Well, I've joined this club in St. Louis, the 4524 Club."

"What kind of a club, is it? Do they play cards? What do they do?" I felt like some interrogating lawyer bearing down on some recalcitrant witness.

"No, it's not anything like that," he replied, "It's a group of men and women who have stopped drinking. It's Alcoholics Anonymous. Have you ever heard of it?"

"Yes, I think so. But what does the club have to do with it?"

"Well, the club is a place that we go to have meetings and work together to not drink. Understand?" My father's voice was almost at a whisper now. He seemed to be awaiting my approval for what he had done but careful not to be heard by anyone else.

"I see. Will you ever drink again?" I responded.

"No, I don't intend to. I've quit for good."

I was at a loss for words. I had not seen my father sober for most of my adolescent years. While he was never out of control, I always knew that he had been drinking . . . I just knew.

Weakly, I finally said, "That's nice, Dad. That's real nice." Such a response undoubtedly was not what he was expecting, but it was about all I could muster for the moment. "Thanks for coming, Dad. I really appreciate your being here with Mother and me this evening."

Before he could say goodbye, I turned quickly and headed back to the apartment. Suddenly, I stopped and yelled back to my father, "When are you coming back, Dad? Maybe we could go fishing."

"Soon, Son. Soon." He was waving to me as the diesel-powered bus, bellowing its black smoke into the night air, turned onto the badly crumbling concrete driveway to pick up its late night passengers.

I waited there for only a brief moment as he ducked behind the rough idling bus and quickly took his seat among the tired travelers. He opened the window and yelled again to me, "Take good care of your mother, Son. I love you."

"I love you, too, Dad. I love you, too!"

My hopes soared as I walked back to our apartment. My mind raced forward with anticipated pleasures, the complete pleasure that perhaps, just perhaps, my dad and mother would get back together again. With his not drinking anymore, they wouldn't have to argue. They would get along and we could all live together. We could go fishing. For those few, fleeting moments that late evening in the early fall of 1950, I wished so hard that it would happen. Regrettably for me, it never did. It was never to be.

This was the summer of the Eagle, the summer I began to regain love and respect for my father a huge step in my young life.

Typist

Southeast Missouri's hot sweltering summer began to show signs of submission as an unseasonably cool and refreshing breeze offered relief from Labor Day's late afternoon. It was 1950. School would start the next day and I would be a junior at Cape's Central High School.

My summer had been delightful. I spent a month at Boy Scout Camp Lewallen in July and completed my requirements for the Eagle badge, one I would receive later that month. My cup brimmed over with happiness. Life was good.

Mother and I spent a quiet Labor Day together. We both figured it was better to pass up the traditional Labor Day picnic rather than fight the crowds down at the Knights of Columbus' grounds. We decided to stay in our cool, fan-filled three-room apartment. Instead of hot dogs, Mother fried chicken and surprised me with watermelon, my favorite summer desert. Actually, all deserts were my favorite. I was sixteen and most any food placed before me more than satisfied my hunger. I was always hungry.

My happy thoughts turned to the opening of school the next day. "Say Mother, whaddaya think about my taking typing? Do you think I should?"

My previous two years' classes had been directed toward a college curriculum, e.g., Latin, algebra, and geometry. Many had the attitude that typing was a girl's class necessary for those who wanted to become secretaries in an office somewhere. Just taking typing, I knew, would be heavily criticized and thought of as "sissified" in my friends' eyes.

"I think that would be a good idea, Gene," Mother replied. "You will be able to use it all your life. Knowing how to type gave me a much better job opportunity. I type every day for the Bert Strubinger Insurance Agency."

"When did you learn to type?"

"Don't you remember? Don't you remember having that big sheet with the typewriter keyboard printed on it and having it displayed in our living room in Benton?"

"Yes, I think so. I remember that big paper keyboard plastered against the wall and listening to you striking its keys slowly at first, but getting better and faster each day. I remember now. Do you still have that big typing sheet? Wait a minute. We don't have a typewriter here. I'll need one, won't I?"

My queries brought another smile to Mother's face. "No, I don't have the big sheet anymore, but you won't need it. As a matter of fact, you can go to my office and practice there on my typewriter on Saturdays. Besides, you can probably get all the practice you need in the class. I doubt if any of the other students have typewriters at home. You'll be okay."

Hearing Mother's encouraging words buoyed my outlook, but I knew what my friends would say when they found out I was going to take typing. They all thought typing was for girls and I'm sure it was their mind-set at that time as I entered my junior year.

Students hangin' out outside of Cape Central High School in the spring of 1951. Pictured from left to right are Carolyn Beckwith, Jane McNeely, Mary Alice Bauerle, Alice Jean Porritt, and Gene Munger.

The first day back in high school after summer vacation was always exciting. Everyone seemed to be in good spirits. The girls looked their best wearing chic summer clothes with their hair done in the latest styles. Most of my friends were reluctant to dress stylishly although most had no money to do so. Instead, they donned their classic attire of blue jeans and T-shirts. There was a whole lot of catching up since we hadn't stayed that close during the summer. Aside from a few vacation trips with parents, the gang hadn't done anything too exciting, mostly baseball and swimming. This was the new school year, and we were going to be juniors, not quite as important as mighty seniors, but much more important than lowly freshmen and sophomores.

"Hey, Gene, are you going to take physics this year?" Al Huter's serious well-modulated voice pierced the cacophony and babbling voices emerging from Central's crowded sidewalks. During good weather, this was the usual meeting place. As the days grew colder with winter's omnipresent rain and snow, we fled the outdoors and jammed ourselves into the narrow halls where our wall-lined lockers prevailed among prodigious laughter and discordant conversations.

Al was a brain. He seemed to know a lot about chemistry, anything science related. He was the antithesis of a sports-minded person like me. I knew I was going to college, but I wasn't too keen on taking advanced science courses. Taking the General Science course looked to me about right, although, I figured I would eventually take chemistry and physics in my senior year.

"Naww, Al. I don't think so. You?"

"Oh, yeah, I can't wait to take physics. Mr. Blumenberg is a great teacher and I'm also taking chemistry. He's teaching that, too. Say, what will you be taking?"

"Err, uh, I think, English, government." I was sure that response would bring a frown to Al's face since no science courses were being considered. It did.

"Yeah, but what else?" Al added in a somewhat disbelieving tone of voice.

I was afraid to tell him I was thinking seriously about taking typing, but I figured it wouldn't hurt. In an almost inaudible whisper, I said, "I'm thinking about taking typing."

Al's uncharacteristic strident response to my choice was met with "Typing? Surely, you're kidding. Typing is for girls."

Just then, one of my basketball teammates, Walter Joe "Doc" Ford moved in between Al and me and exploded in a thunderous voice, "Typing? You're going to take typing, Mung? I can't believe it!"

Hearing my plans didn't quiet him at all as he turned to others standing by him and yelled, "Mung's taking typing. Did you hear? He's taking typing. Hey, isn't that a girl's class? Will you be wearin' a dress to class, Mung?" Heads turned, both boys and girls, at the sound of Doc's loudmouthed voice. I wanted to disappear from view and escape to another planet.

"What do you know about typing, Doc? The reason I'm taking it is because I need it in college when I start typing all those term papers. Besides, it will be fun to learn." I was proud of my response, but I wasn't quite sure it was making a strong case for him and others.

"Well, go ahead. You'll look swell, really swell in a dress, Mung." Others around us howled with laughter.

Undaunted, I made plans to enroll in typing class. I would show them that learning to type was no exclusive girl's thing. I was determined. The remainder of the morning was spent registering for the first semester's classes. Since I had done well in geometry, I also chose Trigonometry and to my satisfaction, typing.

Word traveled swiftly among my friends that I had signed up for Typing I. Their incessant ribbing followed me throughout the halls and after school. I felt like some pioneer about to take the first orbit around the moon.

Band practice on Monday, Wednesday and Friday and orchestra on Tuesday and Thursday at the school's annex started each day, always a pleasure for me and my French horn. Could I do it? What would the girls think? Would I be able to keep up with them? I would soon find out. The second period bell prompted me to stow my horn and realize my time had come.

Out the door, I then walked up the annex's steps to typing class on the second floor. I cautiously entered the spacious room. It was crowded just as I knew it would be, all girls. Each table contained a single typewriter and formed even rows across the room, front and back.

Miss Adams, our teacher, stood smiling as she faced the class for the first time. A typewriter keyboard painted on what looked like an oil cloth stretched on the blackboard across the front of the room.

"Good morning, class. I'm Miss Adams. Welcome to Typing I." She was a well-groomed attractive woman with graying hair combed neatly back from her soft face. Although rather diminutive in size, she presented a regal figure as she peered though her wire rim glasses at her neophyte charges.

Slowly and distinctly, she called roll from a stack of registration cards. When she reached my name, she paused briefly and pronounced my name loudly and clearly. My face turned red as heads turned and snickers spread around the room. "Gene, it's good to have you with us. I believe that you're the only boy in the class." Such an observation was unnecessary. It was very obvious I was.

"Yes, ma'am. I think so," I answered in a quiet, almost mumbling manner. All eyes continued to gawk at me as if I were some headliner in a carnival's freak show.

In a few sessions, I began to realize that learning to type was a process only between you and the typewriter. You couldn't depend on anybody else. My worst habit was to look at the keyboard when typing. This was strictly a no-no in Miss Adam's class.

What would happen when a student was caught peeping at the keyboard? Our teacher had uncanny eyesight. She could spot a cheater from any point in the room. She never called the culprit's name, but gave a quiet, direct rebuke to all, "Class, don't look at the keyboard when you type. You'll never get any better if you continue to do that." Those words always produced a bevy of heads snapping upward like army recruits being called to attention by a demanding drill sergeant.

After a rather uneven beginning, my long skinny fingers began to fit nicely on the Royal's manual typewriter keys. As my speed increased, I became comfortable, and a constant syncopated rhythm took over from my earlier clumsy efforts. With increasing progress, I could imagine how a cool jazz pianist would feel improvising driving riffs and chords.

I looked forward to typing each morning and enjoyed the challenge of the daily speed tests Miss Adams administered. I was pleased with my newly found skills, approaching nearly 60 words per minute and with good accuracy. I knew I wasn't the fastest or the most proficient in the class, certainly not the prettiest, but I was more than holding my own.

On final exam day, I took my last speed test. Most had decided to continue with Typing II, me included. I probably didn't need it, but what did I have to lose? I stuck it out for the rest of the year. I never got any faster or more accurate, but with the newly acquired skill, I gained enormous confidence. I was now ready to continue my quest to learn and develop more advanced secretarial skills. I would take the next step, which was shorthand and the ability to take more copious notes in college classes.

My friends ceased teasing me about typing class, and when I announced to them at the beginning of my senior year I was going to take shorthand, the jokes essentially stopped. Their silence really made me feel vindicated.

The shorthand's classroom also was the second floor of the school's annex, next door to where I learned to type. With great confidence and a little cockiness, I swaggered into my first class, ten girls and I. To my surprise, my shorthand career was essentially over before it began.

Miss Gockel, our teacher, welcomed the class and, to my embarrassment, praised me for my appearance. With class starting, I had never been so confused and baffled in all my life. I was miserable. I felt miscast and knew that I was completely over my head. Even mastering Egyptian hieroglyphics would be easier. How could anyone ever understand what she was teaching? Maybe the girls could, but certainly not me!

After the second day of class, I quietly eased down the steps, said nothing to anyone, dropped the course and started seriously considering taking physics with the respected and beloved Mr. Blumenberg. Who knew? Maybe, I could become a scientist. I certainly wasn't good enough to become a secretary.

Author's Note:

As it turned out, for me typing was probably the most practical course taught in high school. It not only served me well in college, but in the Navy and my personal life. I cringe today when some person hunts and pecks as they wade through some computer's keyboard. If only Miss Adams had been a part of their high school curriculum!

Salesman

Cape's Thanksgiving Day in 1950 had been unseasonably warm. Under a cloudless azure sky, the temperature reached nearly 70 degrees and life appeared to perk up once again in the sleepy town along the Mississippi River.

Winter-like weather had been with us since mid-November and the dramatic change offered good prospects of a pleasant four-day school holiday. The previous week of cold and dreary days had lingered persistently like a thick, gray wool blanket hung in a window shielding the sun from the outside world.

Earlier in the day, Mother and I drove down to Bernie, Missouri, a small rural town about 45 miles southwest of Cape, to have Thanksgiving dinner with my sister, Martel, and her family. After leaving around 5 pm, turkey torpor finally overcame me, and I slept most of the drive home.

Despite the better weather and a good dinner, I wasn't very happy. My immediate problem was money. Christmas was less than a month away and I needed to find a job, any job. I could then buy the most important gift of all, a string of pearls for Alice Jean Porritt, my steady girlfriend since starting my junior year.

Her best friend, Jeanette Hosea, had told me what Alice wanted when I asked her nearly two weeks before. She even told me where I could buy them. The pearls were at Hechts, Cape's most chic boutique and women's fine dress store. A lot of our crowd shopped there, but only a few were able to afford to buy. The pearls cost almost $15, a sum that was far beyond any kind of money that I had on hand. But I was determined to buy those pearls!

We lived in a third floor apartment, recently converted from part of an attic. At the flat's east-end was a long, narrow living room, newly paneled with a light oak stain. A large window gave us an unobstructed and panoramic view of the Mississippi River which flowed majestically less than a quarter mile away. A small kitchen, dining room and Mother's bedroom—really an alcove without a door—crossed and divided the living room and my bedroom.

Having my own private bedroom was very special to me since it was the first privacy I had had since Mother separated from my father nearly five years before. Our first two apartments in Cape were hardly big enough to even turn around in. Our new address, despite the three flights of stairs, was a welcome change. My mother's unselfishness in giving me privacy meant a lot. A 16-year-old adolescent boy needed a closed door to live out his fantasies.

Before going to bed that evening, Mother and I lingered awhile in the dark living room, sitting quietly and watching the river boats valiantly pushing their load of barges toward St. Louis, about 120 miles to the north, against a stiff downstream current.

Through the room's shadows, I could see that Mother was tired from the long day. Friday would be no holiday for her as she had to get up and open the insurance adjustor's office where she worked as a secretary 9-5 Monday through Friday and 8-12 on Saturday, making a monthly salary of $100.00. I could sleep in . . . no school until Monday!

Thinking about my financial problems, I ended the evening's quiet and explained to her why I was so anxious about the upcoming holiday season.

"Mother, I really, really need a job. Christmas is comin', and I don't have any money." Mother seemed unmoved at the angst in my voice.

"Well, Son," she said quietly, "Where do you think you can find a job?" Her soft yet strong voice was not in a sarcastic or mocking way. It was sincere. She knew me well and knew I was anxious about my situation.

"I really don't know where to start. The basketball team will be playing in the Christmas Tournament, so the only time I could work would be on Saturdays. Do you think somebody will hire me for just Saturdays?"

"Why wouldn't they? You never know until you ask. Why not go down to Main Street first thing in the morning and start asking? Then go up Broadway. You'll never know what you might find. I would imagine that with Christmas around the corner some store in town might need a part time person to work on Saturdays." Mother's well-measured and confident voice was therapeutic. I began to feel better about my prospects.

She continued, "I would imagine that Montgomery-Ward's could use a part time person during the holiday season. You know Jewell Ryan. She works in their office down there. Go see her. She might be able to help you."

"Sure, I know Mrs. Ryan. Maybe, she could. But, what could I do at Wards?"

"Oh, there's lots of things that you could do, like uh, a stock boy, maybe even a sales clerk. You'll just have to see."

"A sales clerk? Me? What could I sell? Underwear? Socks? Shirts? I've never done that. Do you think I could?"

"I know you can. Why not? Now, let's get to bed. It's been a long day, and I have to get up in the morning. You'll want to start knocking on doors and filling out applications when the stores open."

Despite her counsel and encouragement and my excitement over the improved prospects of finding a job, I slept late, awakening just before noon. Mother tried to wake me when she left just before 8 am, but I couldn't make the early move. I was, after all, on vacation.

I wolfed down two bowls of cereal, had a quick bath, put on a pair of freshly ironed khakis, slipped on a long-sleeved cotton shirt, eased into a pair of penny loafers, and bounded out of the apartment toward Main Street, only three short blocks away. The warm weather stayed with us over the night, but a strong southerly wind was blowing autumn's few remaining leaves off the trees, presenting an early view of the winter drabness ahead.

The Montgomery-Ward store was the biggest department store in town. It offered shoppers everything from men's suits to breakfast dinettes, and what wasn't there, you could order from their massive catalogue. The store was housed in a huge three-story barn-like building occupying nearly half a Main Street block. In addition to Cape's customers, it also served the southern-most tip of Illinois, especially along the river, and the rolling Missouri farmland communities surrounding the town.

I boldly walked into the store's wide swinging doors, down the narrow aisles that contained men's underwear, socks, shirts and ties, and up the wide steps to the second floor where the general offices were located. It was around 1:30 pm, and the store was jammed with post-Thanksgiving shoppers. It was the beginning of the Christmas season. It seemed obvious to me that this was a good place to get a job.

Jewell Ryan was standing behind a huge wooden counter running north to south, dividing the room from the customers and the office staff. She was a lady with a lovely smile and dressed to perfection. Her two-piece Navy blue wool suit was a sharp contrast to most of the less stylishly dressed shoppers crowding the store.

"Hi, Mrs. Ryan!" I yelled. "How are you?"

"Why, Gene Munger. What are you doing here?" She was an avid Cape Central basketball fan. Her husband, Gene, and his brother, Rich, had both played for Central. She and Gene never missed any of our games, and when we saw each other, she'd always say hello.

"I'm looking for a job. Do you have any?" My direct approach and precocious naiveté must have amused her greatly.

"What kind of job are you looking for, Gene?"

"Oh, anything, just anything. You see, I'm looking for Saturday work to get some extra money for Christmas. I thought Wards might be able to use me."

"Well, we might, but let's start with your filling out an application." She reached underneath the big counter, pulled out a blank job application, gave me a ball point pen and asked me to sit down at one of the chairs lined up against the bare wall.

"Fill it out the best you can, and we'll look it over. I can't promise you anything, but we'll see what we can do."

"Thank you, Mrs. Ryan. Thank you very much." With pen in hand, I eagerly started to fill in the blanks. My job experience was not too impressive, but I was at least able to list three jobs: working last summer at Boy Scout Camp Lewallen as the Assistant Waterfront Director, caddying at the Cape Girardeau Country Club, and setting pins at the Lutheran School Bowling Alley.

Finishing the task a few minutes later, I handed my application to Mrs. Ryan and waited for her positive response. She studied the form carefully and then with a wide grin on her beaming face she responded, "Well, we'll look this over, and if there's an opening, we'll call you. Say, how's the team going to do this year? Are you getting excited about the Christmas Tournament?"

"Yes ma'am! We're going to be a lot better than last year, I think. We should do pretty good in the tournament, just as long as we don't have to play Sikeston in the first round. They're tough. Say, Mrs. Ryan, when do you think you'll be calling me? Soon?"

"We'll let you know, Gene. Thanks for coming down. It was good to see you!"

I went no further with my job search that day. I was confident that Wards would call me and I would be working soon. I hadn't bothered to ask what they would pay me, as the thought had never entered my mind. When you have nothing, a little bit can mean a whole lot!

I went back to the apartment and tried to phone and connect with some friends to see what was going on, but to no avail. It seemed that everybody was either out of town or out shopping. I spent the rest of the afternoon with my nose in the *Sporting News* hoping to read about my Cardinals.

At about 5 pm, the phone rang. I hoped that it was Mrs. Ryan calling about my job. To my delight, it was.

"Hello." My voice was restrained, as I tried to remain cool.

"Gene, this is Jewel Ryan. I have good news for you. We have a job for you. Can you start tomorrow?"

"Tomorrow? Tomorrow? Yeah, I can start tomorrow. What time?"

"The store opens at 9 am. Please report to me here at 8:30. You'll be working in the toy department. Okay?"

"Great! I'll be there."

I couldn't have been more excited. I had a job and was going to make some money. I knew nothing about selling toys, but I figured I could learn. I quickly dialed my mother at her office. No answer. She had to be on her way home.

Just then, Mother came up the steep, narrow steps leading to the third floor apartment. She appeared exhausted as she finished the remaining few steps with a slow, painful shuffle.

"Mother! Mother! 'Monkey' Wards has given me a job! They want me to start tomorrow in their toy department."

"That's wonderful. How much are they going to pay you?" She asked as she removed her raincoat from her thin shoulders and headed for the closet.

"Pay me? I didn't ask. How much do you think they'll pay me?"

"I don't have any idea, but you can find that out tomorrow. I'll iron your white shirt tonight and you can wear your bow tie with your blue suit. Be sure to have your shoes shined."

I slept fitfully most of the night, waking up for the last time at 6 am. Such an early hour usually found me listless and semi-drugged, but not this day. I leaped out of bed, took a bath and dressed carefully. Like a school day, Mother had my cereal and orange juice waiting for me.

Just as I made my departure down the steps, Mother stopped me and clipped on my bow tie, kissed me lightly on the cheek and looked directly into my eyes.

"I know you'll do well, Gene. I am very proud of you, and Daddy'll be proud, too. You must call him tomorrow and let him know."

Arriving at the store, I reported to Mrs. Ryan in the office. She gave me a card and showed me how to punch in and out on the time clock. She pointed out that it wouldn't be necessary to wear a suit jacket on the sales floor and pointed to the office closet where I could hang it.

Before I even asked, Mrs. Ryan advised me that my wages would be set at $.75 per hour. At that rate, I could get Alice Jean's pearls in just three Saturdays and still have enough left for the family. Besides that, I could set pins at the bowling alley on Sunday afternoons and pick up even more money. I was feeling pretty good about my change of fortune.

She then led me up the wide steps to the third floor's toy department. That floor was usually filled with furniture, linoleum, and kitchen appliances. However, since toys were the going thing during the holiday season, a lot of the floor's merchandise was carried off to the warehouse to make room.

About one-fourth of the third floor now contained toys, all kinds and lots of them crammed and overflowing on portable shelves with a voluminous assortment of dolls, games, gun and holster sets, stuffed animals, and so on. Ward's was definitely the place you came to buy toys when you went Christmas shopping in Cape Girardeau.

Mrs. Ryan introduced me to the toy department supervisor, Moe Brady. I knew Mr. Brady's son, Wynn, a trumpet player in the band and orchestra who had graduated from Central a couple of years earlier. Normally, Brady was the appliance department's manager. However, during the holiday season, he was relegated to managing the toy department, a position he treated with great disdain.

Each December he was given the call to move from his sales of high commissioned stoves and refrigerators to switch to the wonderful world of teddy bears and dollies. He mightily resented the change, letting everyone on the store's sales staff know just how unfair and demeaning it was for him to take such a humiliating assignment.

"Moe, this is Gene Munger. He'll be working in your department on Saturdays between now and Christmas."

Brady, a small and slightly built man, shook my hand warmly and said, "Oh, Hi, Gene. It's nice to meet you. I've seen you play basketball. Do you know my son, Wynn?"

"Yes, Sir, I do. He used to play trumpet in the band and orchestra, and he was good, too! He's up on the hill now at Cape State, isn't he?"

Mr. Brady nodded his head and beamed at the positive report of his son. He then asked, "Have you ever worked here, err in the toy department before?"

"No, Sir, but I have caddied at the country club." How caddying and working in a retail department store had any connection to the job at hand hadn't occurred to me. I was already nervous, and his question about my qualifications only made it worse.

"Oh, I'm sure you'll do fine, Gene. Let me show you how the cash register works. You ring up different kinds of sales and fill out forms. Any sale you make during the day has to be written down on your sales card. You'll then turn it in to Dave Graves, the store manager, at the end of the day."

Brady went on to describe Graves and his manner. "He's big and tall, always dressed in a suit. There's no question that he's the store manager here. He barely speaks to anybody, but he seems to be always looking down at you like a hawk ready to pounce on a rabbit. And he'll get really upset if he sees any merchandise out of place or not priced. Woe be to the clerk who's standing around and doing nothing. He'll come right over and chew you out in plain sight of everybody. He just can't stand the sight of a dawdler working in his store."

From what I had heard so far, I was sure that I wanted to avoid Mr. Graves at all costs. He certainly didn't sound like someone I wanted to be around. But, I had already met his daughter Carol, a pretty, blue-eyed freshman, and she was delightful. Always upbeat and animated, Carol wore very classy clothes. This was a true, tell-tale sign to me and my friends that her father must be really rich.

"Don't worry about Graves. He won't bother you. You're just working here during the holidays. Now, let's get to work."

Brady then started going through all of the sales forms and procedures I needed to know about selling toys. He rattled off strange terms like "will call," "lay away" and "credit" in rapid-fire order. My mind went temporarily blank at the barrage of strange new words thrown in my direction. The only real exposure to retail sales that I had ever experienced was the intermittent selling of soda pop, candy bars, and ice cream at Camp Lewallen's store the past summer. This sure wasn't Camp Lewallen!

At 9 am, the first customers started to trickle up to the third floor. Cash customers were relatively simple to serve, and as such, I was beginning to get over my anxiety about being a toy salesman.

This respite continued for only a short time. By some silent signal, a herd of customers came thundering up the steps and descended upon me and Brady. A third toy department salesperson was due to come in later that afternoon, but we needed help immediately. The enemy had landed!

To describe the scene of Ward's toy department at that moment would be to compare it to a meat market during World War II rationing when the butcher advertised that sirloin steak would be available for the special sale price of $.29 a pound. Everybody wanted to be waited on and everybody was in a hurry. In a word, it was pure chaos as parents hurried through their annual shopping ritual hoping to complete shopping for their children before their patience and money—not necessarily in that order—ran out.

I was totally intimidated by what I experienced. I tried to recall what Brady had told me, but it didn't work. I felt a siege of paralysis coming over me. I just stood there gawking at the oncoming horde of shoppers. Just then, an enormously sized woman with a semi-crazed look confronted me with a series of determined thrusts against my chest.

"Will you please wait on me, young man? I have to get some toys for my children." She then took me by the hand as if I were one of her children and started sliding through the aisles picking and choosing toys, loading me down with her choices, and finally hustling me back to the sales counter.

"Now, Son. I cain't pay for all of these toys today. Here's $5 you can put down on lay-away. I'll come back next Saturday and pay for them all. Okay?"

"Lay-away? Sure, but just a minute." I excused myself and went over to my supervisor and asked, "Mr. Brady, this lady just told me that she couldn't pay for all the toys she bought, but she wants to give me $5.00 and wants me to put 'em on lay-away 'til next Saturday when she can pay. You went over that thing with me, but I forgot. I'm sorry. How do I do that? What do I do? Where do I lay 'em away?"

Brady, too, was already at his stress point by now. I imagine he had started the day at that level. He snapped back, "Well, write it up on Form S-134, take her money and give her a receipt, wrap 'em up, and take 'em to the will-call room through those swinging doors over there."

Still completely puzzled, I returned to the lady, started rummaging through all of the other customer's toys bunched up on the counter, found hers, carefully wrote her name and address on the form, noted the toys purchased, took her money, thanked her, and clumsily packaged her toys in brown wrapping paper. I then secured them with light twine and plodded forward to the will call room trying not to drop her precious purchases.

The retail fervor continued throughout the day, but I was adjusting well in my new surroundings. Despite the frenetic behavior, most shoppers were courteous and forgiving with my awkwardness in filling out sales forms and wrapping weirdly shaped packages. I had taken only 20 minutes for lunch, slipping down the street to grab a quick hamburger. I felt that I needed to get back and help Brady hold back the roaring tide.

The expected arrival of another salesperson never came to pass. Brady was irritated with that and complained bitterly to me about the shortage. Unfortunately, that void didn't deter the continuing show of anxious shoppers coming to the third floor.

Mr. Graves showed up on the floor several times that morning, but never said anything. He just glared at me and Brady from the top of the stairs with a serious, scowling look. Although I had been forewarned, Graves' presence intimidated me. Was I not working hard? Was I not being a good salesman? Did I need my suit jacket? Would I have a job at the end of the day?

By mid-afternoon, despite the insecurity and paranoia caused by Graves' demeanor, I had gotten fairly comfortable with the retail toy scene. I was actually beginning to feel like I belonged there. Every now and then, I would botch bundling a load of toys so badly that they ended up slipping from my grasp and scattering in all directions on the floor. The crowds queuing around the cash register didn't seem to notice.

Brady suggested that I take a break for dinner. That surprised me since I figured I would work only until 5 pm.

"I thought I would be leaving by now, Mr. Brady," I said.

"No, Gene, the store closes at 8. You need to get a bite to eat now. It'll still be busy until at least 7, but then we'll spend the rest of the day cleaning up all this mess."

"If you don't mind, Mr. Brady, I'll work straight through 'til closing time. I'm really not that hungry and, besides, one person on the floor is not enough." I was beginning to sound like a true partisan member of the toy sales team.

My decision to skip dinner was based strictly on economics, not on restoring energy for the hours ahead. I determined that with all the hours I worked that day, I'd make about $8.00. At that rate, I could buy Alice Jean's present after next week's work. Why, I was half-way finished with my mission!

For the rest of the evening, the time flew by quickly. Most of the customers had departed, only a few browsers picked their way through the department, mostly killing time, it seemed.

At closing time, Brady thanked me for my helping him survive the season's first bombardment of toy shoppers. "You did a good job today, Gene. We need to get some more help, though. Two people are not enough to take care of this mob. I'll talk to Graves about that. We'll be better organized next Saturday. I'll see you then."

"Thank you, Mr. Brady, I enjoyed working for you. I hope I didn't mess up too much. I'll do better next week."

I recovered my coat from the second floor office closet, slowly and carefully added up all my sales on the card (over $500 dollars), and jauntily made my way down the second floor's steps to encounter Mr.Graves before I went home for the evening.

Brady had forewarned me about Graves' daily closing ceremony of checking each sales clerk's scorecard, but advised to pay it no mind. It was only Graves' way of intimidating his workers. Needless to say, I wasn't looking forward to that meeting. The day's round of ominous looks he had given me was very unnerving, but I had had a successful sales day, and he surely would be proud of my effort. Nevertheless, I had no idea what his reaction would be when we finally met face to face. I was obviously concerned.

Approaching the store manager at the door, I could see that I was the only employee in sight. It was going to be a classic me-against-him or as we would say in basketball speak, one-on-one! I figured I would have to take the initiative to get the upper hand. Straightening my bow tie, sliding my hand over my short brush haircut and taking a deep breath, I moved forward toward the target with the panache of a high-stepping drum major leading the town's drum and bugle corps at the head of the Fourth of July parade.

"Hi, Mr. Graves. I'm Gene Munger." Before he could say anything, I reached forward and clutched his cold, somewhat lifeless hand. "I started working today in the toy department. Here's my sales card."

Graves stared at me, frowned deeply, and growled, "Yeah, I know who you are. I've seen you play basketball." He then looked down at the card through his bifocal glasses perched awkwardly on his oversized nose. Showing only a small sign of emotion, he mumbled in a pleasant voice, "Not bad, not bad at all. I would suspect that you'll do better next week."

Totally surprised by his rather positive and approving response, I quickly replied, "Yes, Sir, I will. I really will. Besides, this job's gonna help me make some money for Christmas to buy some nice presents for my girlfriend and family."

"And what are you going to get me?" He asked. A broad smile filled his large face. The man was actually smiling!

"Pardon me, Sir?" I didn't really know how to answer him. I blinked furiously and tried to answer, "Why, err, uh, I don't know, Mr. Graves. I don't know. What would you like to have?"

"Oh, why don't you just surprise me? I like to be surprised at Christmas, don't you?"

"Yes, Sir, I do. I really do. And, yes Sir, I'll try to surprise you. I really will."

How in the world did I know what he wanted for Christmas? Maybe I could ask his daughter, Carol, next week at school. She might be able to help me. But what if he wanted something that cost a lot of money? What would I do then?

Now, totally shaken and barely able to speak, I uttered a weak, limpid "Goodnight, Mr. Graves," and shook his hand once again. This time the grip was much firmer, like he enjoyed the experience.

Walking into the rapidly cooling November night air, I could hear him burst out laughing, deep and long. Was he laughing at me? Was he teasing me? Was he serious? I'd have to ask Mr. Brady about that next Saturday. He'd know for sure.

Author's Note:

I can't remember whether I bought Alice Jean a pearl necklace that Christmas or not. I probably did. Like a lot of high school romances, we might have "broken up" just before Christmas. Boys and girls that time and age have a propensity to do that, you know.

After the 1950 holiday season had ended, I continued to work in Ward's furniture department on Saturdays during the remainder of basketball season and after school throughout my junior and senior high school years. Yes, and I always was assigned to the toy department during Christmas.

Mr. Graves' gruff and officious manner pretty much stayed the same over that time, but beneath that exterior, he was a most caring man. He was an ardent Central basketball fan, although he never ever mentioned that he saw any of the games. I don't think he ever missed any of them. Later on, he inquired about my plans for college, academic interests, and so on. He even suggested strongly that after college graduation I should consider going to work for Ward's as a management trainee. I never pursued that path. Retailing, especially in a closed environment like a Montgomery-Ward's store, was never that appealing. However, the experience working there with and encountering such an eclectic group of people those junior and senior high school years was invaluable.

■ ■ ■ ■ ■

Musician

Music was always such a big part of my life, starting at an early age. One of my favorite radio programs was *The Cities Services Bands of America's* Monday night concert conducted by Paul Laval. It was from that program that I first became interested in playing some instrument.

I was well into the fifth grade in the fall of 1944 when my teacher, Mrs. Jackson, announced to her class that Sister Agneta was coming over from nearby Oran to start a band at our Benton grade school. I had no idea who Sister Agneta was or for that matter, why a nun would want to do that. But, Mrs. Jackson seemed very excited about it, and her enthusiasm spread over the rest of our class like the prospect of ice cream served during lunch.

After school, I rushed home that day to tell my mother that the Sister was coming over to start a band. Before I had even reached the top of the steps to our second floor apartment, I started yelling at the top of my voice, "Hey,

Mother, there's going to be a band at school! I want to be in it! Can I? Can I?"

My mother, the daughter of a Methodist minister, had a solid background in music. She learned to play the piano at an early age, and as all ministers in those days relied on a piano to add passion and enthusiasm to their services, her minister father eagerly recruited her to do just that. I had often heard her say that when the church doors opened, she always played—at prayer meetings and Sunday morning and evening services. She even bragged that it was she who had taught the great jazz pianist, Jess Stacy, how to "play jazz" in the basement of Malden, Missouri's Methodist Church. Needless to say, she was very accomplished regardless of what or when she was asked to play, church music, jazz, even classical. So, she, too, was excited about her son entering the world of music as a musician.

"Well, Gene, that's really good news. What do you want to play in the band?"

"I guess I'd like to learn how to play the trumpet, Mother," I replied. "I'd like to be able to play like Harry James." I really didn't know who Harry James was, but I had heard my parents talk about how well he played the trumpet and that he had married Betty Grable. That made him very special since I knew who she was. I had seen her picture pinned on my best friend Dick's bedroom wall scantily dressed in a bathing suit and looking very pretty. I loved that picture.

While I favored playing the trumpet, I was somewhat afraid as to whether or not I would be able to manage its three keys. It looked very hard. But, at the first general meeting where Sister Agneta demonstrated the various instruments that the band would be playing, the fingering actually looked easy. Each note required no more than two fingers, and some notes required none. I had never actually blown a trumpet, but that didn't bother me. I knew I could play it, but I had to have one to play first. That meant I would have to ask my dad to get me one, and I wasted no time that evening to make my plea.

"Daddy, could you get me a trumpet? I'm going to start playing in the band, and I need one to play." I'm sure he must have gotten a big charge out of seeing his 10-year-old son asking for something that he had never played nor knew little or nothing about.

"Well, son, I'll see what I can do. You know trumpets are very expensive. How much money do you have?" He replied with a broad grin on his face.

"I don't have much, but I will pay you back," I said. As to how much trumpets cost was way, way beyond my experience, but once I got my trumpet, I'd worry about paying him back.

"I'll see what I can do, Son. Give me a few days. I'll see what I can do."

Like magic, he brought home a used Conn trumpet for me the next week. I found out later that he had a client who had once played that horn, and in a chance conversation, Dad discovered that the man not only had one, but was willing to sell it to him for the tidy sum of $15. To me, the horn was worth a million dollars. With Dad giving me some silver polish and a soft cloth, I spent the entire evening polishing my new horn. It was just like a new one! All I had to do now was to learn how to play it. And I did, practicing daily afternoons and evenings much to the consternation of our downstairs neighbors.

My trumpet career progressed very rapidly. My parents arranged for me to take private lessons from Sister Agneta, and in less than seven months, I played a solo at her annual spring recital. I wasn't playing like Harry James, but I was playing quite well for a 10-year-old boy. Later on, I played taps as the "echo trumpet" for my father's American Legion Post as it supplied the honor burial guard for those Scott County service men killed in action.

Although my playing improved, relations between my parents were spiraling rapidly downward. Their marriage, after so many years, had reached a dead end, and they agreed to separate. My mother and I moved to Cape in August 1946. Obviously, I feared moving to such a large town and was devastated at the break-up of my parents. I had just entered the seventh grade, and I was leaving my friends and home of the past five years. Would I be able to survive there? Would I still be able to play my trumpet? Ah, the uncertain feeling of a young lad about to enter adolescence!

To my delight, my new school, Lorimier, had a band and orchestra, and in no time, I was elevated to first chair in the trumpet section. Having that honor really didn't mean much to the rest of the students, but being on the softball and basketball team gave me much more recognition than playing a horn.

I continued to practice daily, although living in a small duplex apartment and blowing my trumpet didn't set too well with our landlords, an older couple burdened with a son, daughter, and an older married son with wife and child all living in three small rooms and a bantam, penned-in space in the basement. Even playing with a mute didn't seem to help. They were always complaining about the "noise" I was making.

As I moved into Central High School in the fall of 1948, my trumpet playing went with me. But, by this time, basketball had taken over as the main focus in my young life, although, my music was a very close second. I tried the marching band, but I hated it. My real love was the concert band and orchestra. Our rehearsals were at 8:00 am on Monday, Wednesday, and Friday for band and Tuesday and Thursday for orchestra. I truly looked forward to those sessions as they started each school day for me in a most positive way.

I found that attaining first chair in the trumpet section by a fresh-faced freshman was not that easy. I settled down into a routine of third chair one week and fourth chair the next. Competition was fierce, and I struggled just to keep up. I complained to my mother that there were players better than I. While I practiced diligently, I was nowhere near attaining first chair status. How could I get there? She had an idea.

For years, Mother had purchased her shoes at Cape's best department store, Buckner- Ragsdale. Her longtime shoe salesman was Homer Gilbert. Homer, in addition to being a very capable shoe salesman, was, also, a professional musician and a trumpet player. He played in southeast Missouri and southern Illinois' best orchestras and probably would have had a good career on the road with the big bands of that time. That was not to be. He had a wife and a whole flock of children and felt that it was more important to be with them rather than playing in one-night stands spending his sleeping time on some dilapidated bus or car crunched in between snoring, liquor-filled fellow band members.

Homer also supplemented his income by giving trumpet lessons. Mother's idea was that he would give me lessons so that perhaps I could eventually become first chair in Central's band and orchestra. His fee was $5.00 per lesson, a whole lot of money for a woman who was making less than $100 a month as a secretary for an insurance adjustor.

While I knew Homer (he sold me my shoes, too), I always addressed him as Mr. Gilbert. He seemed pleased to start giving me lessons, but unfortunately, the lessons were not that much fun. Instead of playing songs, he had me playing scales and more scales until I was sick of it.

"Gene, the only way that you'll ever really be good at playing the trumpet is to play scales and practice them. Practice them and practice them again." Homer would repeat this mantra continuously. I hated scale playing, all I wanted to do was play songs.

Finally one day, I announced to him in a bold voice, "Mr. Gilbert, I would really like to play *The Carnival of Venice.* Can I?"

"Of course, you can, but I don't think you're really ready to play that yet," he replied. "It requires double tonguing . . . triple tonguing, and you're not into that yet."

"But, I think I can. Let me try it. Please."

With his long thin face nodding slowly back and forth, he said, "Okay, but go home and practice first. Come back next week, and we'll give it a try."

At last I had a piece of sheet music to practice with no more scales! I practiced vigorously throughout the week, much to the annoyance of our ever complaining landlords. Even Mother helped me with the intricate passages of the piece, but once I got to the harder parts, double and triple tonguing, I had continuing difficulty in mastering it. But, I was determined.

On my lesson day, I carefully fitted my horn into its case and gently placed it in my bicycle's basket. Thanks to my dad, the bicycle had been completely overhauled, new tires, brakes and chain. It was like new. The wire basket, larger than anyone else's in the neighborhood, seemed out of place for my fenderless bike, but it held my trumpet case quite nicely.

I pedaled the short distance down to Mr.Gilbert's, resting my bike gently on the curb in front of his house. I bounded briskly up the steps and onto his front porch, knocked twice on the screen door, and responded to my teacher's voice to come in. I pushed ahead, removing my trumpet from its case as I entered the front room.

With great confidence, I eased my music onto the stand and before Mr.Gilbert had a chance to speak, got out the music to the *Carnival of Venice*. I was determined to show him that I was more than capable of playing this difficult piece.

"Hold it, Gene. Hold it. Let's play some scales before you get into that. Okay?"

"But, I want you to hear it, Mr. Gilbert. I've been practicing all week."

"Well, all right, but like I said, I don't think you're ready for it." There was no sign of confidence in his voice, but I certainly had lots of it.

And so the great boy trumpeter began to play. It was not a memorable or auspicious debut. I struggled valiantly to get through the opening, a fairly easy prelude to the more difficult part of the number. The more I played, the worse it sounded. One would have thought I had just picked up a horn for the first time. In embarrassment and frustration, I removed the horn from my lips, said nothing, and bowed my head as if ready to pray. Mr. Gilbert only looked at me with a pained expression.

He finally broke the silence and said quietly, "Well, let's get back to the scales. We can always come back to this later . . . after you've played more scales."

The rest of the lesson went even more poorly. I had lost my concentration completely. I no longer had any confidence in my playing. I hated scales, and it seemed like I was destined to a lifetime of scales. I just wanted to play songs. That's all . . . songs!

At the lesson's close, I reached into my blue jean pocket and handed Mr.Gilbert his five dollars. I thanked him and with my trumpet in its case, started walking down the steep, double tiered steps to the street. What I saw then was an awful sight, so fitting to this terrible day.

My reconditioned bicycle still lay on it side, but someone, some car, maybe even a truck, had run over the front wheel while I was inside completely destroying it and my precious basket. I was crushed. What more could go wrong?

I tried to walk my demolished bike home, but with the front wheel twisted like some contortionist showing his skills to a curious circus crowd. I literally dragged it, trumpet clutched close to my side, back to the apartment. It was truly one of the worst days of my life.

Discouraged, but consoled by my mother, I tried to forget the disappointment and frustration of not being able to play to my expectations. I had reached the sorry conclusion that the trumpet was really not the instrument for me. Perhaps, I would change to the French horn. It was probably a little easier to play. And anyway, I could still be an important part of Central's concert band and orchestra. My mother appeared to understand my feelings and agreed with me to make the change.

Later, I approached our band director, Tony Carosello, and asked if it would be all right for me to change over to the French horn.

Mr. Carosello, a professional trumpeter himself and very popular with all his students, appeared to be taken aback by my request. "Why would you want to do that?" His stern, brown eyes seemed to stare right through me. "You're doing well in the trumpet section."

"Oh, I just think I'd be better off playing the French horn. Besides, there's only one other horn player in the orchestra, and I think you need two of 'em," I replied

"Yes, we could use another horn player, but have you ever played a French horn, Gene?"

"No, but I know I can. It's the same fingering like a trumpet, isn't it?"

"Right, it is, but the horn is not an easy instrument to play. You'll have to adjust to it; it'll take a lot of practice. Are you willing to do that?"

"Oh, sure. I practice all the time," I said. Pains of doubt and confusion pierced my stomach as I listened to my words. Maybe, I *should* stick with the trumpet. But, I *knew* no matter how much I would practice, I would never be able to master triple tonguing, even double tonguing. And I was sure that horn players would never have to do that.

So my trumpet lessons stopped and I moved into the chair as one of the French horn players in the concert band and orchestra. I was right. No triple or double tonguing required, and I really began to flourish with my new instrument, so much so that I soon became first chair in both groups. Besides, I had a direct, unobstructed view to my high school sweetheart, Alice Jean Porritt. She played the saxophone in concert band, the violin in orchestra. My first hour class in the morning continued to be the highlight of the day!

My favorites to play? Beethoven's *Egmont Overture* and Von Suppe's *The Light Calvary Overture* always reassured me that I had done the right thing by leaving the trumpet and taking up the horn.

Gene, as first chair with his French horn in the 1952 Cape Central High School Orchestra.

Soon after graduating from Central in the spring of 1952, I was thrilled when I received a call from Fritz Heim, the municipal band director and the college's orchestra director, inviting me to attend a rehearsal with the city's concert band at their forthcoming practice. Every Wednesday evening this band, composed of the city's best musicians, played concerts throughout the summer at the band shell in the Common Pleas Courthouse Park. To be a part of that group exceeded any previous recognition that I had ever received as a French horn player in my high school's band and orchestra. I had been elevated to a new plateau. My mother was ecstatic. I beamed throughout the rest of the day.

We lived only a few blocks from the park, and with a horn borrowed from the high school, I strode haughtily up the Lorimier Street hill the next evening and met Mr. Heim as other members began to assemble in the shell. We shook hands, exchanged a few pleasantries, and I took my place with the other horn player, Burwell Fox. A Southeast Missouri College faculty member, he was recognized as the best horn player in the area. What a thrill it was to be able to sit beside him and play at summer band concerts!

Seated next to me was Ed Rudert. Ed, the auto mechanic teacher at Central, was a short, portly man, known for his pithy humor and one of the school's beloved. He also, was a longtime tuba player in the concert band.

"Hello, Mr. Rudert, how are you?"

"Hi Gene. Are you gonna play with us this evening?"

"Yes Sir, I am. At least, I'm gonna try," I said as I started removing my horn from its case.

"Oh, you'll do just fine, I'm sure," he replied.

One of the band's members started passing out sheet music for the first piece we were going to practice. That long-forgotten stomach pain of doubt and confusion returned. I had never seen music like this before. It made anything I had ever played look easy. This was going to be a real challenge.

With a sweep of his baton held tightly in his right hand, the conductor brought the band's members to attention. They responded as if consumed by some mystical force. Strange and discordant sounds began to drift harshly toward the conductor's ears. The band, too, was having problems with Heim's new and obviously difficult offering.

Embarrassed, I couldn't even make a sound with my horn. The music before me was just too difficult to play. I faked playing hoping that no one would notice.

After a period of less than a minute, the conductor dropped his baton and signaled his band to stop playing. He started shaking his head like some child spurning his mother's urging to try brussel sprouts at least once and said in a most discouraging fashion, "No, no, I don't think we're going to play this one next Wednesday evening. We'll just have to wait awhile. Maybe later this summer."

Grunts of approval filled the shell as the musicians cast aside that horrible piece of music. I felt vindicated. At least I wasn't alone in my inability to master it.

Ed Rudert sat staring quietly at the sheet of music before him. He made no move to remove it from his stand. Brushing away his long, silvery mane of hair from his wrinkled brow, he sighed heavily and in an almost inaudible voice peered out over the musicians in front of him and said, "They haven't made the goddamned horn yet that can play that music."

I never went back to play with the Municipal Band. I realized that I had probably reached the highest level of my competence, fairly good, but not good enough. Playing my trumpet and my French horn will always be a cherished memory of my youth, one that has stayed with me, not only as a player, but as a lover of classical music and those who have the talent to play it.

Author's Note:

Now in retirement, I am inclined to once again pick up a French horn and resume playing. It's been more than 50 years since I played, but I imagine that there are still many scales remaining that are yet to be played. As you read in the story, I always hated scales, but unless you play them, you're more than likely going to end up feeling like Ed Rudert.

Bunk

John S. Cobb High School was the all-colored school located only a block east of Cape Central and only a block north of the parochial high school, St. Mary's. Both Cape Central and St. Mary's had always been totally segregated and all-white. Despite having good, competitive basketball squads and being practically within eyesight of each other, Cobb's teams never played Central or St. Mary's, nor interacted in any way academically.

Throughout Missouri and the rest of the South, colored people weren't permitted to go to school with whites. They had their own schools and their own teams. That was the way it was in those days, that's the way it had always been. At Central, students never questioned such a discriminatory social order. We accepted segregation without a thought or protest.

During my freshman year, my mother and I moved from our duplex on South Middle to a much more comfortable modern red-brick duplex on Ellis Street that even had central heat! My bed was squeezed into the corner of the apartment's front room to allow space for a blue, tapestry-covered couch. My bedroom was also, the living room. A narrow hallway off the front room offered access to my mother's bedroom, a tiny bathroom and finally a kitchen, barely large enough to hold a small, wooden table, two chairs and a pre-1940's GE model electric stove. The apartment's heavy masonry walls were all painted off-white. There was no wall paper to break up the monotony.

Scanning the *Missourian's* sports page on a dreadfully cold, late February Saturday afternoon, 1951, my watchful eyes caught the box score of Friday night's Cobb's and New Madrid, Missouri's basketball game.

"Wheeee! Hey, Mother, my friend Bunk scored 22 points last night against New Madrid. That means they're still undefeated." My high-pitched voice must have sounded like a screeching owl as it vibrated through our apartment's narrow halls into the dwarfish kitchen where my mother was quietly preparing dinner.

"Who's Bunk?" she responded in a somewhat preoccupied voice. Her five and one-half day work week at the insurance adjustor's office had ended at noon and feeding a hungry teenager had become her priority.

"You know. Bunk! He's the colored fellow I play with over at the St. Mary's courts. He's the star player on the Cobb team."

I don't suppose that I *had* ever mentioned him. He didn't go to school with me. We only played basketball together on weekends.

"Well," I continued, "I sure wish we had him playing for our team. He's probably the best high school basketball player in town, but he plays for Cobb."

"Where did you meet Bunk? What's his real name?" Mother said as she walked into the living room where I was sprawled out on the sofa reading the paper through the failing light of the dull February afternoon.

"Oh, I don't know what his real name is, all I know is Bunk. I met him last year, about the time school started. He and his friends were playing up the street at St. Mary's grade school one day, and I was watching on the side. They asked me if I wanted to play, so I joined 'em. They were pretty good, but Bunk was by far the best. From then on, I played with 'em off and on, first there, then over at the high school behind the Catholic Church on Sprigg Street. You know, Mother, that's a much better court over there. The blacktop at the grade school tears up your gym shoes. On the high school's outdoor court, it's dirt, well, not really dirt, but it looks like dirt 'cept it's gray, kind of a packed dirt, and there's a net on the basket. It's much better."

"Where does Bunk live?" Mother asked. Tall and statuesque, she was still dressed in what she had worn to work that day, a black wool skirt, white blouse, and a light blue cardigan sweater. A white cotton apron fit snugly around her thin waist. Her graying hair was fashioned in a neat, brushed-back stylish manner. She was, indeed, a beautiful lady with her soft liquid blue eyes and smooth skin showing little or no aging.

"Uh, I don't really know, over on Frederick, I guess. Maybe somewhere on the south side. Why do you ask?"

How in the world would I know where he lived? Bunk would just show up on the court, we'd play, and then he'd leave and we wouldn't see each other until the next time.

"Well, maybe, you should invite him over to have lunch or dinner with you sometime. Would you like that?"

"Why, I've never thought about that. Do you think he'd come?"

"I imagine so. Next time you play over there with him, why not ask him?"

I had never had a colored friend over to my house nor had I ever been asked to theirs. There was never any socializing between us after playing. We usually departed with a "see 'ya later" but I never gave much thought to extending our relationship any further than that. Our schools were segregated, our lives were, too, and white boys hung around together. Colored boys did the same but never together.

"Okay, I might. Next time I play with him, I'll ask." Mother's graciousness confused me somewhat since none of my buddies ever even hinted at such a thing as having a colored boy over for lunch or dinner. Why, colored people couldn't even go to the movies with us. I didn't know where they went, but never with us.

I knew they had their own church. I remembered living on South Middle and seeing them all dressed up on Sunday mornings filing into that church on Frederick Street, and then I'd walk by and hear them singing, sometimes wailing loudly, hands clapping. It sure sounded different from my church, Centenary Methodist . . . a lot different.

Cape Central's basketball season wore on for the rest of the month. Our team wasn't very good. We finished with about a .500 record and were eliminated from regional tournament play in early March. I was on the squad and played enough to receive my letter, but being 6' 3", weighing only 140 pounds, I wasn't much of a threat. While our team floundered, Bunk was leading his team to the state championship for colored high schools.

Winter had pretty much had its final fling by mid-March. Warmer weather began to return as budding trees, daffodils, and tiny sprouts of grass began to show life in the lawns around town. With the change, we again gravitated to the outdoor courts around St. Mary's every afternoon after school and on the weekend. Baskctball had become my all consuming passion by that time. Playing baseball, my first love since a kid, was only a pleasant memory of younger days.

I dressed quickly that Saturday morning. The weather promised to be good with clear skies and temperatures in the mid-60's. I knew that there would be games going on over at the St. Mary's court. I wanted to be part of them, and besides, I might run into Bunk. I hadn't seen him in more than a month, and Cobb had won the state championship.

With Central's season over, I was allowed to keep my white Converse basketball shoes which were much better than the ones most wore on the outdoor courts. Bunk and his friends all played with tennis shoes that were long past their prime—shoes held together with friction tape and shoe strings knotted so frequently they resembled tassels hanging loosely off some ancient prince's slippers.

Crossing the intersection of Sprigg and William Streets only a block from our apartment, I headed south on Sprigg toward the court. I walked confidently toward the gleeful sounds of boys playing basketball below the street on the dirt court. A game was already in progress and it was just after 9 am.

I slid under the iron guard rails separating the church and the school and leaped down to the sloping playground. I walked slowly to where the action was. Bunk was there, and he waved to me as I positioned myself behind the wooden backboard held securely by a large, iron post.

Play stopped and Bunk walked over to where I was standing. "Hi, Mung. How've you been? Long time, no see," he said in a warm, friendly voice. Bunk was a little above six feet, light-skinned with almost perfect features. A wide smile showed flawless, pearly teeth. Long, lean hands joined to his well-muscled arms hung gracefully out from the short sleeves of a faded, multi-colored T-shirt.

"Good, Bunk. Congratulations on winning the state tournament. Nice goin'!" I extended my hand to his and shook it warmly as his colored teammates watched me with cautious stares.

"When somebody else comes along, maybe I can play. But not on your side. I wanna win!" I laughed loudly at my sarcastic remark, but no one else did.

They didn't seem to understand that my comment was made in jest. After all, Bunk was their idol, an icon, an all-state basketball player, probably the best basketball player Cobb ever had. To them, I was just another white boy who thought that he was better than any of them playing, and that included Bunk.

The game continued, and I watched with awe as my colored friend showed his graceful, creamy smooth moves. He was artistry in motion shooting the ball with unerring accuracy. Why, he could even "dunk" the ball, a feat that the rest of us believed was reserved for only the likes of the much taller pros. But, Bunk did it with ease. He seemed to do everything that way.

A few minutes later, one of Bunk's opponents decided he needed a rest. Bunk motioned for me to join the other team. He leaned back, smiled and pointed his finger at me, "Okay Mung, now's your chance. Let's see what you can do, and you're my man and you ain't goin' to get a point!"

I had played with and against Bunk many times, but for some reason, I was somewhat intimidated by his challenge and his taunting. All I wanted to do was play some basketball, not engage in some serious one-on-one confrontation with my champion.

For the next hour, we went at it, playing as if the game was the finals of the state tournament. Trying to contain Bunk and compete against a person of his ability was a special thing for me. It always had been, and I always tried to meet the challenge.

The match between him and me really wasn't that much to see, at least from my part. Yes, I scored some points as I was able to rebound a few errant shots under the basket, but it was impossible for me to drive around Bunk. Most of my jump shots were at such long range that only a couple swished the net. As for Bunk, he gave me a lesson scoring more or less whenever he wanted. I was clearly overmatched despite my concentrating totally on the task at hand. He was too much for my inexperience and lesser strength.

We took a break just before noon and plopped ourselves on the ground, our backs leaning up against the grade school wall warmed by the March sun. The others, all colored, stood quietly to one side, muttering softly, but occasionally glaring in our direction. I couldn't understand their stand-offishness because I had played with them before. They knew that Bunk and I were friends. Since I was the only white guy playing with them that morning, it shouldn't have made any difference, but it seemed to.

"Bunk, do you think you'll be going to college somewhere?" I asked expecting that a basketball scholarship was a sure thing for him.

"Nawww, Gene, I don't think so. I believe I'll go join the Army. I don't think college's for me." Bunk rolled his dark, liquid brown eyes upward toward the sky as if college were only a dream in somebody else's world . . . definitely not in his.

"Whaddaya mean, Bunk? You're an all-state player. You could get a scholarship, I'm sure you could." At that point, I figured that it was time to extend an invitation to have lunch at my house. "Say, Bunk, 'ya wanna go home with me and have some lunch? I only live a block away. Want to?"

"Do what? Go have lunch with you? You serious? I couldn't do that." Bunk turned away from me and watched at his friends who were beginning to amble off the court.

"Why not? I just live a block away. Let's go," I replied as I boosted myself up from my resting place. Bunk remained stationary. He pawed aimlessly at the dirt surrounding him. I gazed quietly at his departing friends.

"I just couldn't do that, Mung, I just couldn't. Don't you see?"

I pressed him harder. "Why can't you? My mother would be happy to feed us. She's talked about it. Come on!"

"Nawww, I need to get goin'. Besides, I'm not hungry," he said as he jumped up quickly and headed over to join his friends who were sauntering up the alley to Good Hope Street. They weren't looking back.

"But, you will sometime, won't you Bunk? Won't you?" I yelled.

Not looking back, Bunk mumbled, "Yeah, maybe sometime, but not today. It just wouldn't be right."

"Okay, Bunk, but some other time, right?"

"Right. Some other time."

The court was now empty. All the players had gone along with their basketball. There was no reason for me to sit there contemplating my friend's refusal to join me for lunch. There'd be another time. At least, I had offered. I left and walked slowly back to the apartment.

The warm day had taken its toll. I was still hot from the morning's scrimmage, my tee shirt and blue jeans covered with the court's dust and grime. I took a hot bath and felt better. Mother would be along soon. Perhaps it was preferable that Bunk hadn't come home with me. She wouldn't have been home anyway, and I would have had to fix lunch. Besides, he said that he wasn't hungry. That was probably the real reason he chose not to come.

Thirty minutes or so later, Mother entered from the back door where she had parked her car in the two-car garage behind the duplex. She carried a single bag of groceries which she placed on the counter by the antiquated stove.

"Mother, I've been over at St. Mary's all morning. Bunk was there and we played together, but on different teams. I did pretty well against him, but, gee, he's so much better than I am."

"Well, you have to remember that he's a year or so older than you. You'll catch up next season, I bet." Mother's encouraging words and her look of approval helped bolster my spirits.

"Mother, I asked Bunk to come back to the house and have lunch with me. I forgot that you weren't here. He didn't come anyway . . . said he wasn't hungry."

"Maybe, he had something else planned. Did you ask him to come another time?"

"Yeah, I did. And that's what he said, 'Some other time.' Wonder when that'll be? Soon?"

As my mother turned toward me to answer, her face took on an understanding, sympathetic look. "Soon? I hope so. It may take a long time, but when it comes, we'll be proud to have him join us."

As for my mother sitting down with me at that time and discussing the outrage and idiocy of segregation, she never did. Fortunately, I figured it out by myself. That was always her way.

Author's Note:

Bunk Petit and I continued to be friends and played lots of basketball on the outdoor courts around St. Mary's until school was out. Our conversations generally focused on basketball, very little on other things. While I asked him to join me and my mother for lunch or dinner many times, he always declined giving one excuse after another. I was too immature, too restricted to the status quo of the times to even think that his presence, as a young African American in my house would be too embarrassing or uncomfortable for him.

As I recall, he joined the Army during my senior year, a year that our basketball team ended up in the state's Class A Tournament and lasted until the quarterfinals. I later heard that Bunk had been sent to Korea. Whether he ever returned or ever went to college, I don't know. Had he played in today's non-segregated athletic competition, he surely would have led any team that he played on, high school or college, to a series of championship seasons. Nevertheless, he was one of my youth's early champions. I never saw or played with a better high school basketball player.

▟ ▟ ▟ ▟ ▟

Briarwood

It was the summer of 1951, another hot, humid and insufferable time of year in southeast Missouri where one wished he lived in the cool and refreshing mountain air of the Colorado Rockies.

Although just about to turn seventeen, I was hired as Scout Camp Lewallen's Assistant Waterfront Director with primary duties of teaching young scouts the skills necessary to acquire the canoeing and rowing merit badges. While my teaching capacity had yet to be tested, I felt confident that I had the basic know how to demonstrate the proper way to do the "J stroke" in a canoe and perform the "port pivot" in a row boat. Teaching became easier as the summer went along, despite my frustrations with mostly poorly coordinated scouts who should have spent their time studying birds rather than rowing a boat or paddling a canoe.

With camp ending in early August, I was anxious to get home. My senior year at Central High School started right after Labor Day and being a mighty senior at Central was a big deal, at least to a 17-year-old.

After my mother spent the better part of a day trying to wash out the two-month's accumulation of dirt and dust from my clothes, I decided to call my good friend, Andy Juden, also a senior-to-be. Since I had been out of contact with my Cape friends for the summer, I needed to get caught up as to "who's going with whom" and all those things that were so important in the life of a teenager.

Andy lived about a block away from my mother and me, an easy walk up Lorimier Street. He had been working that summer for his dad helping to manage the family's farming and business interests. While only six months or so older than I, Andy acted more like an adult, performing duties for his father that would never fall on an adolescent's shoulders. My waterfront duties paled in comparison to what he was doing that summer. Andy supervised men, even drove a truck. I paddled a canoe and led songs around the campfire!

My primary passion, next to girls, was the St. Louis Cardinal's baseball team. Being at camp, I had essentially lost contact with my team for the summer, not knowing whether they were in first place, last place, or any place. So, when Andy suggested that we go out to Briarwood to watch the Cardinals on television, I was ecstatic. I had seen television a few times while visiting my father in St. Louis, but never a baseball game, never a baseball game featuring my beloved Cardinals.

As we motored out to Briarwood west of Cape along Gordonville Road, Andy began to tell me a little history about the place. In his staccato-like delivery, he rattled off Briarwood's genesis, built by Andy's maternal grandfather in 1904.

I interrupted his incessant prattle and asked about the Houck family. I knew that the football stadium at Southeast Missouri State College was named Houck Stadium. My mother had also told me that Mr. Houck was related to the Judens.

"Now, who was Mr. Houck and what did he have to do with Briarwood?" I asked as Andy sped along the winding two-lane asphalt road in his olive green four-door Ford automobile.

"Well, my maternal grandmother, Irma Houck, was Louis Houck and Mary Hunter Giboney's daughter. Great Grandfather Houck was of German descent, a lawyer, railroad builder and the man instrumental in getting the college here in Cape. He also wrote a three-volume history of Missouri and a two-volume set of the Spanish Regime."

"Is he living today?"

"Oh, no, he died many years ago. But my grandfather, Papa Charlie, is still living. You've met him, haven't you?"

"I think so, but what did Papa Charlie do?"

"Well, he did a lot of things. Mostly, he owned farmland all over southeast Missouri and used to travel from one to the other on horseback. See, we're turning into the road which leads up to the house."

The narrow road was covered with white chat as it led up a slight elevation towards Briarwood. Giant oak and elm trees covered the surrounding woods making the three-storied white house almost invisible until we were practically upon it.

As we walked up the steep steps to the circular front porch and into the house, Andy went on with his running narrative of Briarwood. "See the grand staircase as it winds up to the upstairs floors? It was made from the timber growing here. But, let me show you something else. See here. Under the dining room table, there's a foot button where my grandmother would either signal the kitchen for the next dish to be served or buzz the kitchen that the table needed to be cleared. Even the upstairs rooms were connected to the kitchen by the buzzer."

"Yeah, Andy, but where's the television set?" I had heard enough about Briarwood. I wanted to see my Cardinals.

"Oh, the TV's in the parlor, but first, I've got to go upstairs and work the rotor to change the direction of the antenna. You never know just where the picture or the sound is coming from, either Memphis or St. Louis."

His explanation puzzled me. All I wanted to see was the baseball game. Memphis or St. Louis? I didn't care. We climbed the stairs to the third floor where Andy started turning the rotor. "There, I think that'll do it," he said as he led me back down the stairs to the parlor.

I positioned myself on the elegant Persian rug in front of the console as Andy turned on the set. Looking around the room, my eye caught a lovely old fireplace and some glass fronted shelves filled with old books. I had never seen such a beautiful room.

The sound of the broadcaster's voice filled the room as he described the beautiful baseball day in St. Louis. But I couldn't see Sportsman's Park or any of the Cardinal players. Was it snowing in either St. Louis or Memphis?

"Oh, look, Andy, I can almost see the players," I screamed as I began to see the faint outline of their bodies.

"No, I can do better than that," replied Andy as he bounded from the parlor and scurried up the stairs to the third floor. He again turned the antenna to seek better reception. "How's that?" He cried from his upward perch. "Any better?"

"I don't think so, but it's okay." I can still see the players. I can hear Dizzy Dean. The Cardinals are batting in the first. It's okay."

And there I stayed throughout the entire game, mesmerized, spread out on the rug looking happily at the set, snow filling the screen with an occasional glimpse of Stan Musial and other Cardinals' ghost-like images peering at me. I was enchanted and I was thrilled to see my team on television.

Despite my enthrallment, Andy made countless trips upstairs to work the antenna trying to get a clear and lucid picture from St. Louis or Memphis. It never got any better. Even if there was a blizzard, I couldn't have cared less.

I didn't return to Briarwood again until my senior prom. Andy and his long-time steady, Jeanette Hosea, and my date from Sikeston, Aletha Pitts, neither long-time nor steady, went out to Briarwood to park after the senior prom.

Driving out there, I recalled Andy's historical reminiscence of Briarwood the summer before as I began to parrot in animated fashion what I remembered about his great-grandfather and grandfather, the house, my first television experience in Cape and so on.

Gene with his date, Althea at the 1952 Cape Central High School Senior Prom.

No one said a word or seemed to care . . . not even that I was going to be Camp Lewallen's Waterfront Director that summer. I wondered why.

▚ ▚ ▚ ▚ ▚

Apples

Cape Central High School senior, Gene Munger, in the fall of 1951.

It was in the late fall of 1951, and a chilling northeastern evening breeze blew hard against my tall, skinny body as I made the short trip up Lorimier Street to Andy Juden's house. It wasn't winter yet, but it felt like it. Hunching over to buoy myself against the frigid air, I pulled my windbreaker collar tightly against the back of my neck and quickened my pace.

Andy was one of my best friends, a relationship that had grown over the past summer. My other pals couldn't figure out why I was friends with him. He wasn't a basketball player. It didn't matter, he was my friend, and I enjoyed his company.

He and his two sisters, Jill and Julia, lived with their parents in one of the more prominent houses in town, an imposing three-story brick structure set on a huge lot, replete with a badminton court and well-kept yard on the corner of Lorimier and Independence streets.

Andy drove a new car, a 1951 four-door Ford, and we managed to do a lot of things together. Sometimes, we'd just go cruising up and down Broadway along Main Street by the Mississippi River. We'd play the radio and just hang out. During our junior and senior years, we'd double date with our respective girlfriends, going to movies, football games, and whatever else we found to do. Going up to his house was always a treat for me. There was always plenty to eat, and we would go up to his third floor room which was paneled in rich walnut, complete with a full bathroom, even a shower. We'd play records and I'd hear his exciting stories about his going to camp in Colorado and visiting Chicago with his parents, all things that I had never done.

I skipped up the steep steps to the huge oak front door of the Juden residence and knocked twice. My knuckles stung with the effort. A few seconds later, the door opened widely and Andy's father stood there looking at me.

"Well, Hi, Gene. Good evening," he said. "Andy will be down in a minute. Come sit down." Although it was only about 8 pm and he was obviously home for the evening, Mr. Juden still wore a white shirt, with tie, a brown cardigan sweater and brown wool slacks. Seeing such formality on a week night impressed me.

He withdrew to a chair, high-backed and covered in black leather that seemed to be reserved for kings. Indeed, in my young eyes, Mr. Juden was a king! A relatively short man, he stood very erect and proud. He was balding with thin strands of graying hair combed neatly over a pate that showed the effects of a man who spent a lot of hours outdoors. All I knew, and Andy tried to explain it to me, was that his dad owned and managed property on Main Street, had a farm, and liked to hunt geese with big-time and important people across the river in southern Illinois.

I took a seat in their living room on their long, pillow-filled sofa and watched as Mr. Juden settled back in his chair, adjusted his glasses over his bulbous nose and resumed his reading. He read under a tall floor lamp whose light, hooded by an immense pale green shade, flooded directly and grandly over him.

Two large brass lamps rested majestically on the end tables by the sofa. A huge, oval shaped coffee table, at least three feet in diameter laden with a gigantic crystal ashtray, sat a few feet in front of me. The room itself was spacious, and one of its walls was adorned with built-in shelves holding a multitude of books. Several oil paintings of brightly colored flowers and ocean landscapes blended nicely with a luxurious Persian rug covering most of the parquet floor.

"Mr. Juden, what are you reading?" I asked.

"*The New Yorker*," he replied without looking up at me.

"*The New Yorker*? What's that?" I replied. I didn't ask why he would be reading some magazine about New York when he lived in Missouri.

"Well, Gene, it's kind of hard to explain," he replied as he removed his glasses and gazed directly at me. "It's not exactly about New York. Yes, some stories dwell on the city, but there are articles on national, even international subjects. But it's more than that. There are poetry, short stories, and cartoons. Really, it's, uh, uh . . . well, you'll just have to read it to get a feel for it. You might like it. I happen to think it's the best magazine in the world."

Mr. Juden then gave me an understanding smile and waited for a response from a 17-year-old lad whose magazine experience mostly amounted to reading *Boy's Life.*

"Oh, I'll have to read it sometime . . . if it's that good." I was embarrassed by my ignorance in the presence of one of the town's leading citizens.

"I'll give you this copy when I've finished with it. You might enjoy it." He then returned to his reading. I was simply awed by his presence.

Andy seemed to be especially anxious that fall evening as he rushed down the stairs from his third floor room. Like his father, he was always well dressed. He wore crisply pressed khaki trousers and a shirt, carried a brown gabardine jacket over his right arm, and resembled some big game hunter.

Acknowledging his father in a somewhat formal manner, he passed through the living room quickly, with me at his heels. With a wave back to his dad, he said a quick good bye which I echoed, and we went through the adjoining dining room into the kitchen, and out to the back yard where his car was parked.

"Come on, Mung, we're going to have some fun this evening," he said sliding easily into the front seat of his dark blue car, a sleek thing with overdrive, whatever that was, and a radio that could even pick up New Orleans late at night.

"Where we goin'?" I asked.

"You'll see," he replied as he started the car, backed it toward an empty garage that seemed never to be used and moved swiftly onto Lorimier Street and north up the steep hill towards Broadway, two blocks away.

Saying nothing, he then drove west on Broadway through town and out by Capaha Park where he stopped at another friend's house, Otis Williams, known to his friends as Hokey.

Hokey was a senior, too, and one of Andy's close friends. Two long beeps from the car's horn brought him running out of his house and alongside the car. He was dressed in blue jeans and a red wool shirt. A blue Mackinaw jacket draped loosely over his shoulders. Bigger than Andy, he was a husky fellow with a square, craggy face and walked somewhat arrogantly with a bear-like swagger.

"Ready to go?" Andy asked. "Yeah, let's do it," Hokey replied as he opened the car's back door, crawled in the seat and started chatting with Andy. Finally, he realized that there was someone else in the car.

In a surprised tone of a voice, he said, "Mung, what are you doing here? I didn't know you were going with us."

"Hi, Hokey," I answered. "I don't know where we're goin'. Andy won't tell me."

"And don't tell him, either!" Andy snapped, "It's a surprise!"

Andy jammed the car into gear and sped away from the curb, continuing west on Broadway to Kingshighway. He then turned north for about a quarter mile and angled eastward on Cape Rock Drive. The Drive was a meandering asphalt road that went around the northwestern end of Cape's more influential homes, then by a massive apple orchard and oak and maple woods, taking a southward direction along the Mississippi River and back towards town.

Cape Rock was also a popular spin for us "cruisers" or a convenient place to park and watch the "submarines race" with our dates up on the river's bluffs.

A full moon lighted the road ahead of us, so bright that the car's headlights seemed unnecessary. Abruptly, Andy left the paved road and pulled over on the small shoulder. Looking out of the car's window, all I could see were trees with branches laden with apples resembling Christmas trees trimmed with yellow shining ornaments. We had stopped in front of Och's orchard.

My friends hopped out and rushed around the car to open the trunk. I sat still without saying a word, bewildered by what was going on. I then flipped open my door and to my surprise, saw an empty bushel basket perched at an awkward angle on the side of the drainage ditch separating the road from the wire fence guarding the orchard.

"Hey, look! There's a bushel basket by the side of the road. Where did it come from?" I asked in a puzzled voice.

"Whaddya expect, Dummy. Of course, it's there. That's what I got out of the trunk." Andy's exasperated voice lifted over the increasingly gusting wind as he tossed the empty basket over the fence. He and Hokey followed in hot pursuit.

All I could see was a flurry of flailing arms as the steady sound of apples hitting the bottom of the basket. In a few minutes, both guys, beads of sweat glistening from their perspiring faces, approached me with the mother lode.

"Give us a hand, Mung, so we can get out of here." Andy's tone of voice emulated that of some Hessian general barking orders to his troops.

"Sure, Andy, but what are we going to do with all those apples?" I asked as I lifted the bounty from their outstretched arms. The weight surprised me and my knees buckled from the unanticipated heavy load.

"Don't worry about it. We'll show you later," he said.

I couldn't imagine our eating all of those apples. They were ripe golden delicious, and this was plainly stealing, but perhaps not really stealing. I rationalized that Mr. Ochs would never ever know, probably wouldn't care, that anyone had taken apples that had fallen from the tree. They wouldn't be picked anyway. They'd just rot there. Perhaps, we were doing him a favor. That clearly was not stealing. I felt somewhat better.

"Let's get out of here," cried Hokey from the front seat, "It's getting late."

Instead of continuing eastward around Cape Rock Drive, Andy did a quick U-turn and headed back toward Kingshighway and into town. No one said a word. I felt like I was on some clandestine mission in which the country's national security was at stake.

Speeding east on Broadway through town, Andy turned left up the high hill to Bellevue Street, made a sharp right turn and proceeded one block until the road abruptly ended.

"Hey, this is Fort A, isn't it?" I asked.

Fort A was known to be a small fort used during the Civil War by the Confederate forces. It lay on a high bluff overlooking the river and provided an excellent point of defense against federal troops using the river as an entry into the town. Fort A, however, produced minimal tourist interest, and its preservation and care reflected that, a heavily overgrown area of neglected weeds, high grass and brush.

"Right," Andy answered, "and now, we're going to have some fun."

"Doing what?" I responded. "Just what are we going to do?"

"Follow us, I'll show you," said Hokey as he filled his loose Mackinaw's pockets with apples. Andy did the same and pointed for me to follow.

I edged forward with the boys to the edge of the bluff overlooking the river, now fully visible by the full moon's light. Main Street, Cape's primary north-south commercial roadway, loomed almost straight down from our position on the limestone cliffs. The brisk chilly wind coming off the river continued to blow unrelentingly through us as we peered motionless at the passing cars below.

Blowing hard into his clenched fists to warm his hands, Andy broke the night's silence and said, "Let's get this guy coming. See him?" A car was moving slowly toward us in a northerly direction.

"Steady . . . steady . . . now fire! Let him have it!" Like mortar shells being rained on troops in battle, they unloaded their apples from their pockets and flung them mightily in a series of arching throws on the unsuspecting car below. I edged back from the bluff and waited to see what would happen. The wait seemed endless.

The missiles reached their target heralded by a staccato-like sound of victory. Thump, thump, as they found their marks on the vehicle's hood and top. The mortar men howled with delight. Their aim had been perfect.

"Let's do it again!" Hokey yelled excitedly. "Let's do it again!"

"Okay," replied Andy. "But let's hurry and load back up. We don't need those folks we hit to come after us. Wait a minute, Mung, you didn't throw your apples?   How come?"

"Oh, I just wanted to watch. I didn't want to throw any," I said. Andy's angry response was predictable.

"Watch? We didn't bring you up here to watch. Now, go back to the car and get some apples. Hurry up!"

I really didn't want to throw apples at cars, but it did look like a lot of fun. Why not? Apples couldn't hurt anybody.

I ran back to the car, crammed both pockets with apples, and returned to the bluff. As I joined my friends, another car was coming, this time from the north.

"Ready . . . Aim . . . Fire!" our general ordered. Lingering silence, then the sweet sound of another victory filled the air, "Thump . . . thump . . . thump!" Another direct hit on the innocent, unprepared, and obviously startled driver below sounded. Bullseye!

Our commander growled out the order to retreat, one not necessary as we all were galloping back to the car to safety and a quick departure from an angry motorist who, at the very moment, could be tearing up the Broadway hill to find the thugs who had banged his car and scared the blue blazes out of him.

But the attack team wasn't content to leave the scene without giving it one more shot. Andy stopped the car right in the middle of the intersection of Bellevue and Lorimier. Both he and Hokey leaped from their seats and whipped back to the trunk. With a quick twist of the key, Andy opened the trunk. Hokey leaned over and picked up the half-filled basket of apples and carried it over to the crest of the steep Lorimier Hill.

Andy quickly caught up with him and together in one concerted motion, they heaved the remaining apples down the long hill to a quiet Broadway. As the two warriors watched their once mighty cache of arms rolling helter-skelter between parked cars and curbs, they stood quietly and proudly for a few beats before returning to the car.

I could not believe what *they*—what *we* had done. My body tingled all over with the excitement of doing something so wrong! First we stole apples.   Then we took our larcenous loot to make an unwarranted assault on some poor driver who had done nothing to warrant such an unnecessary and irresponsible act and then trashing one of our town's streets with the remainder of our unfired ammunition. And no one had caught us . . . no one would ever know!

Speeding down Broadway, Andy celebrated our victory by turning on the car's radio. Rosie Clooney's *Come On A My House* blared loudly as we headed back toward Hokey's house. All of us babbled incessantly, overcome with the euphoria of our encounter. Andy stopped talking, pulled his comb from his pocket, and quietly started rearranging his wind-blown hair back to its original form and neatness.

Our driver ignored the four-way stop sign at the intersection of Broadway and West End Boulevard. There were no cars in sight. Hokey and I didn't even notice our leader's blunder. We were totally into the bursting Latin rhythms of Rosie's band, bopping along and clapping our hands together.

About that time a city police car came out of nowhere with his red flashing lights looking like some fire engine racing to a burning building. Andy saw it first, realized what he had done and pulled over to the curb immediately. He knew he had been caught.

We glanced back over our shoulders through the rear window and discovered why he had stopped. Our car was the object of a cop's immediate interest. We all became stone silent as Andy flipped off the radio.

The officer, a tall, slender man dressed smartly in his blue gabardine uniform, got out of his squad car and approached ours quickly. My heart was exploding inside me. Suppose he knew what we had done? Had he been alerted to be on the lookout for some guys who were throwing apples on cars along Main Street? Did he know we were the likely culprits? Would we go to jail, maybe to prison? What would my mother and dad think? I wouldn't be able to play basketball anymore. I wouldn't finish high school, couldn't go to college. My whole life would be ruined!

Holding his long-barreled flashlight and peering directly into Andy's face, the policeman said, "Good evening, I suppose you didn't see that stop sign back there at the corner?" His voice was not stern or threatening. Rather, it was almost the voice of a caring parent. I had expected the voice of a tyrant.

Andy answered in a most contrite voice. "I'm sorry, officer, I just wasn't paying attention. I was taking my friend home, and we were talkin' and . . . ."

"May I see your driver's license, please," he said as he bent down and looked through the car's open window. Despite his calm and reassuring voice, he gave us all a threatening sneer, as if we were some suspected criminals who had just pulled off the crime of the century. He then pointed his flashlight directly into Hokey's eyes which appeared scared and wide-eyed from the back seat. His eyes resembled a young fawn caught in the headlights of some advancing car.

Continuing to focus his light on Hokey, the patrolman asked, "Is this your friend you were taking home, or is it the boy in the back seat?" I looked down at the floor. My mouth's inside was too dry to respond. I was virtually paralyzed. I became sick to my stomach.

"Yes, Sir," answered Andy, now sounding a little more confident and in control, "That's Otis Williams, he lives just down the street. That's my other friend, Gene Munger, in the back seat. He lives near me. I'll take him home next, Sir."

The officer examined Andy's license carefully and grunted, "Well, I'm only going to give you a warning this time, young man, but next time, you'll have to pay a fine. In the future, be more careful."

"Yes Sir, officer. I will, err, we will. Thank you, officer. We'll never do it again. Promise!" Only some high priest could have sounded more repentant.

As the policeman drove away, Andy's sigh of relief filled the car. I was still too frightened to say anything. I only wanted to get home and fast. I'm sure Hokey felt the same way as he abandoned the car before Andy had even stopped at the curb in front of his house. He didn't say good night, he just ran fast up the terraced steps to his front door and disappeared.

Back at Andy's house, I, too, made a rapid exit from the car, ran through the side yard, and down the middle of the street at lightning speed to get home as swiftly as I could. It was now just past 10 pm. Coach Muegge's curfew was an hour earlier. I knew that my mother would be terribly upset that I was out so late on a school night.

Hitting the front porch of the big apartment house like some frightened animal trying to escape the hunter's gun, I flew up the three flights of stairs, two-three steps at a time, to our apartment. Mother was waiting. She wasn't happy. Her pale, blue eyes pierced my anxious face like the lashing beam of a laser.

"Where have you been? Why didn't you call me? I was worried. I called Mr. Juden, and he said that you had gone out driving with Andy and you shouldn't be too late. Where were you?"

"I'm sorry, Mother, I should have called you. We were just driving around—me, Andy, and Hokey Williams. That's all. We weren't doing anything, really." I couldn't look her in the eyes. She would know I wasn't telling her the truth. She knew me too well.

To my relief, she didn't press me for any further explanation or amplification of my evening's whereabouts and shenanigans. "Well, it's late now, and you need to be in bed," she said in a still somewhat agitated voice.

Suddenly, her tone turned sweet and caring, "I baked you an apple pie, but I guess you'll have to wait and have some tomorrow."

"Oh, that's good. I'll have some tomorrow." It just didn't seem quite right to bring any more apples into my life that evening.

■■■■■

Tigers! Tigers! Yes . . . We Are the Tigers!

No one, including a rather apathetic student body, was too excited about Central's basketball team as it prepared itself for its first game in early December, 1951. Our previous season year was lackluster in most respects, with a 13-12 record led by senior players whose talents were minimal but dedicated juniors whose talents were still in the discovery stage.

The previous year's B team made up of some promising freshmen and sophomores had shown some dash and encouragement, but they were young, green and didn't expect to add much to the total mix. In other words, the 1951-52 season was expected to come and go with a yawn, a sigh and "wait 'til next year" when some of the young kids would get a bit more exposure and learn to play better.

Central's first close victory of the season occurred in early December at Illmo-Fornfelt, 59-57. The opening season's game was a loss to nearby Jackson, our arch-rival. Things seemed to improve as the team won the "Big 4" Tournament handily in mid-December beating Sikeston, Popular Bluff, and Jackson, all "bigger" schools in southeast Missouri. While Central had a respectable record of 4-1 after the tournament victory, there were no predictions of greatness or glory for the Tiger's season. After all, we had not beaten anyone of significance. Further, our starting five was made up of two seniors, two juniors, and a sophomore, hardly a line-up that stirred anybody's imagination.

Dave Howard, a junior forward, was by far the best player of the group. He was an excellent shooter, although only about 6'2" in height and slightly built.

The other junior was Walter "Doc" Ford, a feisty, aggressive 5'7" guard, fairly well built and totally confident that he was better than anyone who ever played. Despite sometimes erratic floor play and inconsistent scoring, Doc was a gamer, hated losing, and spared no one from his acerbic wit and candor. He was, also, one of my best friends.

Paul "Herk" Stehr was the sophomore starting guard. Thin, but wiry, Herk's 6' frame brought forth nothing but hustle and determination. Unusually mature for his age and experience, he brought a kind of quiet leadership to the team that grew as the season progressed.

Don "Petty" Pettigrew, was the other senior and starting forward. About 6'2", Petty was fundamentally sound, mechanical in execution and steady under pressure. Only an average shot maker, but sometimes prolific, he rebounded well and blended well with the others.

Our 6th man was C. W. "Dub" aka "Gobbler" Suedekum. A sophomore, Dub, was still growing, although his nearly 6'3" body fell far short of trying to keep up with his neck, which was elongated enough to earn him his nickname. At the season's start, Dub was still having trouble getting his feet and the rest of his body in sync, but before the season had ended, he had developed into a valuable, reliable team member.

The letterman of the 1951-1952 Cape Central High School Basketball season. From left to right, <u>front row</u>: Walter Ford, Jim Miller, Paul Stehr, Ranney Young, and Gary Metje; <u>second row</u>: Don Pettigrew, Jack Fowler, Gene Munger, C. W. Suedekum, Dave Howard, and Tom Cushman.

I was the starting center, all 6'4" and 165 pounds of me. Being left-handed, this served me well with those opponents not accustomed to guarding "southpaws" in the post. I basically had one move, a fake left—a quick dribble around my unsuspecting guard and an easy lay-up for a basket. In time, opponents caught on fairly well to that move, but with coaching, I soon developed an average jump shot around the key of the circle which helped overcome my fairly weak right handed move.

I couldn't jump very well and was certainly not physical with such a tall, thin frame. My size 15 feet would occasionally interfere with my forward progress causing me to fall sometimes headlong onto the hard floor with no opponent within 10 feet. Such an act, particularly evident during my sophomore and junior years, had earned me the well-deserved and certainly accurate sobriquet of "Paddlefoot."

I've written about Coach Louis Muegge in other reminisces of my adolescence. He was definitely a saint to me, my mentor, my surrogate father. Since high school, my life had been enormously affected by his influence, more so than any man before or since.

The Tigers' early success was overshadowed, however, by St. Mary's Catholic High School, which, in late November, had stunned southeast Missouri's sports fans with a last second, upset win over mighty Puxico, a small school of less than 200 students. This team of country boys ran the legs off of every school in its path, and won the Class B State Tournament in 1951. The St. Mary's Bulldogs were the toast of the town, and few people gave Central any chance to beat the "giant killers" in its forthcoming December 20th game.

That game was pivotal in setting the stage for the rest of the season. The final score, 56-24, obviously shocked the *Southeast Missourian's* sports page readers the next afternoon . . . "Central Turns Hot to Defeat St. Mary's Before Big Crowd."

Emmet "Scoop" Kelly, the long-time writer for the paper, captured the tenor of the game in his most inimitable style:

> A hopped-up band of Central High Tigers had a firm grasp on one leg of the mythical city basketball championship today by virtue of a brilliant, more-or-less unexpected victory over the St. Mary's High Bulldogs at the Arena Building Thursday night.
>
> It was one of those furious, devil-take-the-hindmost contests that saw the 1,199 fans on their feet as often as they were in their seats as they almost raised the roof with their unrestrained cheers.
>
> Central won because the Tigers carried the battle to the Bulldogs all the way.
>
> Mick Shannon, a comer if there ever was one, was held to one field goal as the usual scoring star found the going tough because of Central's Gene Munger, who carried out a big assignment in grand style, and offensively racked up 14 points himself to lead the field.
>
> Another luminary in this star-packed encounter was Tiger guard Don Pettigrew, whose work on the backboards was particularly outstanding.
>
> All in all St. Mary's made only nine field goals, and this by a team that has been scoring at the rate of two points per minute.

Such a victory was totally intoxicating for the team, the school, and even the town. Our guys were for real! For me, someone who had never really been recognized as a star, my performance temporarily brought forth generous outpourings of praise, adulation and recognition from young and old. Sudden fame is a fickle thing, but to a 17-year-old kid, it was totally awesome. But fame had its downside as I was quick to discover.

Central's next challenge was Cape's College High School's Annual Christmas Tournament. Because of our victory over St. Mary's, we were seeded second, with Puxico seeded first. The whole town anxiously awaited the final game, knowing that Puxico and Central would definitely be there.

We made it, tearing through three opponents, Delta, Illmo-Fornfelt and College High School into the finals with Puxico. Fan interest was at a feverish pitch. The game promised to be one for the ages. Would upstart Central put the farm boys in their place once and for all, or would the farm boys return the city slickers to cruisin' in their fancy cars and hangin' out at Wimpy's?

To the team's and the town's disappointment, Puxico's gave us slickers a real lesson. I played horribly and was totally outclassed. The whole team did likewise except for the gutty, inspired play of Stehr. He scored more than 16 points in a cause that was hopeless after about the first 10 minutes which mercifully ended in at least a 20 point defeat. My previous meteoric rise to stardom fell like an asteroid out of the heavens, crashing with a heavy thud onto the field house's floor in front of more than 3,500 disappointed and disenchanted fans.

Porter's Prattle, a column written by Lee Porter for the *Cape Girardeau News*, summed it up very succinctly for readers in his January 3, 1952 column, to wit:

ALL-STAR SELECTIONS STILL TOSS-UP

The on-again, off-again performances of the city's high school basketeers in the past two weeks have really put the race for berths on the city's first All-Star Team into a scramble. While talking with a couple members of the *Cape News'* panel, we confided that every position was still a toss-up as far as we were concerned. They expressed similar ideas. Central's Gene Munger is one example to illustrate the idea.

In Central's early season game with St. Mary's, Munger's work—especially defensively—was as good as has been seen on a basketball court by these eyes. In holding Shannon to two points, he displayed poise, alertness and hustle. He really looked good. Then, in the finale of the Christmas Tournament against Puxico, Gene couldn't seem to do anything right. He particularly had trouble holding onto passes, and in general, bore no resemblance to the Munger that played so flawlessly against St. Mary's.

Porter went on to point out additional deteriorating play from College High's Gary Rust and St. Mary's Mickey Shannon. He closed his column by writing:

Perhaps, and we sincerely hope, the boys will round back into their early season form and treat the fans to some of the hardwood wizardry they showed previously.

I was devastated by the column, but, Porter was right. I had really stunk up the place against Puxico, and I had completely let my teammates down.

At the first of the year, we were unbeatable, but we nearly were upset by College High School in late January. This was a team we had beaten by 24 points in the Christmas Tournament, but in this one, we barely escaped, winning on a last minute free throw by Stehr, 50-49. I really received my comeuppance in this game.

The Preps had Burk Elrod as its center. Burk was tall, about 6'3", uncoordinated, a somewhat clumsy player who more or less played like the proverbial robotic man, showing no finesse or style. Everyone knew that Burk couldn't jump, could be faked easily and was no threat to score.

The first time the Preps brought the ball down the floor, I was ready for him. He had one shot—a quick turn-around jump shot, always going to his right, always.

As the ball was passed into him, he crouched and faked left. I knew he would then move right and get off his jump shot. I would then jam it down his throat. He did, and I jumped straight up, as if launched from a powerful Zeus rocket to block the shot. Instead of shooting, he only pump-faked and then quickly dribbled past my skyrocketing body into the basket for the goal. I had never been so outfoxed in my life. I was humiliated. Their fans howled with laughter. Our fans only groaned at the spectacle of seeing their starting center made into a bumbling buffoon. Burk caught fire after that playing perhaps the finest game of his high school career and scored 16 points.

Area basketball fans were anticipating the next match up between St. Mary's and Central. By early February, our record had soared to 15-2, but January's schedule had not been too challenging and we beat most of our opponents by more than 20-25 points. Still, St. Mary's was no pushover despite our ridiculously easy victory over them in late December: 56-24. We all knew that this game would be different. The Dogs would be hungry.

Central's play that evening was a far cry from its December massacre of St. Mary's. The Tigers had their hands full from the very tip-off. Probably of all the games I ever played at Central, this was the one that local basketball fans have likely remembered and talked about since: "the night Munger beat St. Mary's while flat on his back." Kelly's coverage went like this:

TIGERS GRAB OFF ST. MARY'S GAME
Late Minutes in Contest Tell Tale

Central High School snatched the fat from the fire Friday night at the Arena, surging ahead in the last minute of play to defeat this intra-city rival, St. Mary's High, 38 to 36.

St. Mary's played superb basketball against the erratic Tigers, who ran in on-again, off-again spurts. The Bulldogs were rebounding off both boards consistently, while Central at times couldn't miss taking the ball and at others needed a magnet to locate it.

Don Pettigrew tied the score, 30 to 30, with a half minute played in the fourth quarter. Bounding Bob Miller, Earl Blechle and Glenn Farrar pushed six points through while the Tigers were idle. There the score stood when St. Mary's put on a freeze.

Dave Howard was fouled in a melee, sank the free throw, then made a setup as Walter Ford drove through to gain the ball and passed off to him. Ford booted the score to 36-35 with a field goal and with a minute and 15 second to go, Gene Munger sank a free throw to tie it.

Both teams then had to shoot, and Central got the ball. Munger, under the basket, was propelled backward. As he fell, he pushed the ball under-handed up to the goal. It fell through and Central led, 38 to 36. That was the game.

Our team was less than pleased with its performance. It was lucky to win and indeed, a lucky shot had pulled it out for us. Coach Muegge was furious afterwards. The next day, he chewed us out with well-chosen expletives and berated us one-by-one for our lackluster, uneven performance.

He accused us of being too complacent, cocky if you will, and not willing to fully commit ourselves to being the best we could be. He then strongly suggested that our minds were on other things, like girls (God forbid!) and warned, "you guys better quit playing with yourselves, and give that up until the end of the season."

All of us were crushed. We felt bad. We had let the Coach, our fans, and ourselves down. There was no private team meeting, but each of us more or less came to the conclusion that we would concentrate fully on basketball, and while we weren't going to quit thinking about girls (just how much sacrifice did one have to make?), we would stop playing with ourselves. We'd do anything for the coach and the team.

The St. Mary's thing and Coach Muegge's blistering put-down of his Tigers helped the team refocus positively for the Regional Basketball Class A tournament to be played February 26-29 at our home court, the Arena. The winner would go on to the State Class A Tournament in Columbia, Missouri.

On February 13, we buried the College High School Preps, our intra-city rival, 66-35, which was sweet vindication for our narrow victory in early January. Burk Elrod, who earlier had reduced my defense to no defense, scored a mere two points, both on free throws.

We blew Sikeston and Delta away by 27 and 36 points respectively in our last two regular season games as the Tigers entered the tournament with a record of 20-2. With that record, we were seeded first, although, the only team in the tournament we had played previously that season was the Perryville Pirates, a team we had beaten by 26 points in early January.

The *Cape News* announced its "City All-Star Team" on February 21. I was a unanimous choice, with Doc Ford and Dave Howard also named. Herk Stehr and Don Pettigrew made the second team, which meant that all of Central's starting five made either first or second team all-stars.

Our first tournament game was against Fredericktown. After some early tournament jitters, we gathered ourselves together and won in a romp 60-40.

Our next game was against a tough DeSoto team. Scoop's reporting read like this:

> The game between the Central High School Tigers and the DeSoto Dragons was as good a high school game as has been seen here for a long time. The large crowd got its money's worth.
>
> The Tigers and the Dragons fought a great battle, with the outcome in doubt throughout.
>
> In the third quarter the Tigers had a 41 to 35 advantage but DeSoto rallied to cut down the margin to 41 to 39 as the period closed.

Opening the final quarter, Bob Parmeley tied the score at 41 to 41 on a field goal but Walter Ford sent Central in the lead, 43 to 41, a moment later, which they held for the remainder of the playoff game.

The final score was 48 to 44 in Central's favor with Dave Howard being the Tigers' big gun with 21 points on 10 field goals and one free toss.

In the final game, Central totally outclassed a good Flat River team 52-34. I vividly remembered a brief moment with Coach Muegge prior to the game. He had us all in the dressing room for a last minute team session before we took the court against the Bears.

I don't recollect any stirring or impassioned speech by Coach. He was not wont to do that. He quietly reminded us that while we had had a good season, it would not be a great season unless we won and went to state. Of course, we knew that and with a mad scramble out the door, we ran out to finish the task, confident, pumped, and ready to play.

I lagged behind a bit and walked out of the locker room door with the coach. I wanted to tell him that we were going to win this game for him, that he could count on it, but I felt that such a dramatic statement at that time would be hokey. I said it anyway. I knew it was going to happen!

He smiled and put his huge, muscular arm around my neck and said, "I know that, Mung. I know that." And we did just that before 1,200 screaming fans. Petty accepted the first place trophy for the Tigers. We were going to state!

One of the biggest things about the trip to Columbia was that we got to stay in a motel, away from home. Coach Muegge had us bedded down in the All States Village Motel, a sprawling series of white painted dingy cabins joined together in groups of two. The team shared six cabins.

The Missourian reported:

> A caller in mid-afternoon Tuesday at its All-State Village quarters found the Central squad a studious lot. In one cabin, big Gene Munger was poring over his trigonometry. Walter Joe "Doc" Ford was curled up with a copy of *The Count of Monte Cristo*, a required book for English. Most of the others were similarly engaged.

Our first game that evening was with Jefferson City, a team that had not been figured to make it to state. We knew nothing about them and how they played. It wasn't important because we knew we were going to win anyway.

We played in Brewer Field House, a cavernous barn of a building on the University of Missouri campus where the big school's Tigers played their home basketball games. Taking the floor that Tuesday evening was terrifying, especially with the field house filled to capacity. I had never played in front of that many people, estimated to be at least 5,000. If my other teammates held similar fears and anxieties, they didn't seem to show it. Doc Ford was at his most irreverent best, needling, cajoling, and insulting each and every one of us. By game time, we were loose and ready to play.

And play we did! We took charge early and routed the Jays 52-30 in rather easy fashion. Bud Thies, the *St. Louis Globe Democrat's* sports writer described the victory:

> Jefferson City's Jays found the high-class company of the state finals too rough and bowed to Cape Central, 52-30. Central grabbed a 10-5 lead in the initial period and kept it growing. At halftime, it was 25-11 and going into the final period, 40-21.
>
> Joe Kretschmar was a one-man team for the losers. He generaled the team and used his push-shot from outside for 14 points. Gene Munger, Cape's tall pivotman, pivoted nicely to outsmart the box defense around him

and rack up 22 points, 10 of them on sit-ups
as his catlike quickness left the Jays standing.

After Tuesday night's game, we didn't have to play again
until Thursday afternoon at 2 pm. Miles away in Cape
Girardeau, the fans and the student body were in a frenzy
making plans to charter buses, take cars, or hitch hike,
finding any way they could manage to get to Columbia and
watch their beloved Tigers play their second state
tournament game.

In the meantime, our team was getting the royal
treatment as one of the state's final Class A teams. We had
an honorary coach, Dick Barnett, chairman of the Chamber
of Commerce committee and owner of a men's store. He
gave each team member a brown checked pork pie hat which
each of us wore proudly as we ambled together, cocky and
proud, through downtown Columbia stores.

Our Thursday afternoon opponent was University City, a
St. Louis suburb. We had seen them play in the tournament
and knew that these big city boys were going to be tough, but
after our easy victory against Jeff City, we knew that we
were more than up to the challenge.

On that late Thursday morning, right after we had
returned from our pre-game meal, New Year's Eve came to
the All States Village! At least 200 well wishers, including
cheerleaders and students from two chartered buses
descended on the Tiger team. Even my best fan, my
wonderful mother, who never missed a game the entire
season, was there. With this mob scene, the entire team
totally lost its concentration for the game we were about to
play leaving any hope to win on the slushy snow-covered
grounds of the motel's grounds firmly mired among the
spontaneous cheers and yells generated by the Central fans.

Prior to the game, Coach Muegge told me that my play
against the Jays had piqued the interest of the Missouri
University basketball coaching staff, and if I continued to
play well, I could expect a scholarship offer. This bit of
intelligence brought a huge lump in my throat. Up to that
point, I had never figured I would even be considered to play
basketball at the University of Missouri. Wow!

The Tigers were never really in the quarter final game with the University City Indians. We were flat, mentally exhausted from the unexpected outpour of fan fervor and support of two hours ago. Our B Team would have given a better performance. From a personal standpoint, I was never any factor in the game. For that matter, no one was, although Dub Suedekum came off the bench. He scored 8 points, his high for the season, and only a prelude to his receiving All-State honors in his senior year when the Tigers won the Class A State Tournament.

Bud Thies, the *Globe's* sports writer filed this game report:

U. CITY, ST. LOUIS, DE ANDREIS GAIN STATE SEMI-FINALS

De Andreis, University City and St. Louis U. High made it safely through the first three quarter-final games of the Class A state high school basketball tournament.

University City's Indians won 54 to 37.

The Indians broke away mid-way in the second period after a hard-fought first quarter found them in the red. It was floor errors on the part of the Tigers which permitted the breakthrough.

Sauer and Cristal of U. City and Gene Munger of Cape were outstanding. Sauer held Munger to five points the first three periods and then it didn't matter that the big pivot man broke away for 10 more. Munger, on the other hand, held the U. City pivot man practically scoreless.

With our tails between our legs, our heads drooping, we ate our post game meal and went back to the Village. We had gotten our butts beat! The season was over, and we had disappointed our fans and ourselves with a bummer of a game similar to our ignominious defeat at the hands of Puxico in the

Christmas Tournament. That seemed like such a long time ago with 14 straight victories in between.

None of us wanted to see that evening's quarter final games. We had overdosed on basketball, our season was over. Instead, we hung around the motel, danced in the rooms with our girlfriends and those other students who had made the trip. Despite losing, one would have thought we had won the world's basketball championship. We were having a party!

1951-1952 Central High School Basketball Squad. From left to right, <u>Front Row</u>: Earl Macke, Don Alba, Paul Masterson, Louis Meisenheimer, Dave Young, Eric Mount, Donald Nanney, Bob Hunt, Tom Womack, and Arthur Welch; <u>Middle Row</u>: Gary Tomlinson, Jack Boswell, Gerald Hinton, Jerry Erlbacher, Don Koch, Wood McComb, Jim Miller, Walter Ford, Gary Metje, and Russell Withers; <u>Back Row</u>: Paul Heuring, Don Pettigrew, Jack Fowler, Gene Munger, C. W. Suedekeum, Dave Howard, Tom Cushman, Paul Stehr, and Ranny Young.

My English teacher, Alene Sadler, sent me this note right before the team traveled to Columbia. The note said:

> Gene,
> May I add my wish for the best of luck to you. We're right proud of you, and I do hope you go right on winning.
> A. Sadler

Following Miss Sadler's letter was my father's letter, hand written on both sides of a single yellow legal-sized sheet of paper. He had separated from my mother and me at the start of 7th grade. The letter was written at 10:30 pm on that fateful Thursday when the Tigers lost the final game.

My dear boy,

This to congratulate a real basketeer and a marvelous player and sportsman in the fullest. That's my boy!

I'm ever so proud of you and all you've done—quietly, seriously, and without any fanfare and selfishness—your record for Cape will be remembered, and you bear in the school itself proof positive of the high standards of accomplishments a student can achieve.

Remember today's disappointment had to come—there is always the limit—a time when victory is snatched from us regardless of all we undeniably put into the game, whether basketball or the trial of a law suit. It was not a loss chargeable to you individually. It was a team loss and you all bore it well. Your season made all of us swell with pride.

Your game was marvelous throughout the season and it proves that you not only play basketball but better still, you've begun to learn and master the job assigned to you. There will be other jobs to do in your life, and you will do them well.

I am so pleased, Son, and happy, too, that it was possible for Mother to see the game, enjoy the little vacation, and be with you in your hour of well-earned recognition. She is so rightfully proud of her Little Boy.

Get your rest . . . both of you.

Love,

Daddy

To reminisce over other events in my life that took place more than 50 years ago is a very moving thing. I obviously couldn't remember everything. Some names, etc., are probably not correct, but, I think I remembered the most important things, at least to me.

How blessed I was to have had those experiences, to have shared them with my peers, my teammates, who for all purposes, most have faded completely out of my life to do their thing, hopefully bigger and better after that magnificent championship season.

▌ ▌ ▌ ▌ ▌

Pepper Martin

The first weekend in March 1952 had turned unseasonably warm for southeast Missouri. A strong southern wind had blown its way from the Gulf. Cape Girardeau was getting a welcome respite from the usual cold and unforgiving blasts of frigid air that normally stayed around until early April.

It was also the first Saturday since the Cape Central Tigers had lost their quarter final game to University City, Missouri in the Class A State Basketball Tournament. Our team had returned home on Friday, disappointed, but proud upon getting to the tournament after losing only two games the entire season. To my surprise, I had been selected to be on the second all-tournament team. Further, my basketball play during the tournament had caused "Sparky" Stalcup, the University of Missouri's basketball coach, to suggest to Coach Muegge I had a promising future there. To play basketball at the university would be special.

My spirits were extraordinarily high that balmy weekend, about as euphoric as a high school senior could be. Life couldn't have been any better for me. Good things appeared to be ready to happen.

My high school sweetheart, Alice Jean Porritt and I had gotten back together after a brief separation caused by some forgettable misunderstanding. Rather than seek immediate and sane reconciliation, we let our pride and obstinacy take over. When we lost the last game, however, we made up and resumed our steady relationship that had prevailed more or less since we were juniors.

My good friend and teammate, Walter Joe "Doc" Ford and I had spent the day cruising the town in his dad's two-door 1946 Studebaker, a grotesque stylish thing that gave the appearance of looking as if it were either coming or going. One couldn't tell by what they saw. With the afternoon's temperature approaching 70 degrees, we rolled down the window and drove through Cape's streets expecting to see our friends and especially girls.

We could have cared less about the style of his dad's car. Style had no keen interest for us in those days. It was the transportation, the "wheels" that really mattered. And if you didn't have wheels, at least access to some, you really weren't "with it."

The car's back seat was so small that even a dwarf would have been cramped, but its closeness didn't matter either. Doc and I would double date in that heap, regardless of my tall, gangling 6'4" frame. I always managed to tuck myself into the confining space.

Doc had played point guard on the team and was our playmaker. Only a junior, he had been selected to play on the All-City basketball team for his aggressive play and leadership. Barely 5'7", he was always looking for a rumble, never backing down from any of our teammates or opponents. On the basketball court, he was in control. Doc, always driven with an intense, competitive drive, was known for having no patience with those who gave less than their best.

We had been friends since I moved to Cape in 1946. He was probably initially fearful that I would take his place on the Lorimier Grade School's softball team as its first baseman. My height perhaps threatened him. That fear, however, should have been unfounded, as he was a much better softball player. Although my mother had just purchased me a first baseman's trapper glove, I settled to be the pitcher, one which struck no fear in the hearts of our opponents.

High Noon was playing at the Esquire, Cape's newest theater just up the street and cattycorner from the Broadway which was affectionately known as the "Barn." Prior to the Esquire, the Barn was considered the elite among the Cape's other two theaters: The Rialto, known as the "Rat Hole" and the Orpheum known as the "Perfume." Actually, the Esquire didn't have as many seats as the Broadway, but it was the newest, shiniest, and when it opened in 1951, we high school students abandoned the others in large number. Besides the name Esquire sounded better, a lot classier.

Doc and I had agreed to meet there for the early show starting at 6:30 pm. Neither one of us had a car that evening. His folks were using theirs, and my mother's car, a two-door 1941 Plymouth coupe, was hardly a style setter with a very tiny back seat.

Although the afternoon's spring-like weather had turned a bit nippy as I made the short walk to the movie from our apartment, I was particularly upbeat as I walked with what some would call a swagger. I felt more like a prancing heavyweight champion prize fighter entering the ring to take on a badly outmanned opponent.

As I strutted up Broadway, Cape's primary street running west from the Mississippi River to Highway 61, a steady sound of horns blasted through the early evening's air by cars loaded up with friends. With windows opened, they all seemed to acknowledge my presence. This was a most unusual experience for me. I had walked Broadway many times in the past, and barely anyone had even noticed or seemed to care. I guess I had become a celebrity, and it sure made me feel good. I tried to take it in stride, to stay cool, but I was bursting inside with pride.

I arrived at the Esquire, but Doc was nowhere to be seen. Knowing him, he would show up in a few minutes. Moving past the theater, I stood next door in front of the Emporium, Cape's answer to an upscale pool hall. Many friends continued to ride by. They waved, I waved. Would this magical evening never end?

I then noticed a couple of my friends standing a few feet from me, also hangin' out, watching the traffic, hoping to see someone they knew, maybe to hook up with a couple of dateless girls. They had graduated a year ago, but I was still in high school.

"Hi Mung. You guys almost made it all the way!" Larry "Burf" Burford's husky voice rose above the night's bumper-to-bumper traffic along the town's main drag. A light blue windbreaker fit tightly over his well-developed shoulders and a jet black baseball hat rested awkwardly on his brutish head. Burf was no one to mess around with. He had lettered in basketball and baseball at Central, but had decided not to go to college.

"Thanks, Burf. We did pretty good, but we sure didn't have a very good game against U. City. At least I didn't. I think we could have taken 'em, but we didn't. For sure, we'll never know now 'cause the season's over."

Larry's best buddy, Jerry McCullough, also a 1951 graduate and former linebacker on the football team, joined in on the conversation. Known to his friends as "Mac," his football reputation was that of a hard-hitter and totally fearless. He weighed about 140 pounds, stood 5'10" tall, and when he tackled his opponents, they thought a freight train had just run over them. He had a full head of sandy hair, with a ruddy complexion and a profusion of freckles scattered unevenly over his thin face.

Mac asked, "Mung, where are you goin' to college? I imagine there'll be lots of offers from all over. How 'bout Mizzou?"

"I don't know, Mac. Coach Muegge told me that Mizzou might be interested, but I just don't know." My rather blasé response was a vain attempt to shield my true feelings about getting an athletic scholarship to play basketball. I was now totally confident I would.

I fully expected to be courted by at least one, perhaps two colleges or universities. The hometown college, Cape State, wouldn't be that attractive to me. I wanted to play basketball away from home.

It was nearly show time and still no Doc. "Have you seen Doc Ford, Burf? We're goin' to see *High Noon*."

"Nope. I haven't," he replied. Turning again to Mac, Burf asked in his strong voice loud enough for me to hear. "Mac, do you think Mung would want to go with us to see

Pepper Martin?" Larry's craggy pockmarked face evolved into a broad grin.

My head snapped back as I heard the name of my mother's baseball hero, Pepper Martin.

"Did you say Pepper Martin? Where is he?" I shouted.

"Over at Cairo. Wanna go?" Burf waited for my answer as he wiped his strong right hand across his face in a futile effort to erase the smile on his face. Mac stood by with his hand in his khaki trousers and just smiled impishly at me.

"Would I? Would I? Sure I wanna go see him. Yes!" I was ecstatic over the prospect of seeing Pepper Martin, but I needed to call my mother and get her permission.

Just then, Doc sauntered up to the three of us. "Ready to go to the show, Mung? I heard it's a good one. Burf, Mac, how are you?"

I was so glad to see my best friend. I knew he would want to go with us. "Doc, guess what! Pepper Martin's over at Cairo. Mac and Burf have asked me to go over with them."

I then turned to my two older friends and asked, "Can Doc go with us?"

"Sure, Mung, if he wants to. We'd love to have him, the more the merrier!"

Doc responded quickly. "Are you talking about Pepper Martin, the old Cardinal baseball player? How do you know he's there? Are you sure?" Doc's questioning voice threw me off guard. He didn't appear to believe what he had heard.

"Of course, we're sure." Burf replied in an indignant impatient voice. "Do you wanna go, or don't you?"

"Nawww, I don't think so, guys. I'd rather go to the show." Doc turned abruptly away from us and walked straight over to the Esquire's ticket booth.

Naturally, I was disappointed at my friend's reluctance to join us, but it only reaffirmed my previous commitment. "Well I wanna go," I said, "But I have to call my mother and see if it's okay."

I slipped in to the Emporium and walked past the six pool tables occupied by active and anxious players. Others stood by awaiting their turn at the game. Occasionally, a whoop and holler filled the room as a ball found the right pocket. Now and then, a loud groan would take over as a player's easy shot missed its mark.

Easing through the crowd, I spotted a pay phone at the end of the long, rectangular room, shoved a nickel into the phone and carefully dialed our apartment's number. I listened anxiously to the three short rings. My mother's soft voice answered, "Hello?"

"Mother, I have a chance to go see Pepper Martin." She could tell from my voice that I was very excited.

"Pepper Martin? Where is he? Is he in town?" Her voice seemed to be as disbelieving as Doc's.

"No, Mother, he's over at Cairo. I've got a ride over to see him. May I go?"

"Are you sure? Who are you going with?"

"Yes, I'm sure. Larry Burford and Jerry McCullough are goin' to take me. They'll be back before midnight. May I go, please?"

There was a long pause from my mother's voice, one that seemed an eternity. "Well, I guess, but make sure you're back here by midnight," she said haltingly.

"Oh, thank you. I will and I'll try to get his autograph. Okay?"

"Fine, and please be careful. I love you."

I just knew Mother would have liked to go with us. She had gotten on Pepper's bandwagon in 1934 when he practically single-handedly beat the Philadelphia Athletics in the World Series. He batted over .600 and literally drove the A's crazy with his daring base running and head-first slides.

Sportswriters dubbed him the "Wild Horse of the Osage." A native Oklahoman, he was notorious for his reckless abandon in which he played the game. His uniform was always dirty with diamond dirt and the omnipresent tobacco juice that oozed uncontrolled and shamelessly from his mouth.

The Cardinals were then known as the Gas House gang, the zaniest bunch of baseball players ever to play the game, and Pepper Martin was their leader. When a reporter once asked where Pepper had learned to run the way he did, he responded, "Well Sir, growin' up in Oklahoma, when you're there as a runner, there ain't nothin' to stop you."

Grantland Rice, one of America's greatest sportswriters wrote about him, "Pepper Martin was no great outfielder, no great infielder, but he is a great baseball player."

And I was going to get to see him, maybe even shake his hand and talk to him. I couldn't have been more excited.

The three of us piled into Larry's 1948 Packard and headed over the Cape Bridge with its toll of 50 cents, spanning the Mississippi River and along the river bottom of southern Illinois.

I couldn't stop talking about Pepper Martin as we sped over farmland along Highway One, south toward Cairo, about 12 miles away. Since he was Mother's idol, he also became mine. I could even recite statistics and milestones in his multiyear career. Although he had retired and was no longer in baseball, he ranked higher on my list than Stan Musial, the Cardinal's all-star outfielder at the time.

Burf and Mac said nothing as I babbled away. Every now and then, I would pause to get my breath and could hear them snickering. What was so funny? To me, this was serious business. I was going to see Pepper Martin.

Burf turned on the big Packard's radio as a weapon to neutralize my enthusiasm and chatter, turned the dial to hear music from New Orleans's 24-hour station, WWL-AM and Russ Morgan's orchestra broadcasting from the Roosevelt Hotel's Blue Room. Listening earlier at night in my room, I had often fantasized about being there and dancing with Alice Jean, but not tonight. I was going to see Pepper Martin.

The car started slowing down as we entered Cairo's outskirts. A string of flickering lights marked the first sign of civilized activity since we had passed the Colony Club and turned south some 12 miles back. The Colony Club and the Purple Crackle Club, just over the bridge, were only a few miles apart and a welcome oasis for southeast Missouri residents who eagerly sought liquor by the drink, live music, and of course, gambling. Everyone knew that "goin' across the river" meant an evening of song and fun.

But hardly anyone ever went to Cairo to party. Cairo was considered too wild and risqué for most folks. It was a wide open town known for its prostitution, bars, and strip joints. At the confluence of the Ohio and Mississippi Rivers, the town was certainly no place for high school boys, most sheltered all of their lives from such debauchery. Surely Pepper would not be in those terrible places, perhaps at a community hall, hotel, probably a high school gym.

To my surprise, the Packard pulled into an unpaved parking lot next to a place that looked like it might be a night club. A small, multi-lighted sign hanging down from a dull white stucco building flashed on and off showing "El Patio" to all interested visitors and travelers.

From the back seat, I blurted out, "El Patio? Why are we stopping here? It looks like a night club, a beer joint. Pepper Martin's not here, is he?"

Burf and Mac looked back at me and started laughing uproariously. Still not speaking, they got out of the car and made their way toward the club's front door, their heads bobbing up and down in joyous amusement.

"Hey, wait," they cried, "Pepper is here, hurry up. You'll miss him."

Spirits refreshed, I quickly opened the vehicle's back door, slid out from the ragged cloth seat covers and followed the guys into El Patio. Peeking into the club's dark interior, I could barely see anything. Gradually my eyes acclimated to the dim room, as I saw scattered lamps set against unpainted concrete blank walls. Cigarette smoke hovered over the room full of lively revelers. My eyes began to water from the foul putrid air.

There were no tables available for us. A scantily clad cocktail waitress—dressed in a Spanish gaucho's costume replete with a green felt hat festooned with a red tassel hanging from its side—led us through the crowded tables and pointed to a small opening at the bar.

"Sorry, senors," she said in a distinctly familiar southern twang. "There ain't no tables for ya for the show, but have a drink at the bar. The place'll thin out after the first show and we'll find ya a table then."

I followed closely at her heels. She stopped suddenly, spun around and pointed her long thin forefinger at me. All I could do was focus on those long crimson painted fingernails. I had never seen such. I stood gaping at her and she said, "My, my, I never noticed your letter sweater, Sweet Thang. Did ya play somewhere?"

"Yes, ma'am, I played basketball at Cape Girardeau Central High School."

The waitress then moved even closer to me, took her hand and rubbed my beardless chin in gentle, stroking movements. "Yeah, honey, and I betcha you were gooooood, too!" I didn't say a word. I was scared to death.

The three of us perched ourselves onto the bar stools as I gazed at the long bar overloaded with massive numbers of beer bottles, shot glasses and half-empty high-balls. Along with us, impatient customers waited for something to happen. At this stage, I couldn't imagine that these guzzlers were there to hear Pepper Martin talk about his audacious base stealing during the 1930s, and the 1934 World Series.

Suddenly, a smooth, rich baritone voice boomed mightily from behind a green curtain looming wide and full across the stage fronted by a cheering crowd sitting erect over their small tables. One would think they were getting ready to listen to some pastor's sermon on the ravages of sin.

"And now, ladies and gentlemen, direct from Chicago, Illinois, the one, the only, America's greatest dancer, Pepper Martin!"

The curtain parted quickly. A four-piece band containing a trumpet, sax, clarinet, and snare drum opened the act with loud and steadily pulsating music fit for Salome herself. But Salome did not appear. Pepper Martin did!

Wearing a flowing black evening gown, the exotic dancer with two of the longest, most shapely legs I had ever seen started her number with a series of suggestive moves that brought the male-dominated crowd to its feet clapping and screaming.

Pepper had a full head of auburn red hair that fell loosely over her shoulders and down her long arched back. She was certainly attractive by my young standards, but, also a beautiful woman who danced very well. The rising and falling crowd wasn't there for Pepper's dancing. Even I had figured that out by now.

As the band increased its tempo, Pepper began to slowly, almost artistically, remove her gown. The crowd was at a feverish state as she swirled around the full surging swing music. "Take it off! Take it off!" the chant continued military-like and precisely.

The crowd was so excited by then that they gave her performance a long, standing ovation. Kings and queens would have been proud at such outpouring love and appreciation from their devoted subjects.

Pepper's show lasted, I guess, maybe 10 minutes. As she took her leave, the baritone voice once again filled the room, "Pepper will be back at 11 and 1. We hope you stay with us." The crowd roared again its approval. Indeed, based on their response, it pretty well confirmed they were willing to stay forever.

After the show, Mac turned to me and said, "Well, Mung, whaddaya think? Ever seen anything like that before?"

I didn't really know how to respond. Obviously, I was moved by Pepper's exhibition, really moved, but now, I just wanted to get out of there and go home. I was so embarrassed that I had been so naive, so stupid to think that going to Cairo, that wicked city, was to see and hear one of my baseball heroes.

"Yeah, it was okay, I guess. But I think we better go on back. I promised my mother that I would be home by midnight. Can we go now?"

"Go? Whaddaya mean go? Let's stay for the next show. We'll now get a table and . . . ."

"No really, Mac, I gotta go. I really do. Maybe we can come back next weekend and spend more time. Maybe we can even get here for all three shows. Okay?"

Burf nodded to Mac and headed toward the door, "Yeah, let's go. Mung, we can come back next week and take it all in." Burf wasted little time as he started his car and left the graveled parking lot behind in swirling dust and flying gravel. He kept the radio on the whole trip. None of us had much to say.

I finally broke through the trip's silence just as we were turning west for the remaining three miles to the bridge and the Missouri side.

"'Ya know, I've been thinking guys. Do you think, just maybe, that the dancer, that stripper, well I mean, could she be related, maybe even be Pepper Martin's daughter? You think she could, huh?"

"Naww, Mung, don't think so, but she might. Next week, when we go back, we'll ask her. Okay?"

500

Ceremonies for the 1952 Central High School graduating class had ended on that warm, muggy May evening. Four years at CHS were over . . . four glorious years filled with special memories, good times and wonderful friends. A current offer of a basketball scholarship to the University of Missouri and a summer job at Camp Lewallen as its Waterfront Director awaited me. Life couldn't be better!

After hearing the State College's Dr. McGill challenge our class in his graduation address "to always seek the high ground in whatever you do," we scurried over to Dixie Lou Bader's spacious house on William Street for a graduation party. Mrs. Bader had taken up the rugs, and we danced throughout the evening to the music of Glenn Miller, Ray Anthony, and Rosie Clooney's *Tenderly* in her sweet, rapturous style.

As the night wore on, midnight passed and small groups sprawled on the floor and reminisced about their life and times at CHS. Most were going on to college. If there was fear or anxiety about going, such was far from any of our thoughts. Tired and way past my bedtime, I slipped upstairs, found an empty bed and quickly went into dreamland. I guess I was having guilt pangs for staying up so late knowing that my basketball coach, Coach Muegge, would not have been pleased.

As the sun's early morning rays began to lighten up the bedroom, soft, but quiet, enthusiastic voices awakened me from my peaceful reverie. Sitting on the edge of my bed, two of my classmates, names I can't recall, were extolling the sheer comforts of their strapless bras. Having no desire to join in *that* conversation, I abruptly rose, looked disgustingly at the girls, grunted a weak "good morning" in their direction, and made my way swiftly down the stairs.

Really hungry now, almost ravenous, I enticed Tom Cushman to drive us down to get some doughnuts at the Dixie Creme Donut Shop at the corner of Independence and Spanish Streets. Gobbling down six of those delicacies in rapid-fire order, I felt refreshed and yes, somewhat stuffed.

That afternoon, I took my physical examination for scout camp. I had been the assistant waterfront director at Camp Lewellan the year before and this year I would be the director. Although I wouldn't turn 18 until the end of June, it never really occurred to me that such a responsibility should be assumed by someone a lot older. My confidence was never higher!

A few days later, my doctor called Mother and expressed concern that "Gene appears to have an abnormal amount of sugar in his blood." Somewhat anxious, Mother questioned me if "I knew what could be the cause?"

I explained that it was probably my donut caper. She snickered at her son's medical opinion. I was right on the money.

Although camp didn't open until mid-June, I was scheduled to attend the June 1 National Aquatic School at Osage Beach, Missouri for waterfront director training. Andy Juden, my close friend and classmate (the guy who convinced me that going to bed at 9:00 pm every night wasn't too cool) asked me to go with him to the Indianapolis 500 motor race on Memorial Day, May 30. Hokey Williams and Bill Mabry, all CHS classmates, were invited also. My knowledge of car racing was a total void, but I agreed to go with the condition that we would be back on the 31st.

Andy responded positively to my demand. "We can do that, Mung. We'll leave on the 29th, go to the Sports Car

Club of America's show that afternoon, sleep in the park, see the race, and drive back afterwards."

Assured that the trip would work out and still allow me to leave for camp on the 31st, I received Mother's approval and waited anxiously to make the trip. We left early on the 29th in Andy's father's 1952 four-door Ford. Andy was a superb driver, although he pushed it pretty hard over the 350-mile stretch. Despite our screaming at him to stop at any of the many frozen custard stands along the highway, Andy ignored us continuously, always countering with "It's on the wrong side of the road." So much for frozen custard on the way to Indianapolis.

Nearing Indianapolis, Andy became a walking and talking encyclopedia providing us with facts about the race, the Motor Speedway, the drivers, their incredible speeds and so on. In his staccato-like repartee, he explained, "The race is 500 miles long, 200 laps on a 2.5 mile oval. It's called the Brickyard because it was once paved with 3.2 million bricks. It's always run on Memorial Day. There are time trials during May, and the fastest driver gets the pole position."

"Pole position? What does that mean?" I asked.

Interrupting his surgical treatment of the race, Andy responded tersely, "That means it's in the front row, on the inside. They're three cars across, and 33 cars will be racing. Eleven rows of cars, get it?"

"How fast will they go?" queried Hokey.

"Well, at least 125 miles per hour." Andy was on a roll.

"That fast? Can a Ford or Chevrolet go that fast?" I chimed in.

"No, no, no. These are racing cars. One of the fastest cars is the Kuzman-Offenhauser. A lot of drivers will be in those. But, really, Fords or Chevrolets? No way."

"Who do you think'll win?" Bill questioned.

"I believe Bill Vukovich had the fastest time trial, and he'll have the pole position. I guess he'll be the favorite." Andy was probably more psyched about this race than the rest of us, since he really knew what he was talking about. We were just a few shades behind him in our enthusiasm. This was really going to be something.

We arrived in Indianapolis around 3 pm that afternoon. It was one of the biggest cities that I had ever seen, and it looked as large as St. Louis, even Memphis. Its size didn't seem to bother Andy. He had been to Chicago many times and without a map, he seemed to know exactly where the sports car show was located. Eureka! Before we knew it, we were in the park, out of the car and strolling through the exposition hall.

Andy continued his line of expertise. He knew sports cars. We would follow him like adoring children as he explained the positive features of the more than 100 cars being exhibited. Where in the world did he know all that? He was simply amazing.

Leaving the park, we knew we would return to spend the night. We had no idea it was illegal to sleep there, especially in a car, but the thought of staying in a hotel was out of the question. Between us, we probably had only $50 and no credit cards. They didn't exist in those days.

Driving into downtown Indianapolis, the city was alive with race fans. Streets were jammed with early evening revelers. It was a real happening. Andy wanted us to go by the Antler's Hotel where a friend of his parents was supposedly staying. Antler's Hotel? What a funny name for a hotel. Of course, people probably thought that Cape's Idan-Ha Hotel was kind of strange, too.

With all of the people swarming around, we thought it would be a good place to meet girls. After all, we were nearly 18 years old, and surely there must be girls our age that would be dyin' to meet us. No chance. Of course, our group obviously wasn't being sought out by anybody, especially girls.

Around 9:30, we headed back to the park to spend the night. Four young men spending the night in a 1952 Ford wasn't exactly like sleeping at the Ritz. My three friends were of normal size, but my 6'4" skinny frame, with size 15 shoes was no match for the close quarters presented by the Ford. Needless to say, I didn't sleep much, possibly from the anticipation of the race, but more likely from the fact that "putting two pounds of sand in a one pound bag" was bound to be a bit uncomfortable. It was!

Up early, when awakened by a park guard, we were asked rather discourteously to leave and leave NOW. We did and rapidly. Although not thoroughly rested, we didn't mind. We were going to see the Indianapolis 500 race. We would leave sleep for another time.

After breakfast, Andy continued his remarkable ability to weave his way through city streets and arrive around 9:30 am at the Speedway. What a place! I had never seen so many people in my life, all kinds, all shapes and sizes, rich and poor, old and young. Excitement abounded aplenty throughout the Speedway as we took our seats. I couldn't really appreciate where our seats were. They were strategically placed at the first curve of the track, about five rows up from the rail. Not bad for a bunch of southeast Missouri high school graduates! Thank you, Mr. Juden!

We browsed thoughtfully through the race's program looking carefully at the track's history, previous winners, cars racing, time trials results, and a myriad of facts about the race. Since we had such an excellent briefing from Andy, we felt rather cocky that we were only mildly supplementing our race knowledge. We weren't exactly experts, but from those around us eavesdropping on our conversations, they probably thought we sounded well informed.

Nearing the start of the race, the strains of *Back Home In Indiana* flowed majestically over the massive crowd, at least 150,000 fans. Some tenor sang the national anthem followed by Wilbur Shaw's husky baritone voice bellowing the traditional "Gentlemen, start your engines." Almost instantaneously, the collective roar of 33 racing cars propelled us off our seats. The crowd's following yells of approval were deafening.

Still standing, we watched the cars take their customary three laps before the race officially started. Like a symmetrical flock of Canada geese flying undisturbed over Midwestern fields, the finely tuned cars gradually increased their speed as they approached the race's starting line. All of us fans stayed on our feet as the race began. I had never seen anything so exciting. It was truly magical.

In a short time, most everybody returned to their seats. I didn't. I was totally captivated by the spectacle.

Unfortunately, others were not so captivated by the tall, skinny kid standing in front of them blocking their view of the race.

"Sit down, kid. Will you please sit down?" Around the third lap of the race, their cries turned somewhat violent, no longer politely asking, now demanding. I finally got it and sat down. At our position in the stands, we would catch the rubber, grime, and fumes of the cars speeding around the first curve. To some, this was an almost holy experience. After about 50 laps into the race, reality replaced holiness as our clothes and bodies became filthy.

As young men, always hungry, we decided after a while that eating our lunch, sandwiches and cokes we had purchased earlier, was more important than watching 33 cars speeding around a 2.5 mile track. Actually, the race at that point was somewhat boring notwithstanding the unexcelled excitement of the start.

And true to form, keeping with tradition and a longtime habit, I began to nod off. In no time, I fell asleep around Lap 100 despite the incessant roar of the racers' cars and the crowd urging them on. Between the painful few hours of sleep I had in the park and the monotony of the race at that stage, sleep probably presented the best remedy for me.

Andy's hard jolt to my ribs aroused me quickly from my nap. The race had about 20 laps to go, and it was apparent that Bill Vukovich was going to be the winner. Andy suggested that we "beat the crowd" and leave early. After all, we knew who was going to win the race.

With only nine laps to go, Vukovich crashed his car and 22-year-old Troy Ruttman came through to win the race at an electrifying speed of almost 129 miles per hour. He was the youngest driver ever to win that race. Of course, we didn't see the dramatic finish. We were racing back to Cape. We never looked back on our premature exit. We had a full share of joy and pleasure that Memorial Day.

Back in Cape around 11 pm, I bid farewell to Andy and the boys and wished them a good summer. Just as Andy was pulling away from the curb, he yelled, "Hey, Mung, wanna go again next year?"

"Well, maybe. But if we do, can we stay in a hotel?"

Laughing heartily as he moved his car toward Broadway, he replied, "Well, maybe it would be better if we just brought a cot for you to take to the race. You think?"

I gave no reply as I bounded up the three flights of steps to the apartment. Mother greeted me at the door. My bags were packed and I'd be heading to Osage Beach in a few hours. Truly, the Indianapolis 500 race was an unforgettable experience, always to be cherished and never to be forgotten.

Rush

Graduation from Central High School in May 1952 arrived with the giddy anticipation of going to college with a dual academic and athletic scholarship at the University of Missouri swelling my over-inflated head.

My job for the summer was at Boy Scout Camp Lewallen as its waterfront director, another heady thought since I was still only seventeen and not turning eighteen until late June. Life at that time was beautiful!

Boy Scout Camp Lewallen Waterfront Director, Gene Munger, in the summer of 1952.

Both the trip to see the Indianapolis 500 and camp went well for me, and as September loomed, I began to have some apprehension about leaving home and starting my college career. While the camp's experience greatly bolstered my confidence and maturity, there were a few doubts as to whether I would be able to fit in at Mizzou, play varsity basketball, and maybe even join a fraternity.

In my earlier high school years, joining a fraternity was about as far from my mind as anything could be, but as graduation came near, I started getting letters from fraternities at Mizzou inviting me to rush week. Andy, much wiser to the world of fraternities than I, explained the ins and outs of rush, what it would be like and so on. He had an older cousin, a member of Phi Gamma Delta, who had briefed him and Andy's steel trap mind—he never forgot anything—worked his magic with me. Indeed, I wanted to go to rush, and perhaps, join a fraternity knowing neither its costs nor most anything else.

With bags packed, and a goodbye to Mother, Andy picked me up the week after Labor Day and we headed to Columbia. Not going to college was never really an option for me. It had always been taken for granted I would go. The question was where? When Mizzou offered me a basketball scholarship, it was easy to say yes and eliminate my hometown college, Southeast Missouri State, from the list. Comparing Big 8 basketball to the quality played in the MIAA (Missouri Intercollegiate Athletic Association) Conference, the choice was easy. I was just too good to play at Cape, at least in my swelled head, I thought so.

Understand I had never experienced anything like this since I had been raised in small towns in southeast Missouri—Chaffee, Sikeston, and Benton. Moving to Cape when I was turning 12 was one really big step. Cape was hardly big city life, but to me, any town more than 10,000 was just that.

While Andy did a thorough job describing rush, going through it left me with a lot of highs, and unfortunately one big low. He and I arrived on campus and both of us were initially berthed at the Phi Gamma Delta House. We later checked in at Inter-Fraternity Council Headquarters, received our schedule of houses to be visited, and the rush was on!

My first visit during rush was at the Phi Delta Theta House. I dressed appropriately, I guess, sporting gabardine trousers, well-pressed dress shirt, with shoes shined. Andy hadn't told me what to wear. As I walked in, one of the greeters, dressed smartly in a blue linen sport coat, button-down white cotton shirt with his fraternity's logo presented clearly on a light blue tie and white bucks, met me warmly and introduced me to others: athletes, house president, alumni, etc. Maybe, I should have worn my only suit, a double-breasted blue one.

While I had never met any of them, they knew more about me than I knew myself. It was as if they had been my constant shadow throughout my life. They reviewed and praised my academic scholarship, scouting as an Eagle Scout, scout camp waterfront director, all-state basketball player, lawyer father and grandfather, even that I liked to dance! One would have thought I was some kind of media celebrity as the "brothers" surrounded and peppered me with questions about my life. I was duly impressed.

This routine by the Phi Delta Theta's continued throughout the next three days as I visited Phi Gamma Delta, Sigma Chi, Beta Theta Pi, and Kappa Alpha. All expressed the value of brotherhood one would experience as a member, the valuable contacts one would make with the other brothers who will occupy important and prestigious positions in business. For me, I was so awed by all of this bravado that I was completely confident that being in a fraternity was the absolute and essential key to my future success in the world.

With this type of introduction and bluster, I became very comfortable in each of the houses I visited. Those guys came across as the greatest in the world. They really seemed to like me, and all were emphatic that I considered joining their fraternity. Frankly, I wanted to join 'em all, but I knew I would have to make a decision soon.

As all the prospective pledges went back to headquarters to pick up their bids, I then made my decision. I chose Kappa Alpha. With a certain swagger, I strode forward to meet their representative who awaited me with a broad grin and a firm handshake. He escorted me back to their house where I became "king of the hill" as I made my way into a throng of KA's all shaking my hand and expressing how pleased they were to have me in their pledge class.

When the excitement subsided, the house president advised that I would need $50 for an initiation fee to bind me into the fraternity, to become a pledge. To most pledges, such a fee would not be much of a financial burden, but in my case, I simply didn't have it. I had less than a hundred dollars, but I knew I would need that to buy books and get organized for my forthcoming classes. I was totally ill-prepared to make any kind of financial commitment at that time.

"Oh, I'll have to call my father in St. Louis and he'll send me the money," I said hoping to ward off the embarrassment of being unable to make the necessary deposit at that moment. "May I use your phone?"

Calling his law office, I hoped he would be there, and there would be no problem having him send me a money order. He instantly wanted to know how rush week had gone for me.

My spirits rose and I told him what had gone on and my selection for Kappa Alpha. "And Dad, I need $50 so I can become an active pledge."

There was a long, lingering silence on the other end of the line. He finally answered, "$50? Did you say $50? Well, Son, I, I don't have it. I just can't help you at this time. I'm sorry."

"But Dad, I need it. I have to have it in order to join Kappa Alpha. Can't you just borrow it? I can pay you back, I promise. Please? Don't you see, without the money, I can't join the fraternity." I wanted to cry out loud with my disappointment, but I kept control. To me, this was the most important thing in my life, and my father couldn't help me. I knew my mother was in no position either. I felt so alone and helpless at that point.

"I know, Son. But I just don't have it. Things are a little tight right now. Perhaps, you can tell your group you will be able to join in the future. I'm sure they will understand."

"All right, Dad. I'll do that. Maybe they will, maybe they will." I hung up the phone, took a deep breath, and went back to the president and gave him the bad news. He was sympathetic, but advised, "At this time, you can't be a pledge. You'd have to wait until the second semester, but we still want you in the fraternity."

I guess his encouraging remarks made me feel somewhat better, but I couldn't wait to leave. I didn't even say goodbye to the rest of the group. I walked slowly back the two blocks to the Phi Gam house where they were getting ready to have a party honoring their new pledge class. Wanting none of that, I slipped upstairs and fell into a deep sleep, hoping that I wouldn't wake up, ever. I was heartbroken.

Later, one of the Phi Gams came to my room and invited me down to the party. It was in full blast. I really didn't want to join the group, but I did and attempted to be sociable explaining that "At the last minute, I decided to wait until the next semester before joining a fraternity. I needed more time."

The humiliation and embarrassment I endured eliminated any possibility of joining a fraternity, but as I eased into college life, played freshman basketball, regained my confidence and hopefully, a little maturity, I promised myself I would never be so humiliated again. Obviously, joining a fraternity at that time was not the end-all to end-all, but at the time, it certainly was.

I never forgot it, but I sure got over it.

�▲▲▲▲

Delivery Man

By the autumn of 1953, the 50s were well underway and bringing many lifestyle and cultural changes to America's way of living and thinking. As a relatively immature and naive adolescent, those changes were swiftly and unknowingly passing me by as I departed from my carefree and glorious high school days to an unknown world where what you had done and accomplished meant little or nothing. I was rapidly discovering why Missouri was labeled as the Show-Me State.

I believe it was an Englishman, Lord Asquith, who once said something like, "Youth would be an ideal state if it only came later in life." For me, my youth at that time was anything but an ideal state.

Starting my freshman year at the University of Missouri in Columbia that previous fall had been filled with great expectations and confidence for the future. In a short time, those feelings vanished as the "Good Ship Reality" steamed relentlessly over my fragile craft and washed me painfully into the rocky shore. It was a harsh and brutal landing in a strange and unforgiving place where I had few friends, no nurturing and supporting parents, and scores of faceless people who neither knew me nor cared whether I even existed.

At the end of my freshman year at the University of Missouri, I felt like my life was in a continuing maelstrom of disappointments and delusions. Everything seemed to have fallen apart during the year. Although on an athletic scholarship, my basketball skills were clearly no match for the better and stronger freshman players. I was told that my chances of playing varsity basketball in the 1953-1954 school year were slim to none. My grades were only slightly above average, a far cry from my nearly A average as a high school student. Nothing seemed to be working.

By the end of my freshman year, our country was well into the Korean War, although some simply called it a conflict. Whatever it was called, I knew that I wanted no part of it. The draft board in my home town of Cape

Girardeau kept a watchful eye on those draft age men who were not full-time students, fair game for those drop-outs when discovered. To quit school, accept involuntary enlistment as a soldier and be sent to Ft. Leonard Wood for basic training presented no serious alternative for me. Either I would return to the university, a less than appealing choice, or return to my roots in Cape and enroll at Southeast Missouri State College.

I had a few months to decide and spent the interim summer at southeast Missouri's Boy Scout Council's Camp Lewallen as its Waterfront Director. Located on the tranquil banks of the St. Francis River in the Ozark Mountain foothills, the change in scenery and activity was exactly what I needed. By summer's end, my confidence was restored, my mind was clear and I decided to enroll for my sophomore year at Cape State. The decision, itself, was easy since a return to the university portended more of the same frustration and unhappiness. It was time to go home again.

I realized that a basketball scholarship was probably not available since they were probably all set for the coming season, but at least, I could inquire. I was right. As luck would have it, the State College's Booster Club came to my rescue when they heard that I wanted to return to the Cape and play. Based on what they remembered of me as an all-state high school player at Cape Central, the club pooled their resources—not a lot by today's standards—and established a fund in my behalf. I knew nothing of the Club's efforts. I figured that the college had come up with another scholarship, and I was the lucky beneficiary.

Since I was living at home, the scholarship provided me with tuition and books (all of about $25 per term), my noon meal, and a job at school which would pay about $60 a month. Additionally, the college would try to get me a part-time job during the off season.

Such funding, in retrospect, sounds skimpy, but in 1953, it was a big boost to my welfare. Importantly, it gave me a new start, a chance to finish my college education, hopefully a chance to play varsity basketball in a less competitive but talented conference, and the opportunity to start enjoying life again.

My mother was delighted with my decision to return to my roots. She had missed me madly during my year at Mizzou and seemed excited about my living with her and watching me play basketball again. We had a marvelous relationship, having lived together ever since she and my father had separated in 1946.

As I enrolled in college that fall of 1953, I was a very happy young man, a youth of just nineteen years who had learned in the past year that things didn't always work out as planned. When they don't, change directions, take a new path, and start over again.

Returning to my roots, back to Cape Girardeau, was the right thing to do. While the town was located on rolling hills, as one traveled south, the hills soon dissipated into flat, endless fields of cotton and soy beans. To the west were the beginnings of the Ozark foothills. To the east was Illinois and its nightclubs and casinos across the river where all of us underage could drink illegally without care or question.

Although Cape's primary economy was the state college, it served as an important hub of commerce for the rural communities and farms scattered around it. Its central location made it the place to come shop there by the river on Main Street.

Conservative in its make-up, Republican in its voter choice, Cape, a small city of less than 20,000, was a wonderful place to grow up. It boasted good schools, a preponderance of churches, and virtually no crime. It, indeed, was the quintessential Midwestern town.

My first meeting with Ralph Pink, the college's basketball coach was cordial enough, but somewhat reserved. He was starting his second year there. The first had been successful, no Conference championship, but a winning season. The town's boosters had told me he was a serious, dedicated coach who excelled in planning, not only in well-organized practices, but in preparation for an opposing team.

Pink, tall and physically fit, about 6'3" with light brown receding hair and a pleasant, handsome face, was a disciple of clean living and demanded the same from his athletes. When I was recruited to play for the university in the spring of 1952, Pink had not been hired. Had he been around, I would not have opted to go to State, as my ego and dreams steered me to loftier heights and goals. Therefore, I was not one of his recruits, which probably accounted for his perceived chilliness in the air.

"Welcome, Gene, I'm pleased to have you with us," he said as he thrust his right hand firmly into mine.

I winced at the strength of the man's grip, but was unable to counter much of a retort except to say, "Nice to be here, Coach."

There was no "get acquainted" talk, as he went directly into a lengthy review of the past season, noting who was returning and declaring that the team would be a strong contender for the Conference championship. I acknowledged his optimism and declared that "I would do my best."

His brow stiffened a bit as he looked over my thin body, all 170 pounds and spread over a 6'4" frame, and responded, "I sure hope you can gain some weight. This conference is tough. With your being at home, your mom's home cooking should do the trick."

I countered quickly and looked him squarely in the eye, "Yes Sir, she's a great cook. I'll gain some weight before the season starts. Yes Sir, I will!"

"Fine," he replied, "But you need to put on some pounds. We'll need you under the boards." He then pulled a scrap of paper out of his sport shirt's pocket with a pencil-scrawled phone number. "Let's see, I think we've got a job for you here in town. Have you ever heard of Bierschwal's Market?"

"Yes Sir, I have. It's over on Good Hope Street, not far from where I used to live. In fact, it's not very far from where Mother and I live now. What's the job?"

"They want a man to deliver groceries on Saturdays. They'll pay you $1.00 an hour. You do drive, don't you?"

"Yes Sir, I do drive. However, I've never driven a grocery truck, but I'm sure I can. I've driven trucks before. In fact, I drove the scout camp truck this summer. I did fine." I sounded confident, but the jaded memories of my struggling constantly with the floor shift stick on the camp's 1939 Ford pickup belied my confident air.

"Fine. Why don't you call Mr. Bierschwal today and make an appointment to go over and see him. He needs a man to start right away."

Like a giant bird leaving its familiar nest, Coach then rose from his swiveled office chair and in a broad, sweeping motion with his long, powerful hand pointed to the door. "Sorry, Gene. I gotta go now. Thanks for comin' by. Call me if you need any help, and don't forget to get with Mr. Bierschwal."

"Thanks, Coach. I'll get over there right away. Thanks for everything." I purposely avoided shaking his hand again for fear of feeling again the vice-like grip of my new mentor. He then turned and ambled down the cold, cavernous concrete block halls of Houck Field House in a stoop shouldered saunter that I would see countless times over the next three years.

The field house was only two blocks from Mother's apartment, a spacious two-bedroom second floor jewel of a place renting for only $65 a month. I was thrilled that I had been able to get a job so soon, and it paid $1.00 an hour!

My mother was tickled with the news. When asked if she knew anything about Bierschwal's Market, she replied, "No, I have never traded there. I go to the A&P Store down by the river." She later recalled that she thought it was a small "mom and pop" grocery store that had been around a long time, that it was well known for good meats, and they delivered groceries.

I called Mr. Bierschwal and made an appointment to go over to the store later that afternoon and to talk to him about the job. At exactly 4 pm, I walked into the store. Mother had been right. It was small. However, the shelves were stocked neatly and everything seemed to be in its proper place. A white porcelain meat counter practically filled the entire back of the store and displayed a wide and abundant range of fresh poultry, pork, and beef. A check-out counter stood free on the right side of the store's front. A hand-crank adding machine awaited customers to add up their purchases before departing. While the store's interior had a pleasant enough aroma, one could catch a slight whiff of sawdust in the air.

Bierschwal came out from behind the meat counter and moved quickly in my direction with outstretched arms. I had never met Eddie, but in our opening conversation, he quickly let me know that he was a big booster of State's athletics. His appearance certainly belied the appearance of an athlete or for that matter, one who would be interested in athletics. He stood about 5'6", was half-bald, had a hawk-like nose set on a round, pasty face, and shook hands with infant-like strength. To my delight, he remembered me from high school days and appeared genuinely glad to meet me.

I caught him up on what I had been doing since leaving the Cape, why I had decided to return and above all, how pleased I was to have the opportunity to work for him and deliver his groceries.

"First, Gene, you'll have to get a chauffeur's license. That's easy. Go down to the License Bureau on Broadway and apply and they'll give you one." Despite Eddie's frail appearance, his authoritative and confident voice left no doubt that he was in control. He was the boss, and he seemed to revel in knowing that.

"When do I start?" I asked.

"You can start Saturday but get that license first. Get here around 8 am and I'll show you your route. When you're not delivering groceries, you can make hamburger and stock shelves. We'll try to keep you busy." Eddie talked like I knew how to make hamburger. He never even asked if I had ever driven a truck. We shook hands, and I returned to the apartment. I had a job!

With the required license in hand, I showed up promptly at 8 am that Saturday and jauntily strolled back to the meat counter. Eddie was hunched over carving away at a huge beef hindquarter which was spread over a substantial oak carving block supported by three round legs.

Seeing me standing there, Eddie immediately stopped his work, wiped his small, thin hands on his clean, white apron, and motioned for me to come to the back storeroom where the day's orders had already been filled. Groceries and meats were packed carefully and exclusively in wire-rimmed baskets about twice the size of a shopper's market basket. They lay in two rows, single file, on a long, rectangular wooden table. A mess sergeant would have been proud!

Eddie explained that he had filled the morning's orders earlier, but in the future, this would be my job. He then went over the mechanics of filling each order, being careful to remind me that each customer must get exactly what had been ordered. Then, he got out an old city map and reviewed each customer's location suggesting the fastest, most direct way to get to them.

"You won't have any trouble finding them. You'll have more trouble getting away from them as they really like to talk. But, hurry on back. There's always something to do back here," he said.

We then went out back behind the store in an open alley where I got my first glimpse of Eddie's truck, a paneled 1938 Chevrolet. A one-half ton antiquated piece of machinery that looked like it was once bright orange in color. Now it was showing an anemic yellow hue and badly faded black script lettering read "Bierschwal's Market" on each side of the cab. Mother was right. The market had been around for a while.

Eddie helped me transfer the wire grocery baskets from the table into the back of the old truck. When finished, he slammed the back door sealing my cargo safely until it could be delivered to waiting customers.

"Be careful, Gene. Be careful," he yelled as he returned briskly to his waiting mother lode of beef.

Despite its ancient appearance, even for 1953, the truck was easy to drive, had good pick-up, and the stick shift was no problem. I felt like Captain Midnight on a secret mission. The truck's tinty radio blared out the Saturday sounds of hillbilly music—before country and western, you know— from the local radio station KFVS. It was the only station I could pick up, and while I loathed that music, I drove steadily ahead with a wide, almost arrogant smile on my face. I felt like I was in total control.

Delivering groceries to Eddie's customers turned out to be a very pleasant experience. Most were either shut-ins or those who didn't want to bother with the hassle of driving to a store and shopping. Convenience was the key, I suspected, and I was making it more convenient for them.

My morning route, about twenty miles, covered twelve customers spread throughout the city. My ride took me near the river, larger homes, now apartment houses, through the poorer neighborhoods to the south, cross town to the newer, tidier houses near the college and finally out to the west end of town where new subdivisions were emerging from what were formerly cow pastures and wooded hills.

My experience in serving older people was limited. More than half of the folks on my route were well into their sixties and seventies. Eddie was right, they liked to talk and almost always offered you something to drink and eat. Two couples lived in very small second floor apartments, and entry to them was outside and up steep wooden steps. I never thought much of how difficult it was for them to go up and down those steps. How would a young man in the prime of youth know that?

A few lived in houses they had lived in all their lives, or at least most of their adult lives. Entry was always by the back door, but my knock prompted a quick response and immediate access to their kitchens. The balance, living in the newer and more affluent houses, continued with the same routine: always the back door, never the front.

All of the customers painstakingly checked their list with what was in the basket, noting either the freshness of the vegetables or the beauty of Eddie's meats and poultry. Occasionally, they would grumble slightly about the brand received preferring another and so on. For the most part, I suspected that this latter ritual was part of breaking in the new deliveryman, however, it didn't bother me. In retrospect, I believe that the at-the-door appearance of a young man who was pleasant, courteous, and seemed to care for their welfare was one of the best parts of their day. It soon became that for me.

I almost never received cash, as they deferred payment until Eddie sent out his monthly statements. Price did not appear to be an issue, or at least the price of a good was rarely questioned. From experience, Eddie knew his customers very well and knew what they wanted and at about what price. The thought of my having to later fill baskets for these folks gave me some concern, but I figured that my boss would keep a watchful eye on me to see that I was doing the right thing for his beloved flock.

The first morning's drive went very well. My last delivery point was at a small white, single story wooden house just barely in the city limits on the west side of town away from the river. To get there, I had to drive the truck off the highway and up a winding gravel path overgrown with the last remnants of summer's uncut weeds and grasses. As I pulled up to the house, it did not appear that anybody was at home. There was no car in sight and the window shades were pulled down completely. If there was life inside, they certainly didn't want the outside world to know about it.

Cautiously, I got out of my truck and walked around the house to the back door. The back side of the house had no porch, only two steps supported by concrete blocks led the way to a screen door. I knocked twice. No answer. I knocked again. No answer. The third time, I knocked and yelled, "Bierschwal's Market is here with your groceries."

I heard the sound of shuffling feet coming to the door. The door opened and there standing by the screen door was a lady simply dressed in only a blue chenille bathrobe. Totally unprepared for such a sight, I stood there with my mouth wide open. Gosh, she was simply gorgeous!

Her long blond hair hung wet from her sloping shoulders. She was quite tall, lithe in body with a smooth face accentuated by deep set blue eyes that stared at me like a laser beam. She and those eyes were having an effect. I didn't move.

She smiled impishly, opened the door and said, "Oh, I'm very sorry. I was taking a bath and didn't hear you. Do you have my groceries?"

While seeing her at the screen door had nearly taken my breath away, noticing her defying the restriction of her robe completed the job. I felt asphyxiated, in a non-life-threatening sort of way.

Completely at a loss for words, I tried to recover and responded, "No ma'am, I don't. I mean, I do, but they're in the truck. I have to go get them. I didn't know if anybody was at home. I'll be right back." I backpedaled furiously from the door, stumbled over the first wooden step and fell hard on the ground. I got up quickly, brushed myself off and scurried back to the truck.

I was totally shaken by this unbelievable experience. First, I didn't think anybody was at home. Then, I was at the wrong house. And then I discovered that not only was someone home, but that someone was a beautiful woman dressed only in a bathrobe with apparently nothing on underneath. What was I to do?

At least, I could deliver her groceries, but I sure wasn't going to stick around there, no way. I returned to the back door with her groceries and she was still waiting just inside. "Come on in, please. Could I get you something to drink? How about some iced tea? It's awfully warm outside." She spoke with a deep, husky voice that was about the sexiest thing that I had ever heard. It reminded me of Lizabeth Scott, one of my favorite movie stars.

"Err, I don't think so, ma'am. I've got to get back to the store. Thank you, anyway, ma'am. Maybe next time." I then watched her take her groceries from the basket, neither bothering to verify what she ordered or checking the price of her ticket. She continued to keep those ravishing blue eyes focused directly on me.

"Is something wrong, ma'am?" I asked. My thin, reedy voice must have sounded wimpy to her. It certainly did to me.

"No, nothing. Nothing at all. What's your name?" She asked as she turned directly into me, bumping me lightly with her body. I responded positively to that movement and motion for sure, but I searched desperately for an answer.

"Name? Name? Why, my name is Gene Munger. I just started delivering groceries today for Mr. Bierschwal, Bierschwal's Market. I go to school at the college. I play basketball. I went to high school at Cape Central. I live here. What's yours?" I couldn't face her directly so my eyes focused on the kitchen's linoleum floor covering, a pattern of bright spring flowers.

"Mine's Linda. I just moved here from Malden. Ever heard of Malden? I didn't actually live in Malden, just outside of it on a small farm."

"Yes ma'am, I've heard of Malden. I've even been there. I've taught some of Malden's Boy Scouts how to swim. I worked at scout camp this summer. Why did you move here?" I couldn't believe my brashness, my inquisitiveness in front of this lady. I guess I really wanted to know.

"I moved here because my husband has been sent to Korea. He's an Army Reservist. They called him up this past June. I just couldn't stand living in that small town, so I moved to Cape. I think I'll like it here. I need to find a job, but I haven't really looked." As Linda talked, she edged closer to me. The fragrance of her warm sweet breath and recent bath was like an overpowering aphrodisiac to me. I was aroused beyond anything that had ever happened to me.

"I really must be going, ma'am. I must." I was sure she could see that she was having a significant physical effect on me, and frankly, she seemed to be enjoying my manly reaction to her charm. I was excited, oh, how I was excited, despite there being at least ten years or more difference in our ages. I could not envision my seduction of an older, certainly more experienced woman, not by any stretch of the imagination. My early Methodist morals were being challenged to their fullest, and I was certainly being challenged.

"You don't have to go, now, do you?" Her bathrobe was now hanging completely open. Indeed, she wore nothing underneath. I turned away reluctantly and headed toward the door. My entire body felt charged by a massive overload of high voltage.

"Yes, I do, Linda. I really do." I staggered out the back door, around the house and back to the truck. I had forgotten the basket. I had to return. I did, but I knew I couldn't go back inside. I spoke softly from the backyard, "Linda, would you please hand me my basket? I forgot it." No answer. I yelled a bit louder this time, "Please, ma'am. May I have my basket?"

The basket then appeared through the back screen door held by a long, graceful arm. I paused briefly and went over to get it. At that point, the screen door swung open wide and there she was standing before me, completely naked and smiling. "Are you sure you have to go?"

I was completely disoriented. I couldn't look at her, her beautiful Venus-like body. I just couldn't do it. I covered my eyes, turned my head and reached for the basket, snatching it quickly from her gentle grasp. I said nothing more and shot back to the sanctuary of my truck.

I waited for a few minutes in an attempt to regain some semblance of composure before I started the truck and left her house. It was not easy leaving her in my physical state of rapture. While the early Methodist tapes were swirling around in my head, a much stronger feeling of uncontrolled lust was tempting me mightily to return to her lair and relieve my passion with the older woman. I just couldn't do it. Maybe later, next time, but not now.

The rest of my day, notably the afternoon delivery of only a few more customers, went off without incident. Needless to say, I didn't discuss with Eddie my experience with the lovely Linda, nor would I ever. For that matter, I only shared the experience with two other close friends.

I continued to work for him until basketball practice started, about mid-October, most Saturdays and occasionally a few hours after school. Eddie proudly showed me how to make hamburger, taking the scraps, not necessarily the meatiest, of his butchering process and grinding them up for human consumption. This task was certainly not one that required much skill, but had a satisfying result which people appeared to relish, then and even now. If people saw how most hamburger is made, I'm sure its consumption would decrease.

I continued to deliver Linda her weekly groceries for about 10 weeks that fall, but there was never a repeat, not even a mention of our first encounter. I don't think I could have been so cavalier in responding to a second challenge. Secretly, I wished that I had, although, I didn't have the machismo, the aggressiveness, the courage to force the issue. I'm sure Linda realized that and perhaps she was able to relieve her passion with one who was more experienced and could satisfy her longing and loneliness for a man's company. Selfishly, I hoped that she didn't.

Rather than becoming her lover, I became a friend and a good listener. We shared coffee together every time I delivered her groceries. Sometimes, I would purposely neglect to fill her order completely so I would have an excuse to return in the afternoon to be with her. We would sit and visit in her kitchen, sitting around a small chrome dinette table on vinyl padded chairs. The conversations were usually light, but occasionally during our visits, she would release to me her feelings of loneliness and fear that her husband would not return from Korea. I always assured her that he would.

Formal varsity basketball practice was set for November 15. On my last Saturday at Eddie's, he noted that he had lost a customer, one that he had had only a few months.

"She was a good customer, too, Gene. Very pleasant on the phone and always paid her bill. Said she was moving. Didn't say where."

"Where did she live?" I asked. I had a strong premonition that it was Linda to whom he was referring.

"Out west of town, just about at the city limits."

"Oh, yeah, I know. Nice lady. Her husband was in Korea, a nice lady. Too bad, I really liked her."

As for Linda, I never saw or heard from her again. I presume her husband did return from Korea, and they lived happily ever after. In my eyes and memory, he was a very lucky man.

Scout Master

In May of 1954, I had just finished my sophomore year at Southeast Missouri State College when Steve Limbaugh, the Troop Commissioner of Centenary Methodist's Troop 3 asked me to become the scoutmaster of the troop.

Scouting had been a big part of my young life, as a scout, waterfront director at the district camp, Camp Lewallen, and Voyager Trainer at Region 7's Canoe Base. Initially, I resisted his offer, but he was most persuasive in advising that I could still play varsity basketball, go to college and "run the troop." He explained the meetings would take place on a bimonthly basis in the fall and winter, and even when involved with basketball road trips, there would be other adult leaders to take my place.

Talking to this handsome, persuasive man, the world's greatest salesman, I began to like the idea, the challenge, and the opportunity to continue my involvement with scouting. I hesitated for a few minutes, still questioning the time commitment involved. Finally, I nodded to him and said loudly, "I'll take it on, but under the condition that if my studies and basketball become too much for me to be an effective leader, I will leave." Steve agreed.

I understood fully what a commitment it would take to be the troop's scoutmaster. I also knew I would not be a temporary caretaker to a bunch of young boys. I would give my all and work tirelessly to teach them camping skills and what scouting could bring to their respective lives.

We met later to discuss the troop's inventory of camping supplies. Unfortunately, the cupboard was virtually bare. This would not do. Supplies were needed immediately. Troop 3 was going to be a camping troop! My "wish list" was fairly extensive: Baker tents, band saws, axes, cooking kits, and so on quickly filled our note pad. In no time, the list became a reality.

My first troop meeting took place a week later. Its makeup was essentially from middle to upper middle class families. About a dozen scouts attended our first meeting and most were either Tenderfeet or Second Class in rank.

Jay Mullen was the highest ranked scout, First Class, and my senior patrol leader. Jay's camping skills and leadership qualities were not known, but I was confident he would take his leadership duties seriously. After all, he was the oldest in the troop, and the boys respected him.

One of the senior adult leaders was "Doc" Eugas. He had had a long-term tenure with the troop. He was a most patient man, one whom all the scouts respected completely. The boys listened intently to his excellent instructions on knot-tying, first aid, and so on. I could have never succeeded as the troop's scoutmaster without Doc's leadership. His entire life was dedicated to scouting and those in his presence were so fortunate to have known him.

My first emphasis to the troop was to tell them Troop 3 would be known as the "camping troop." We would go camping at least once a month using the troop's cabin located about 15 plus miles northeast of Cape as our field headquarters. When the weather was good, we'd sleep in tents and when bad, we'd use the cabin.

Since television, video games, etc. had not yet enraptured the boys' lives and most of their hormones had not been fully aroused, at least not the 12-year-olds, I felt, for the most part, camping would be of great interest and fun for them. It was.

Our meetings in Centenary's church basement were spent working on scouting's requirements for their next advancement, some to Second Class, and others to First Class. After a while, the boys became very active in that endeavor. In particular, their semaphore techniques, sending wig-wag messages back and forth across the church basement with speed and accuracy was most impressive. Knot-tying contests often brought on fierce rivalries among the patrols. Competition in all the games was intense, but done in a spirited, fair manner. After a while, the bonding, so necessary to take place in a scout troop was taking hold. Troop 3 was becoming a troop!

The southeast Missouri fall continued to be warm and unseasonable, allowing the troop to camp with tents, prepare meals over a fire, sharpen their axes, sleep on the ground, hike in the woods, and tell stories and sing around the campfire. As the weather turned colder, I would give them the option to sleep in the cabin, but most remained outside in their tents. After a few below freezing nights on winter weekends, their exodus from their tents to the cabin's apparent warmth was swift and complete. Unfortunately, the anticipated relief from the cabin's fireplace provided only minimal improvement. The boys were not happy.

Some innovative juggling took place to work around my college studies, basketball practices and games to continue my scout meetings and take the boys camping. Indeed, it required some adjustments, but it was never that difficult to make it all happen. Classes at college were challenging, and basketball demanded hard work, but meeting with the troop and watching these young men grow and mature made it well worth the effort.

Winter passed and spring brought more camping, advancements, and continued joy and excitement from the young men. Many of the boys had never been to Camp Lewallen, and they looked forward to spending a week in June living in tents, working on merit badges and swimming in the St. Francis River.

With great enthusiasm, the boys' parents loaded up their cars to head to camp with their eager children, bed rolls, uniforms, a few hidden boxes of candy, and a promise from their sons to write to their moms and dads. Homesickness was a looming threat, but as most of us going to camp for the first time had all succumbed, most survived. Troop 3's boys would be no exception.

Many of the troops from the Southeast Missouri Council did not wear the scout uniform during camp. I insisted that all my troop wear the uniform at all times. This rule caused some discomfort, but in time, the young men's swagger and pride in their troop began to bring on a major notice among the other campers. They all were entirely focused and ready to show the camp that Troop 3 was the best.

The troop's first competition took place during Pioneer Days. Each troop engaged in a series of contests to display their prowess in such events as raft, tower and fire building, knife and axe handling, and map reading. Since the past months' camping experience provided excellent training in all of these skills, Troop 3 easily won the competition. Other troop leaders were impressed as to how these young boys had become so proficient in camping skills. I somewhat discounted their success, but I was inwardly bursting with pride.

The Water Carnival took place on Saturday, the next-to-last day of camp. Most of the troop could swim, but none had any experience in rowing or canoeing. How they would do in those racing venues remained to be seen. But after a bit of basic instruction on how to paddle a canoe, I felt confident that the boys would more than hold their own. And they did, barely edging out a Sikeston troop, made up mostly of older scouts. Our troop was ecstatic. They had won Pioneer Days, and now the Water Carnival. Troop 3 was the talk of the camp!

Sunday came all too soon. We were going home now with the boys' heads filled with memories that would last a lifetime. The parents were overjoyed with the boys' successes. None of them had thought about being homesick. None had complained about the mess hall's meals. All wanted to come back next year. First year Papooses, would now return as second year Braves, and third year campers would become Warriors.

As for me, I couldn't have been more proud of my boys. While their camping skills progressed beyond anything I could have ever imagined, these young men were growing up. Camp Lewallen's week further taught them the true value of teamwork, hard work, and fellowship. Hopefully, those lessons learned would stay with them forever.

As my senior year started, I knew advanced accounting courses and basketball had now become more demanding. A decision had to be made. Should I continue as Troop 3's scoutmaster? I felt it would not be fair to the boys to act as their scoutmaster with such a heavy senior year schedule. I just couldn't do justice to these young men. In true sadness, I had to give my resignation. It was not a good day.

Telling the troop at their next meeting of my decision was difficult. The boys took it in stride, some wondering why, but most asking only if they would be able to go camping soon, if they would be going back to Camp

Lewallen next summer, and if I would be able to go with them again.

A replacement scoutmaster would be found, one who would be so lucky to lead this troop. With those scouts, I was assured his experience, like mine, would be most pleasant and fulfilling.

As I said my last good-bye, my thoughts moved far ahead to their future. Where would they end up in their lives? Would their ambitions be realized? What professions would they choose? Would they be successful? Would they become responsible citizens? Would they make their parents proud? I had no doubt. I was so fortunate to have been such a small part of their young lives. Truly I was blessed.

Roundball

At best, my varsity basketball experience at Southeast Missouri State College from 1953-1956 was about average.

Leaving Mizzou at the end of my freshman year and returning to Cape to play basketball energized me completely. Becoming a member of the varsity squad suggested to some of the athletic boosters that I would add a lot to the team. Such optimistic forecasts were certainly a bit overstated. Nevertheless, with my limited skills, I usually held my own in practices and played fairly well in games where I usually entered as the first or second substitute for our starting five. I was never a scoring threat, but on occasion, opponents would be unaware of my being left-handed which allowed me to make quick spin moves to the basket unmolested to score easily.

I still recall with great pleasure the road trips the team took during non-conference and conference games. Some took us to far away places from Cape including eastern New Mexico, Mississippi, Texas, Kansas, and Louisiana. Since I had barely ever been out of Missouri, those trips were something special.

My early teammates at Southeast were a special group, particularly:

Ray "Rip" Rippelmeyer, who had played previously on Southern Illinois University's varsity squad, was a leading scorer. However, Rip, a right-handed pitcher, had signed a professional baseball contract with the Milwaukee Braves thereby making him ineligible to play varsity basketball at SIU, a NCAA restriction. Southeast was a member of the National Association of Intercollegiate Athletics (NAIA), and since baseball was not played in that conference, it had no such restriction. The Valmeyer, Illinois, native wanted to continue to play college basketball, and our school was a logical choice, one which definitely made the Indian's squad much better. Playing in the 1953-54 and 1954-55 seasons, Rip was an All-Conference selection.

Ted "Slewfoot" Henderson was a senior, our starting center, and one of the most aggressive and tireless players on the squad. His offensive skills were not nearly as good as his defense, although, he was no slouch in the pivot. A Flat River native, Slew was our leader, and my appearance on the squad as a potential replacement starter for him was never in question. He was the man. I learned so much from him, particularly in rebounding and defensive techniques. Slew was an All-Conference selection in the 1952-53 season and second team All-Conference in the 1953-54 season.

Elmer "Bud" Balzer, a physical specimen right out of central casting probably should have been in the movies. Extraordinarily handsome, Bud played well as a starting forward in the 1953-54 and 1954-55 seasons. He was a better than average shotmaker and more than held his own on defense.

All three of these athletes were committed to winning, showed maturity way beyond their years, and were excellent teammates, always helping the younger squad members with their fundamentals.

Richard "Ike" Eichhorst and Paul "Cowboy" aka "Trojan" Copeland were the other starters, both sophomores. They had started as freshmen and were returning for their second year of varsity competition.

Hailing from Lemay, Missouri's Hancock High School, Ike had not enrolled in college directly out of high school. A year later, he tried out for the team as a walk on. It wasn't long before he became a starter on a full scholarship. A prolific scorer, he was runner-up to Rip as a junior, the leading scorer in his senior year.

Cowboy had a scholarship. He had been an outstanding point guard at Union, Missouri's high school. His ever present hustle and deadly two-handed set shot made him a starter in his freshman year.

Ike, Cowboy, and I became the best of friends. Traveling with them for those three seasons provided endless stories of laughter and irreverence.

Bill Graham, a smooth shooting guard from Crystal City, had initially attended St. Louis University on a scholarship, but after one season, decided to transfer to Southeast for the 1953-54 season. He played for the next three years, a starter in his junior and senior years. Not particularly fast or physical, he was an excellent shooter, always able to get open on the court and contributed significantly to the team's successes.

Bill "Burr" Sims, a Festus, Missouri high school standout who played at Memphis State University, joined the team at the start of the 1954-55 season. A strong, raw-boned post man, Burr had an enormous wing-span permitting him to become a premier shot blocker. He also could jump with the best of those who played against him. I was marked to be a starter in my senior year, but his talents quickly overcame mine, and Coach Pink placed him into the starting lineup.

My first road trip as a sophomore was to Carbondale, Illinois to play the Salukis of Southern Illinois University. In the fourth quarter, with the score tied and only a few minutes left in the game, coach sent me in. Naturally, I had a bad case of butterflies circling in my stomach, but after a few trips up and down the floor, I settled down and became more engaged in the game. Ike put up a shot which caromed off the backboard to my outstretched hands. No one was around me. In my excitement to shoot a totally unmolested shot, I jumped high and uncharacteristic of my usual soft touch, slammed the ball hard against the backboard and missed the entire rim and basket. From there the Salukis went on to win by a few points. We were defeated in a game we should have won. I had let the team down.

Coach was not happy with my first shot *ever* for the Indians. Putting his arm around me after the game, he said quite stoically, "Gene, you've got to make those shots. It really hurt us." Naturally, I felt badly about my initial performance, but I was at least encouraged he had confidence in me to put me in a close game.

Rolling into December, we played in a Christmas tournament in Ottawa, Kansas. We reached the finals only to lose to Washburn University. Coach was pleased with our performance. I played some, made no mistakes, and scored a few points. I was beginning to feel like a part of the team.

Our coach, Ralph Pink, was in his second year of coaching at Southeast. Pink, a serious man, dedicated to the highest values of college coaching, was the quintessential planner in game preparation. He had played varsity basketball at Northeast Missouri State, served in the Coast Guard and played on one of its championship teams. Coach received his master's degree from the University of Missouri. His initial coaching year at Southeast had been a winning one. His no-nonsense style of coaching sometimes ran contrary to the playful antics of Ike and Cowboy. Since these two players always brought a winning approach to the games, Coach learned early to go with the flow and hoped those two would continue to help the team win with their aggressive and unselfish play. They always did, too!

Conference play commenced in January. Our first road trip was to Rolla to play the Miners. Playing there was always a battle as the Miners and their rowdy student fans whooped and hollered throughout the game played in a "cracker box" of a gym. We eeked out a victory, knowing when they came to Cape, we'd defeat them easily, as we always did.

Our road trip to Springfield, (Southwest Missouri State, now Missouri State) resulted in a defeat, but brought laughter to Ike and Cowboy during a pre-game meal. Our meal was always roast beef, no gravy, a baked potato, no butter, green beans, and hot tea. The waitress brought out our meal, but to our surprise, there was gravy spread heavily on our beef. We couldn't believe it. Perhaps Coach Pink was changing our usual routine.

Just then, Coach came to our table and in a voice filled with great pain and distress said, "Oh, hell, they don't want us to win here in Springfield. They put gravy on our meat." None of us laughed, at least we tried hard not to, but when Coach left the room, we roared.

After the game and in defeat, my roommate, Slew Henderson, and I retired to our room. During our late night conversation, Slew asked me about Cecilia Morgan, one of my friends and classmates from Cape Central. Slew wanted to know more about her, whether she would be interested in meeting and dating.

"Naww, Slew. She wouldn't go out with you. You're a basketball player," I said in a half-snickering manner. "Besides, she was one of the smartest girls in our class. You wouldn't even be able to talk to her."

Slew groaned and responded, "No, I'd just like to meet her and ask her out for a date. That's all."

"Okay, I'll try to fix it up for you, but I'm not sure she'd be interested." I did, they got together, married after his graduation in 1954, and have remained life-long partners ever since.

On a previous occasion, Rip talked to me about Glenda Jones, another classmate from Central and one of the college's cheerleaders. He, too, was interested in meeting and dating her, and wanted me to "fix him up." I did, they got together, married in the fall of 1954 (my first wedding as a groomsman) and have remained life-long partners ever since.

While my sophomore season was undistinguished as a basketball player, I became joined at the hip to my teammates, spending long hours on the bus rides, traveling the southern junket to Springfield (Southwest Missouri State) and Warrensburg (Central Missouri State), and then later in the season on the northern trip to Maryville (Northwest Missouri State) and Kirksville (Northeast Missouri State, now Truman University). Both trips had the team leaving Cape on a Friday, playing Saturday and Monday night games, and returning home on Tuesday afternoon. Those road trips which seemed endless, always ended with a great sigh of relief from all of us.

On these long trips, Hearts and Pinochle became our card games of chance. I preferred Pinochle, lovingly taught to me by Ike and Cowboy. While we probably played hundreds of games, my partners and I always lost against my teachers. Was cheating goin' on? Naww, I just figured it was the bad cards I was dealt. I was so naïve!

Snow was a constant companion when we made the northern trek to Maryville and Kirksville. One of my unforgettable moments was in Kirksville as the team was leaving the restaurant after its pre-game meal. Bill Graham, hiding behind a snow-laden parked car threw a snowball and hit Coach Pink square in the head literally bringing him to his knees. No one laughed as he slowly raised his body from the deep snow. Without a word, he brushed himself off and pointed directly at Cowboy and Ike and sadly shook his head.

"You two never learn, do you? You never learn," he shouted and then picked up a handful of snow and proceeded to fire back at the two innocents. Seeing a significant character change in the coach, the entire team took sides and proceeded to engage in a rousing snowball fight. Unfortunately, our game that day was wasted in the snow, as we later lost that evening.

During the 1954-55 season, we made a road trip to Hammond, Louisiana to play in Southeast Louisiana State's Christmas Tournament. The tournament started on a Monday and Coach held a practice that Sunday evening. While driving hard along the baseline toward the basket, one of my teammates came under me as I leaped forward to shoot causing me to fall heavily to the floor. Pain ripped through my body, particularly into my right hip. The next morning, the school's doctor x-rayed me and revealed, to my surprise, I had a separated shoulder. When the team heard about the diagnosis, Cowboy and Ike kidded me unmercifully, suggesting that "everything was connected to my buns." Consequently, my new nickname became "Buns."

Our first road trip during the 1955-56 season was to play in the Christmas Tournament in Los Portales, New Mexico, with Eastern New Mexico University as the host. We ripped through our earlier opponents, but lost to West Texas State in the finals.

The next morning after our defeat, we were on the road again to play Midwestern University in Wichita Falls, Texas, at least a 10-12 hour trip across the barren plains of the Texas Panhandle. The morning's wake-up call came at 4 am which left most of us sleeping poorly on and off across Texas. We went down to an ugly defeat that evening. No one was happy, and we were exhausted.

In all three of my varsity seasons, we always had winning records, never winning the conference championship, but remaining unbeaten in conference play at home. Coach Pink continued to harp endlessly about our training habits imploring us to avoid cigarettes, alcohol, and donuts and pancakes, and get at least nine hours of sleep during the season and so on. While I judiciously trained, I longed for the day when the season would end and I could party with my friends and slide easily back into regular college life.

My last collegiate game was against Maryville in February, 1956. Coach started his five seniors, four of whom (Ike, Cowboy, Bill and Burr) had been starters for the past two years. Playing there earlier that winter had been an embarrassment to me as I posted a 0-0-5-0 in the box score—no field goals, no free throws, and fouling out of the game with five fouls and no points scored.

This time it was different. I played well, scored 12 points, and gathered in several rebounds as we won easily. In winning, Ike set the teams' record for most points scored in a season. We were delighted with that. He had been our leading scorer, winning All-Conference honors in both his junior and senior years.

After the game, Coach Pink came over and put his arm around me and said softly, "Gene, nice game. I guess I should have been playing you more. I'm sorry I didn't."

The seniors of the 1956 Southeast Missouri State College basketball team in 1956 (above) and 42 years later in 1998 (below). From left to right in both photos are Rich Eichhorst, Bill Graham, Bill Sims, Gene Munger, and Paul Copeland.

Taken aback by his kind and gracious words, I replied, "That's okay, Coach. That's okay." I could have said much more, but I was so happy the season had ended and my basketball career was finished. My last season produced a grand total of 50 points, hardly record-setting totals.

As I walked off the court for the last time, the remaining crowd stood and applauded for us seniors. It made me proud to have been a part of the team for the past three years. I remembered how my basketball career had started at Lorimier School, followed by Church League, then Cape Central, then University of Missouri and ended at Southeast Missouri State. It, also, made me aware of how fortunate I was to have had the strength, talent and will to play high school and college basketball, an opportunity reserved to only a few.

Had my three years of varsity basketball at Cape been worth all of the struggle, the long practices, butt-numbing road trips, disappointing losses, and missing out on so many parties and fun times? Indeed, playing basketball had given me a full-ride scholarship which resulted in a debt free, quality education.

And, too, it brought bonding and lasting friendships which have endured to this day. For those experiences, I shall always be so grateful.

Southeast Missouri State College Basketball Senior Gene Munger in 1956.

Clearwater

Being the son and grandson of lawyers, my father's friends would continuously ask me, "Are you going to be a lawyer like your daddy and granddaddy?" With my burr-head looking down at the ground, I would mumble, "Yes Sir, I am." Being anything else was out of the question, it had already been decided.

As my sophomore year ended at Southeast Missouri State College in May 1954, Jack Ellis, a classmate and an Air Force veteran, asked me if I still intended to be a lawyer, and if I did, "What kind of a lawyer?"

I answered rather cockily, "Why sure, I'm going to go to law school and then go into partnership with my father. Why do you ask?"

He answered, "I would think you would want to be a tax lawyer. They make lots of money."

"A tax lawyer? I'm a history major. What courses would I have to take to be a tax lawyer?"

"Well you gotta start majoring in accounting. After graduation here, you'd go get your Masters in accounting, take the CPA exam and then go to law school. I'm tellin' you, tax lawyers really make a lot of money." If anybody would know, Jack would. After all, he was five years older and a veteran.

I thought he had a good idea, although accounting was far from my mind as I spent that 1954 summer in the northern lakes of Wisconsin working at an Explorer Scout Canoe Base. Starting my junior year, I figured changing my major to accounting would work well and I might as well start to begin my journey to getting rich.

My basic introductory accounting courses went fairly well over my junior year. My professor, (the only one teaching accounting) Bon O. Brown, encouraged me, although he warned me that the Intermediate Accounting course was the one that "separated the men from the boys." That course was taught in summer school, and while I had always enjoyed my summers at scout camps, I knew I had to go to summer school and cram at least five or six more accounting courses in my senior year to complete my major and graduate with my class in May 1956.

Professor Brown was right. Intermediate Accounting was much more difficult than my earlier courses. Fortunately, Al Painton, another accounting major and an Air Force veteran steered me through that course. I shall always be indebted to him. As my final exams ended, I realized accounting wasn't nearly as interesting as history, but I understood that getting rich was going to take some sacrifices I was willing to make.

My father, now practicing law in St. Louis, called me the next day and invited me to go fishing with him over at Clearwater Lake, approximately 90 miles southwest of Cape. While I had never fished the lake, fed by the Black River, I was very familiar with Piedmont, a small town nearby. Those of us who were members of Camp Lewallen's staff would go over there on our night off. The younger staff members and I would usually take in a movie or saunter down the main drag looking to talk to the town's girls.

Dad had given me a 1946 four-door, stick-shift Chevrolet as I started my senior year. He got it as payment in lieu of cash from one of his clients. That car, with the key never removed, became community property for me and my basketball teammates. If only it could have talked about some of its passengers' experiences during that year!

Although I was completely worn out from summer school mentally, certainly not physically, I warily made the trip over to Piedmont the next day although I relished going fishing. My summer was totally void in that area. Frankly, I had no expectation that our already fragile relationship would undergo any improvement during that weekend.

As a lawyer, Dad was most skilled at giving advice and counsel to his clients. His courtroom demeanor was text book and he was widely regarded as an excellent trial lawyer. Unfortunately, we had never been able to develop a meaningful father-son relationship. It was probably due to my parent's separation as I was turning twelve years old when Mother and I moved to Cape.

Dad had already come down from St. Louis, secured a room at a motel and waited for me. We greeted each other warmly, but all I wanted to do was get something to eat and go to bed. Conversation was light and minimal at dinner as I wolfed down a chicken-fried steak dinner and finished off a chocolate sundae in record time.

Retiring to bed early, I slept nearly twelve hours. As an experienced fisherman, Dad knew we should have arisen early to escape the sweltering, humid Missouri summer sun. When I finally awakened, he uttered not a word of disappointment nor criticism, took me to breakfast and when we finally arrived at the lake, it was nearly 11 am.

Seeing my Dad dressed for fishing was a sight to behold. He looked like someone right out of central casting. Freshly pressed cotton trousers, a long-sleeved shirt, and a sharp bolo tie gave him the appearance of someone about to address a summer encampment of fellow lawyers. His broad-brimmed hat nicely protected his bronzed face from the unforgiving sun.

For my dress, shorts, a t-shirt, and a well-worn baseball cap were a sharp contrast to my father's classy apparel. I never gave it a second thought. We were fishing, not dressing for a fashion show.

Dad rented a boat with motor, sought lakeside counsel from one of the storekeepers at the dock and away we went to a spot recommended to be ideal for catching fish, a cove protected from the wind by a large stand of oak trees. Needless to say, at that time of day, any prospect for catching fish was dim, indeed.

As we anchored the boat, there was little or no conversation between us. Finally, I figured something had to give. I asked, "Dad, what was it like growing up in Dexter and Bloomfield when you were a boy? Tell me about being in the Army during World War I, marrying Mother, and you know, becoming a lawyer."

His face grew into a big smile and he began to tell his life's story in a somewhat concise, but chronologically accurate summary. In the past, I had heard some of it in bits and pieces, but filling in the blanks was most interesting, actually compelling to me.

"Well, growing up in Dexter in those days, early 1900s with my brother, Martel, and sister, Mary, was a lot of fun. My dad was a lawyer, but we moved to Bloomfield when I was about 12. When the war broke out, both Martel and I joined up much to my father's chagrin and concern for our safety, but we wanted to fight the Germans. Both of us went to France, me in the Quartermaster's Corps and Martel as an infantryman. Martel was seriously wounded and sent home. I came home after the war ended.

Your mother and Martel were very close and folks just assumed they were going to get married when the war ended. Unfortunately, Martel later died from his war wounds, and your mother was devastated. I felt sorry for her and started dating her. After a while, we became engaged, got married and before long, your sister, Martel, was born. We moved to Chicago where I got my law degree, working during the day at a law office and going to school at night. We returned to Bloomfield, I passed the bar exam, and your grandfather and I started practicing law together."

"How'd that work out?" I asked. "Did you and grandfather get along?"

"No, not really. He knew the law very well, but he was very impatient with me, constantly belittling me for my modern ways of working with clients and preparing for trial. We broke up after a while, and Mother and I moved to Chaffee where I set up a law office. You came along a little later. Martel worked for me as a stenographer. She was really a good one, but I guess I was too impatient with her, too. She tried very hard to please me, but I gave her no slack. It just didn't work out for either of us. From

Gene's sister, Martel Munger, in 1944 in Benton.

Chaffee, we moved to Sikeston for a few years and then to Benton. Well, you know the rest of the story."

For a second or so, he remained quiet and gazed out on the lake in a moment of deep reflection.

I then pressed him for more details, particularly of his Army service and the early days with mother and him in Chicago. He responded excitedly and continued talking, almost without my interrupting him, for more than another half-hour.

Finally, I said, "Dad, I didn't know all of this. Do you think you and Mother will ever get back together?" I had never even broached that question. I surprised myself at even asking such a personal question. I had never ever talked to him about their relationship much less expressed any hope for their reconciliation.

"I don't think so, probably not. I believe she's doing very well without my being in your and her life, but I do miss both of you. She has done such an excellent job of raising you. I am so proud of you, your basketball, good grades . . . you've really done well, and I know how proud your mother must be of all you've been able to accomplish."

I had no answer for his response. Although my Mother had never uttered a harsh or negative word about him since the separation, I knew there was simply no way she would want him back into our lives. She still loved him, but her life was now dedicated to my happiness and future. As far as she was concerned, our life would always be without him or any financial support he could give.

The sun was now bearing down on us from the west and both of us were perspiring heavily. I had had it, and I was ready to call it quits. Dad seemed undeterred from the heat and humidity. He continued talking, this time reminiscing about his experiences with practicing law with his father. It was a very difficult time. The subject abruptly changed to my future, my future as a lawyer.

"You tell me you've switched majors to accounting from history. How's it going?" I could have answered positively, but after a course in business law and getting acquainted with such terms as lessor, assignor, guarantor, etc., I knew the switch wasn't really going as well as I would have liked. Frankly, I found the lexicon of business and accounting boring. I missed history, but getting rich as a tax lawyer still had a lot of appeal particularly based on my current meager financial condition.

"Oh, it's going okay, but my senior year with the advanced accounting courses along with playing varsity basketball is really going to be tough. I can do it, but it won't be easy."

"I know you will do just fine, just fine. Say, it's really getting hot out here, what say we call it a day? We haven't caught any fish, and it looks like those clouds over yonder are going to bring us rain? Let's go!" He restarted the motor and we headed toward the dock. Our fishing day had ended.

Back at the motel, we showered, took a nap and went to dinner, this time enjoying a good steak and listening to my dad reminisce fondly about some of his trials as a country lawyer. As he talked, tables next to us leaned forward to hear him, listening intently to his every word. As a raconteur, the man had no peer!

We went our separate ways the next morning, my suffering from fierce sunburn but feeling a little better about my father. We had somewhat bonded at that point in time, although we needed more time together. One fishing trip wasn't going to be the divining experience for us to become pals, but it was a start. More time would be needed, but at least, I was hopeful. I looked forward to that.

Dad was diagnosed with throat cancer in 1959 and finally died in late 1964. Over the years, he had been a chain smoker of unfiltered Camel cigarettes, five packs a day. During the last few years of his life, we became much closer, sharing experiences, crying, and praying together as his life ended. At last, we had bonded completely as father and son.

■ ■ ■ ■ ■

To Navy Officer Candidates School

It all happened so fast for me. In a scant two months I graduated from college in May 1956, turned down an accounting assistantship at the University of Illinois, left Cape, Mother and friends, moved to St. Louis, took an accounting job with Shell Oil Company and played like I knew what I was doing. I really didn't.

My student deferment ran dry when the local draft board rudely advised me that it had a change of plans for a 22-year-old accountant who was no longer a full-time student. That eventuality had never occurred to me. I was simply having too much fun. My new life was the typical story of a small town boy getting caught up in the fast life of the city. Parties, hangovers, renting the first apartment and getting a pay check every two weeks had all sort of blended together in a confusing but enjoyable change from the past. Being confronted with induction into the Army was something else. I was no draft dodger, but I certainly didn't want to face basic training in the rolling hills of south central Missouri as a recruit. After reporting for my physical in early November, I knew then that the army definitely had me program-med for a two-year dose of shiny buttons and khaki clothing.

Eugene M. Munger, Jr., a senior at Southeast Missouri State College.

I scrambled quickly, and in a matter of days, applied for Naval Officer Candidate School, tested, and was accepted for the January class. At least I would sleep between sheets, not on scratchy wool blankets barely cushioning rocky Ozark soil.

I finally broke the news of my leaving to my supervisor in early December, ended a just beginning relationship with an elementary school teacher and partied frenetically throughout the holiday season.

On the first Thursday in January, I packed my clothes, left my snickering, disbelieving former Marine private roommate and longtime friend, Sam McClanahan, with a messy apartment and promise to write.

The ride home that night to Cape, a trip of a little more than two hours, was lonely. A two-lane, winding road snaked itself over the gentle hills and valleys between the city and home. I had gotten accustomed to the freeways of the city, but this antiquated, narrow road reminded me that progress had not reached these parts.

The January wind, knifing and northerly, cut fiercely through all of the aging doors of my 1946 Chevy. Its overburdened heater was little relief from the unusually frigid temperatures of the past few days. Winter in those hills was normally cold, but that night had to be a record breaker. The car's radio had long ago delivered its final static sound. There was really nothing to occupy my time, but the reflections of what had happened over the past few months.

Dad had taken my decision not to go to law school pretty well. As long as I could remember he was always telling his friends, "The boy is going to be a lawyer just like his dad and grandfather." I'd always go along with that line, but down deep inside I knew that it was not to be.

I had definitely decided that I didn't want any part of the law profession, but it was comfortable to go along with him during my infrequent visits. We hardly had anything to say when we were alone together, at least nothing important.

The drive up to St. Louis that late April to tell him that I would not be going to law school was miserable for me. I had never dreaded anything so much in my life. I parked the car and walked the few blocks over to his downtown Chestnut Street office, an aging multistoried building which was the home for many law firms and insurance companies. His secretary was expecting me and Dad was waiting. We exchanged a few pleasantries before I delivered my message. I expected his worst reaction.

"Dad, I've decided, err, think that I'll not go to law school at, err, this time, but instead, I've, uh, I, uh, want to go ahead and apply for an accounting assistantship at Illinois, then I'll err, go ahead and go to law school and you know, become a lawyer like you." My weak voice and hesitating delivery showed no conviction at all as to my future plans.

Dad looked at me for a beat or two and then leaned back in his handsome leather chair, placed his hands behind his neck, smiled broadly and gazed at me for what seemed like forever.

"I'm delighted, Son. Simply delighted," he said at last. I knew he was disappointed, but his response put me at ease. My heart ached for him as I knew how much he had looked forward to my joining him there in the city after law school. In my mind, the prospect of continuing my family's law legacy had abruptly ended.

Mother was happy with my decision. She had little respect for lawyers, and despite my family's law tradition, she never wanted me to take that course. While she never expressed an opinion to me, she was never encouraging when the subject was brought up. She had raised me and was always there when I needed her through scouting, high school, and college. Dad had done very little to make our life better. Yes, she was bitter, and she resented any possible involvement that I would have with him in the future. In her mind, he did not deserve to be any part of it.

The dim lights formed an irregular crown starting on the rolling hills to the west and rising gently, as I approached Cape after leaving St. Louis earlier that evening. The crown peaked with the long-standing dome light of the college's Academic Hall, one of the highest points in the county.

Although it was nearing midnight, I decided to take one last drive around town before checking in at Mother's apartment. The streets were quiet. Almost nothing was moving.

Cape Girardeau had not changed much over the years. A few of the national fast food chains were cropping up out on the main highway, but basically, the town's features still resembled a quiet river town lost in a time warp of the early 1900s. Merchants still seemed to operate in the same way, occasionally changing their windows displays, never modernizing their stores.

The Mississippi River was Cape's eastern boundary. I had many memories of the river, good and bad. We could always count on the spring floods creating all night vigils of merchants sandbagging their storefronts and praying the waters would recede and spare their businesses from ruin. Eventually nature relented, and the water returned to its banks and concern for a better way to harness the beast faded away in the sweltering summer heat.

But fall was the best time for me to enjoy the river. I would take my college date to the river bank and lie there on my blanket and watch the river barges pass in front of us. Their powerful spotlights would occasionally find us. The vulgar laughs and comments of the crew would always break the spell of our passion.

My midnight ride took me through the old neighborhood where Mother and I had settled when we first moved to Cape in the late 1940s. It was not in the best part of town; however, the grammar school was nearby. I didn't have the slightest concern that my route to school had been along the Frisco railroad tracks.

I remembered where we lived on South Middle. Its walls were paper thin, and the domestic quarreling brought on by a tyrant of a woman and her meek husband introduced me to words I had never heard before. How well I remembered.

I figured I had to go by the high school. Central High and its four years had been a lovely time in my life. All the good things that could happen in high school had happened to me. I had gone steady with the best looking girl in the class, played on the basketball team, was all-state, an honor student, and part of the "in crowd."

It was getting late now, as I pointed my car across town and up the hill toward the college. It was located majestically on the highest hill in the town. It once had been strictly a teachers' college, but it lost that moniker several years ago when it became a state college. Many of its buildings were made with native limestone, and it could have easily passed for an Ivy League school, but in appearance only. It was a small college with some outstanding teachers, particularly in the liberal arts and science. The St. Louis students and their sophisticated ways were a sharp contrast to the soft southern twang and the laid back charm of those coming from the rural towns of the Bootheel.

Down from Academic Hall, I saw the outline of Leming Hall, one of the two women's dorms on campus. I smiled as I remembered those days when I would linger for one more kiss, one more squeeze from my date as I hustled her to the door to meet the 10:30 pm curfew. If she didn't make it, there was always the alternative of boosting her through one of the ground floor windows. Now, that was really daring!

I fell in love more than once, always overwhelmed with sadness and regret at losing the love of my life, but I always recovered nicely to do it over and over again. Ah, the love life of a college student. Those were the days!

I finally reached Mother's apartment about 1 am. She greeted me warmly and offered hot chocolate before I turned in for a few hours of sleep. I was in no mood to talk, but I tried valiantly to respond to each of her continuing questions. I had been her entire life for the past ten years. Now, I was going to leave again, only this time, I would not be a few hours away, but all the way to the East Coast. It would be a new adventure, a new start in what would be a major leap into a world of responsibility and commitment.

We moved into my old room so I could start transferring some of my clothes into a smaller suitcase. I certainly wouldn't need many clothes for Newport, only a few sports clothes for the weekends. I packed light, kissed her gently, and tried to get a little sleep before the train.

My mind wandered. Maybe, I should have gone ahead to Illinois and gotten my Masters, then the CPA, and maybe, tried law school. It was too late to dwell on what might have been. The plan had changed.

The sound of the telephone jolted my body fiercely. The clock by the bed showed 4 am. The train, the train, I was going to miss the train! I was panic stricken. How could I have fallen asleep without setting the alarm?

I ran into the kitchen, snatched the receiver and blurted, "Hello?"

"Where the hell are you?" Ranny Young's high voice exploded. He and Don Rasche, both college classmates, had also been selected for Officer's Candidate School, and we had agreed to go to Newport together.

"Rasche's here. The train'll be here in a minute. Are you coming?"

"Damn, Rann. I overslept. Hold the train. I'll be there in five minutes."

I jumped into my clothes, grabbed the bag and with a "See you. I love you," cry into Mother's bedroom, I roared out into the cold, winter air and into my car.

The tired Chevy hesitated slightly for a heart-stopping second, coughed and then responded to my heavy foot on the accelerator. Bob Stoneman had agreed to buy this relic for $300 and would pick it up at the train station in the morning. It had been a good car, but its future was behind it.

The distance to the station was less than a mile. Broadway, Cape's Main Street, was completely deserted at that time of the morning. For me, it became a raceway.

For some reason, I remembered my scouting days when the troop would get up early on holidays to put up American flags along the town's main streets. This was definitely no holiday, and there were half-frozen scouts scraping their knuckles on corroding iron flag holders as they tried to dress the river town up for the day.

In a few minutes my abused, but reliable, car arrived at the station. My guys and the train were waiting. With one heavy bag banging against my side, I dashed for the train, apologized weakly for holding everybody up and scooted up into the coach car. Panting heavily, I collapsed into my seat.

About that time, the conductor came ambling through the car, calling out for tickets. His freshly pressed uniform showed the shininess of years on the rails. The friendly, familiar, knowing face of "Poppa Frank Morgan," the father of one of my high school chums, filled me with warm confidence.

"Poppa Frank, are you the conductor?" I asked.

"Yes, and you're damned lucky I am. I was barely able to hold this thing until you could get down here. Ranny tells me that you, Rasch and him are going to Newport, to OCS. Right?"

"Yeah, how about that?" I said.

"Well, I sure hope the Navy teaches you to get out of bed, 'cause if they don't, you'll be back here before you know it."

They did, and I never went back.

■ ■ ■ ■ ■
New York, New York

On that early cold morning of Friday, January 4, 1957, the Frisco train limped slowly out of the Cape Girardeau station as it made its way northward toward St. Louis. A cold winter wind blew the big steam engine's belching black smoke eastward toward the Mississippi River only a small distance away.

With my long-time friends, Don Rasche and Ranny Young, I was heading to the U.S. Navy's Officer Candidate School at Newport, Rhode Island, a ride that I nearly missed as I overslept at Mother's apartment.

I wasn't much company during the four-hour trip to the city. I was simply exhausted from the hectic ride down from St. Louis the evening before. I stayed up late to visit with Mother, trying to catch her up on the past couple of weeks and my impending journey to Newport. She was excited, of course, and when I told her the boys and I were going to spend the weekend with Brian Mullen in New York, she was delighted.

Holding down one coach seat all by myself, I slept soundly until the train made a short, jarring stop at Festus, about an hour from St. Louis. Ranny and Don sat together in front of me, their continuous chatter carrying softly over the other sleeping passengers. I figured with the long trip ahead of us, there would be plenty of time for talking. Besides, I needed more sleep!

Arriving in St. Louis' Union Station just before 9 am, we retrieved our bags, made our way over to the station's snack bar, scoffed down some doughnuts, and transferred to the train leaving at 10 am for New York City. We were on our way, a journey that would soon change my life forever.

Crossing the Mississippi, we quickly huddled together in the bar car. Ranny and I ordered a beer, Don refrained. One by one, we tried to catch each other up on our lives since graduating from Southeast Missouri State that previous May. Don had started working as a loan officer at Cape Federal Savings & Loan. His father was a vice president there. He and his long-time sweetheart, Margaret Cleland, married right after college.

Ranny continued to sell shoes at JC Penney, a job he had started while in high school. He and Martha Ann Estes were fairly serious, but no engagement ring adorned her finger.

My rather non-distinguished position as a Treasury Management Trainee at Shell Oil Company's St. Louis Division office had kept me in check, but had not prevented the Army from drafting me. Getting accepted to OCS had spared me from donning khakis for two years. As for any girlfriend in my life, even to write home to, I was completely void in that area.

After several beers, we decided to have lunch in the dining car, an experience that none of us had ever had. We ate ravenously, and naps quickly followed for all of us. Awakening again, this time a bit hazy, I saw that winter's darkness had overcome us as the train entered Ohio. I spent the next hour or so simply looking out the window at the dull, scattered lights peering out from the gray nondescript barren Ohio fields and hills. My thoughts turned to what lay ahead. Could I make it through OCS? Where would they send me? To a ship? Perhaps, shore duty? I knew it would be a significant change in my life, but was I up to it? I just didn't know. My throbbing head from too many beers added little to my reverie.

Our train arrived at Penn Station around 10 pm that same day. A smiling Brian Mullen met us there, a place that made even St. Louis's cavernous Union Station seem small. Although it was late in the evening, the place was swarming with people, commuters hurrying home for the weekend, harried parents tugging and carrying small crying children whose early bedtimes had escaped them. A cold chill overcame me. This was New York City. What was I doing here?

A few years older than I, Brian had finished law school at the University of Missouri, passed the bar, was drafted into the Army and was on duty in the city. His future plans included moving to Oregon and starting a law practice in Medford. While not related, both our grandfathers had been Methodist ministers and were close friends. In our way of thinking, that made us brothers or at least "kissin' cousins." Further, he had rented an apartment with a couple other Army draftees, and when he found out that I was going to OCS, he called and insisted we stay with him before we went up to Newport. For a couple of southeast Missouri boys who had barely ever been out of the state, maybe over to Illinois or Tennessee once or twice, this was pretty cool stuff.

Bags and all, we piled into Brian's four-door '56 Chevy and headed over to his apartment in Queens. While fairly heavy traffic weaving from lane to lane caused us some concern, Brian drove like one of the natives adroitly holding his own and offering a running commentary on the sights around us.

His furnished apartment, a three-bedroom, spacious living room and tiny kitchen, was located on the fifth floor of a building that was one of many such structures which all looked alike. His roommates were away for the weekend which freed up two beds for Don and me leaving Ranny to fend for himself on a couch that had seen much better days.

We talked until after 2 am sharing some of Brian's Rheingold beer and trying to wind down from our long day. In rapid fire conversation, sounding like an enthusiastic tour guide, he gave us the itinerary for the weekend: Empire State Building, the Rockettes at Radio City Music Hall, the Metropolitan Art Museum, the Automat, Fifth Avenue, the Statue of Liberty, the Staten Island ferry, all the places that had once seemed so foreign and far away from the rolling hills around Cape. And he even had fixed me up with a blind date for the next evening!

Sleeping late, we rolled out of bed around 10 am and found Brian already up with the *New York Times* enveloping his full attention. A quick breakfast of bagels and cream cheese (my first ever) and off we went to Manhattan Island to play tourists. Despite a cold, damp wind, we saw the sights, had a mid-afternoon lunch at the Automat, climbed the steps of the Empire State Building, and caught the Rockettes at Radio City. Even the Benton-Clio Follies weren't that good! Late in the afternoon, we returned to the apartment and met Brian's lady, Mary Margaret Culliney, an Irish lass of incredible style and beauty.

She was an absolutely stunning woman, tall, jet-black hair swept up in a tight bun, svelte body wrapped tightly in a black sheath dress, angular face and dark shining eyes that lit up the room. An assistant interior decorator at *Ladies' Home Journal* headquarters, she clearly was one of the most beautiful women I had ever seen. Although from West Virginia, her accent was that of a cosmopolitan New Yorker, not that of a mountain state denizen. After a few pleasantries, she immediately engaged us country boys from southeast Missouri in animated conversation quickly discovering each of our backgrounds, likes, dislikes and so on. We were mesmerized by this awesome woman, and I might add that Brian sat beside her with the look of a man who had just won the lottery. Methinks he was really in love.

Away again in Brian's car, a bit crowded with the five of us, we headed for Times Square to see its marvels and meet my date for the evening, Barbara Shook. Rendezvousing with her in the lobby of the Taft hotel more than made the start of that evening pleasurable. She was a delight, a lovely brunette dressed in a blue taffeta dress with a presence about her that portrayed class. I was smitten at once and struggled mightily to find something to say.

Regaining my composure, I said haltingly, "Where do you work, Barbara? In the city?"

Her soft brown eyes brightened as she replied, "Oh, I work at the *Ladies' Home Journal*, the same place that Mary Margaret works."

"Oh, my goodness," I exclaimed, "My mother subscribes to that magazine. I grew up with the Journal."

I could see somewhat of a frown on her beautiful face and a look of disbelief when she said quietly, "Oh, that's nice." I felt like the proverbial penny waiting on change.

The rest of the evening was magical, my walking hand in hand with Barbara looking at the bright lights of Time Square, listening to jazz from inside the famous Metropole and capping off the evening with a nickel ride on the Staten Island Ferry.

Midnight had passed, but the city didn't seem to care. Cars and taxi cabs continued their rapid ride up and down the city's wide avenues and narrow streets. It might as well have been rush hour. Brian suggested we take Barbara back to her apartment, but she nixed that idea, suggesting instead that she take a cab. Still swooning with the excitement of being with such a lovely lady, I kissed her faintly on her delicate cheek and suggested that perhaps we could see each other again, maybe after I had been commissioned and had a few days' leave. I felt like the man who had everything going his way, not a care in the world. A real big timer I was!

"It was lovely meeting you, Gene," she said as she moved effortlessly into the waiting cab. "If you're back in town, please call me. Mary Margaret has my phone number."

"I will, I will," I shouted as the cab darted quickly into the busy street. "I will!" The ride home back to the apartment left me with very little to say. I had just had the date of my life. I was simply bubbling inside with pride.

The next morning familiarized me to the Sunday edition of the *Times*, one which arrived with no fanfare but only the challenge to read it for the rest of the week. My hometown paper, the *Southeast Missourian*, paled mightily by comparison. Just reading the entertainment section with all the available movies in the city was overwhelming. There were hundreds of choices, while Cape had just three.

Brian continued our weekend odyssey as he drove us around the next day through Central Park, down the West Side Highway, even across the George Washington Bridge, through the Bowery, and Chinatown. Was there no end to what one could see here?

Since we were going to catch an early morning train to Providence, one that luckily made a stop only a block or so from the apartment, we went to bed early, exhausted from our whirlwind visit in this town of wonders.

Awakening early at the harsh sound of an alarm clock that had the potential to raise the dead, I staggered out of bed and peered out the window to see another gray, dreary January day. There was no magic to this morning. The boys and I dressed quickly, donned suits and ties and with our overcoat collars pressed tightly around our necks, bid Brian goodbye and walked slowly to the nearby Queens station lugging our heavy bags.

On time, the train lumbered into the station, and with our tickets held tightly in our hands, we boarded the car which was already filled with tired, silent passengers, many standing and staring impassively at the squalid industrial area passing before us. Was this any way to start one's day?

At the next stop, many passengers left which freed seats for all of us. Ranny and Don sat together. I shared one with a middle-aged lady who whose maid's uniform peeked out under her brown, woolen winter coat. Neither of us spoke much, but she did ask me, "When does this train get to Bridgeport." I wasn't much help as I replied, "Ma'am, I have no idea. I'm going to Newport, Rhode Island to go to the Navy's Officer Candidate School." She nodded. She was not impressed, not in the least.

I was still in a daze from the weekend. My previous hesitant thoughts about OCS and my future left me at Penn Station. Now reality had returned. My stomach turned queasy with fear and doubt. Leaning back on the seat and with a soft sigh, my eyes closed and my mind raced through a myriad of good and bad reminisces: early days living in Chaffee, Sikeston and Benton; my friends, Dick and Johnny; Dad and Mother's separation; moving to Cape Girardeau; Camp Lewallen; Alice Jean, my high school sweetheart; Coach Muegge; my basketball career at Cape Central and Southeast Missouri State; graduation; my first real job with

Shell Oil Company and Mother's many sacrifices along the way.

A new chapter in my life was emerging, one which would eventually bring many changes and challenges far far away from my southeast Missouri roots. I was so fortunate to have been on that next journey. But that's another story.

■ ■ ■ ■ ■

Mungah

Arriving in Newport, Rhode Island on a cold, windy January 4, 1957 afternoon, I wondered whether I was in my right mind. At the time in late November when I took the oath as a naval reservist and committed to attend the Navy's Officer Candidate School, it seemed like a good idea. I wasn't so sure upon my arrival.

At least in the Navy, I'd be on a ship sleeping under and between sheets and not training in the woods of Ft. Leonard Wood, Missouri as an Army recruit carrying an M-16 rifle. After all, the school was only for four months and then I would be commissioned as an ensign and hopefully assigned to a destroyer on the west coast. That thought pleased me, but arriving in the face of Newport's harsh winter gave me some doubts.

When my class of candidates first arrived, we were given a series of battery tests covering mechanics, reasoning, etc. As one whose mechanical aptitude was comparable to some simian trying to operate a tractor, I knew I wasn't going to fare well in this area.

Can you imagine my understanding the steam cycle of a destroyer? I never did, but with significant and patient assistance from my classmates, I stumbled through the engineering course. For the rest of the curriculum, subjects like navigation, seamanship and weapons were new to us, but became relatively easy. Many of my classmates were graduates of elite eastern schools like Harvard and Yale. Two friends from college, Ranny Young and Don Rasche, were in our class, and we more than held our own with this group. Southeast Missouri State College had prepared us well.

After about six weeks into the class, my company officer, Lt. Rumplick, passed the word for me to be in his office at 1600 (4 pm). Somehow, I knew I wasn't being invited to receive the "Good Sailor of the Week" award.

"Mungah, I have reviewed your battery test scores, and it is our recommendation you consider disenrolling from the school immediately. Your mechanical test score was one of the lowest we've ever had here. Obviously, there's no way you can ever get through the engineering class."

Initially, I wanted to correct my CO and tell him my name was Munger, not Mungah. However, in view of hearing the threat of disenrollment, I thought better of the idea. Throughout my naval career, I was never addressed as Munger, always Mungah. I never quite understood that, but in time, I got used to it.

"No, Sir, I'll admit engineering is a challenge, but my instructor is very good. Between him and my classmates, I'm doing all right. I now have a 3.2 grade point average (4.0 is perfect) with only a few weeks to go." I held my breath thinking he wasn't about to believe me.

A heavy frown came over the officer's face as he responded, "Well, Mungah, we're going to watch you very closely. We won't disenroll you, but we're going to keep a close eye on your progress. Dismissed."

I thanked him kindly, repeated my love for the Navy, God, country, motherhood and apple pie, did a clumsy about face and left. My classmates welcomed me back enthusiastically to the barracks believing a visit to the lieutenant's office had been a precursor to being sent to basic training in Bainbridge, Maryland. I had been saved!

The classes went well after that. Adjusting to military life, tests given at every class, study hall every night, inspections, etc. became a matter of routine. 36-hour liberties in Newport for a bunch of highly energized college boys were very welcomed. We couldn't wait to leave and hated to come back.

With about a month to go, hemorrhoids came into my life. The Navy doesn't take kindly to any kind of illness, and when I reported to sick bay for relief, they immediately sent me over to the Navy hospital. The problem would be taken care of with surgery and a month's stay there. I pleaded to the Navy doctor during his bedside visit saying "Please, Doctor, please let me go back to my class. I have only one month to go before I am commissioned, and you can order me back for the operation. Please, pretty please."

To my relief, he approved my request to return to my class. In a few weeks, I was commissioned in May, and for whatever reason, probably because they understood with my mechanical aptitude a ship under my command would find itself grounded in a mud bank somewhere rather than at a pier, I received no orders to return to the hospital. Nor did I receive orders to report to a west-coast-based destroyer. Instead, I was assigned to the headquarters of the Supreme Allied Commander Atlantic, Norfolk, Virginia. The command was the Navy arm of NATO. It was strictly a planning organization, no ships, just a bunch of senior foreign officers enjoying a leisurely billet in Norfolk with their families. My duties were those of a communications watch officer, hardly a stressful assignment which required me to disseminate messages, classified and non-classified, to the senior staff. As an ensign on shore duty, it was about the best I could hope for. Besides, the stress of living with four other bachelor naval officers in Virginia Beach was enough for me.

In April, 1958, about a year into the assignment, I heard that the senior staff was seeking a junior officer to accompany British Admiral Woods and other senior officers to visit those NATO nations, in Europe and Canada, which would be supplying naval support in the event "the balloon went up." That was the code word for "there's a war on!"

Requirements were for the officer to have typing and shorthand skills. I typed well, but as for shorthand, I left that high school class after only four days. Shorthand proved undecipherable.

I really wanted to go, but the shorthand requirement appeared to be an overwhelming obstacle. At the time, I dated a young lady who was a secretary at the Navy's main base. I confessed my problem to her, but she had a solution. She would teach me speedwriting.

"What's speedwriting, Judy? Explain it to me." Needless to say, the speedwriting concept was not difficult to understand. For example: "speed" would be shortened to "spd." I got it; I could do that. I made an appointment for an interview with the admiral's aide, Lcdr. Bonner.

Mr. Bonner was the quintessential British officer, stiff, precise in communications, and very proper. I had met him, but like so many senior officers on the staff, it was not a personal relationship, only as a watch officer delivering messages to a senior officer.

His office was adjacent to the admiral's. Totally organized, his desk was void of any extraneous material. One could conduct a military operation off it. He greeted me formally and said, "Now, Mungah, this assignment is very demanding. You will in effect be the admiral's primary and personal secretary. You will be expected to take dictation from him, anytime he so chooses. All of his work will be designated top secret. You understand, Mungah?"

"Yes Sir!" I more than understood. What in the world was I getting myself into? Would speedwriting carry me? If not, I'd be sent home immediately. My naval career would be ruined.

"Now, tell me Mungah, you do have typing and shorthand skills, don't you?"

"Yes Sir, I do. I type very well, and my shorthand is done with a process called speedwriting."

A puzzled look came over Mr. Bonner's face. "Speedwriting? Please explain, Mungah. Please explain."

Taking a deep breath, I went about attempting to explain the process. Surprisingly, he grasped the concept at once. "Oh, Bully! That's fantastic! I've never heard of that. It'll work. I'll now take steps to get your orders processed. You'll be a member of the team. Well done, Mungah!"

I was ecstatic with being accepted, but I really had to bone up on the speedwriting challenge, and over the next few weeks, Judy and I went into a full court press. I became fairly adept, but only as long as she practiced dictation to me in a slow, steady voice. I had no idea how Admiral Woods would perform, but at least, I felt fairly prepared.

As the team's departure date came for early June, I became excited with the prospect of visiting England, France, Denmark, Portugal, the Netherlands and Canada. At that stage of my life, I had barely gotten out of Missouri; St. Louis was the largest city ever visited in my childhood. Going to Newport, I had the pleasure of seeing New York City, the Big Apple, for the first time in my life. Yes, I was strictly a babe in the woods.

We left around June 10, flying to Paris overnight with a stop in Newfoundland. The fact that I was in a seat between two rather heavy officers was no inconvenience. I didn't care. I would have been happy in the cargo section. I slept not a wink and was completely jazzed. Pareee, here I come!

Our flight arrived in mid-morning of June 11. We checked into our hotel which gave me an opportunity to at least sleep a few hours before dinner. At dinner, the team sat down to a sumptuous French meal. I had bonded with a U.S. Navy commander, R. D. "Buck" Byard. As an enlisted man, he was stationed on the U.S.S. Arizona which was destroyed by Japanese aircraft during the Pearl Harbor attack, December 7, 1941. He subsequently became commissioned, and received his MBA at Harvard. A supply corps officer, his expertise was logistics.

The sommelier came to our place at the table and suggested a wine appropriate for the dinner, a Bordeaux, vintage 1950. Byard agreed and as the man retired to get our wine, I said, "Commander Byard, I don't drink wine."

I thought the commander was going to come right out of his shoes hearing my negative response to drinking wine. "What do you mean, you don't drink wine? Do you realize French wine is the best wine in the world? You will drink this wine, Mungah, and you will enjoy it. Understand?"

"You see, Commander, I once got very sick at a college beer bust where Red Ripple, or maybe it was Thunderbird wine, brought me to my knees. It was red wine, and I haven't touched any wine, particularly red wine since."

Byard laughed loud and long. The room echoed with his laughter as the other officers looked around to find out what was so funny. When he told them what I had said, they joined in the laughing and joking of the moment. "Well, Mungah, you're gonna find there's one helluva difference between the wine we're gonna have and that trash you had in college. Believe me!"

The sommelier brought the wine selection and watched approvingly as Buck savored its bouquet, sipped it gently, nodded positively and said in his minimal French, "Au Bon! Au Bon!" Hearing that, I guess the commander liked it.

While I didn't protest my wine glass being filled, I knew I wasn't going to like it. My memory of the bad experience hung over me like a dark cloud. Slowly, I raised the glass to my lips and I was overwhelmed with the taste. "Oh my goodness, Commander! This is really good, really good!" I was hooked, and have been so ever since.

The next morning, our team motored out to the headquarters of Supreme Allied Commander, Europe. A general was scheduled to present a lecture on the security of Europe under NATO. Mr. Bonner informed me at breakfast that I was to meet with Admiral Woods immediately after the lecture in order that he could dictate his comments covering the presentation. My stomach tightened as I realized my baptism of fire was only a few hours away.

Leaving the presentation, Mr. Bonner escorted me into a secure room where the admiral awaited me. A very kind man, one who had commanded a submarine in World War II, greeted me warmly. "Ah, Mungah, good to have you aboard with us. If you will, get your pad. I want to dictate a memorandum to Jerry." Jerry was the four-star USN Admiral Jerald Wright who held the position of Supreme Allied Commander, Atlantic. Would I ever refer to him as Jerry? No, I barely would address a Lieutenant Junior Grade by his or her first name.

Admiral Woods seated himself behind a long, mahogany table. He began to dictate in a fast, syncopated style. My blood ran cold. I was about to be found as an incompetent, a fraud, an imposter.

"Mungah, this will be a Cosmic Top Secret memorandum to Admiral Jerald Wright, Supreme Allied Commander, Atlantic. Dear Jerry . . . ." I certainly could get that introduction. It was what would come next that terrified me to my core.

"Today, errrr, no Mungah. Let's say this morning, no, let's say at 1100." That was the beginning of his dictation. It was slow, ponderous, and repetitious in a dictation that I could have recorded same in calligraphy.

Suddenly, he stopped and in a somewhat disgusting manner said, "No, Mungah, I don't want to dictate this. Instead, I'll call Jerry on the phone. I presume there's a secure phone I can use here." I'll ask Bonner to get one for me. That will be all for today, Mungah. Thank you for being here."

I stood up from my chair, bracing myself at attention, thanked the admiral, followed him out the room and took a cab back to the hotel. My day had ended. Not in any way I had anticipated, but it had ended. For the rest of the 40-day tour, I never had to take another word of dictation from the admiral. My duties, for the most part, were non-existent save attending receptions given by our foreign hosts and reciprocated by our team. The French champagne was even better than the Bordeaux.

The one duty I had as the team would arrive in another NATO country was that of delivering and placing all classified material in the military's secure vault prior to meetings. Upon leaving the plane, the team would run over to me with their bags in hand and in an almost collective voice and unified thrust say, "Mungah, get my bag."

Getting senior officers' bags was a small price for me, a 22-year-old ensign, to have had the experience of visiting such places as Paris, London, Copenhagen, Lisbon, Amsterdam, and Ottawa, immersing myself in their cultures, discovering French wine, and realizing that speedwriting wasn't nearly as difficult as it could be.

Author's Note:

The remainder of my naval career presented no more trips to Europe and Canada. It was spent entirely in Norfolk at SACLANT where I became a registered publications and security officer. My release from active duty came in May

1960 and a return to civilian life and my previous employer, Shell Oil Co. I remained in the naval reserve for a total of 13 years, attaining the final rank of commander and commanding two Naval Security Group units in St. Louis and New Haven, CT; both received national honors.

All in all, it was an experience I'll always cherish, and one I'll never forget.

■■■■■

50 Year High School Reunion

Attending the 50th reunion of the 1952 class of Central High School on the weekend of September 27, 2002 gave me an opportunity to reunite with many of my classmates whom I had not seen since graduation. These people were a major part of my early life, and several had appeared in my stories. A reunion with them to share so many memories was too important to miss.

As you have read the many stories of my growin' up in southeast Missouri, one of the many boyhood personalities described in those stories was John Brussman. In John's case, I had not seen him since college. We met in the second grade in Benton, played together almost every day until he moved to Cape Girardeau in 1945 with his Uncle John and Aunt Nona Hobbs, two of the most kind and beautiful people I have ever known. We continued our close relationship through Lorimier School and Central, both active in scouting and trying to grow gracefully and somewhat clumsily out of adolescence into manhood.

At college, we grew somewhat apart. I concentrated on history, accounting, and varsity basketball. He in chemistry, but both of us were still aggressively seeking manhood and figuring out what we wanted to do with the rest of our lives. He connected handsomely with a real beauty, Jackie Drui, and they married immediately after his graduation in 1957.

From there, we essentially lost contact with each other, both serving in the military and pursuing a career, John with Anheuser-Busch, me with Shell Oil Company. Later, in my last years with Shell, I heard that John had retired as the Vice President and General Manager of Busch Agricultural Resources, Inc., a subsidiary of Anheuser-Busch. He was responsible for malting, rice milling, hop farming, and contracting. Was this the same skinny Johnny who swam with me in the Mississippi River, set pins at the Lutheran bowling alley, swam in the creek down stream from the Ozark Packing Company, and climbed the rope with no feet at Central? Indeed, it was and I could not have been more proud of his success!

In the late 90s, John and I connected again via e-mail and resumed our relationship electronically. I brought him up-to-date with living in Flagstaff, Arizona, and shared with him my many stories. He shared his lifestyle in Sand Point, Idaho, hunting, dressing in buckskin, and playing the role of a mountain man in the region's annual celebration. Unfortunately, Jackie had passed away, but, John had remarried Martha, Jackie's best friend. Life was good for both of us in Idaho and Arizona respectively. (He and Martha subsequently moved to Reno, Nevada a few years ago where they now live today.)

Both of us were excited to see one another after all those years. The reunion would be perfect for that to happen, returning to our roots, reminiscing over our youthful experiences, catching up on each other's family, and most importantly, seeing and visiting with our former Central classmates.

My wife, Molly, and I met John at the Drury Suites. Martha didn't come to the reunion, but instead remained with her mother in St. Louis. One would think after all those years apart from one of your closest boyhood friends, both pursuing contrasting interests, traveling in different circles, there would be a lingering period of transition. That didn't happen. We were off and running, caught in a time warp . . . it was 1942, not 2002!

We immediately immersed ourselves in memories of yesterday, remembering goin' to the Rialto Theater on

Friday nights, wonderin' if our parents would ever find out we were swimmin' in the Mississippi or who had the best rubber gun on South Middle Street?   Poor Molly was magnificent as she stood by and shook her head at two old friends reliving their salad days. As she said later, "How do you guys remember all those things?" John and I just shook our heads. We just did . . . we always will.

Driving out to Cape's Country Club for the reunion's opening reception, we wondered if we would be able to recognize everyone. Fortunately, the reunion committee had plans to avoid such an embarrassment and name tags for all saved the day.

We would have never recognized some of our classmates. They had changed, though obviously we hadn't! Others, to our amazement, appeared to have changed very little. Good genes were making a statement. Working the room, we tried to meet and greet all there. Pictures of sons, daughters, and grandchildren spread throughout the room. Experiences at Central that were so serious and humiliating at the time brought hearty laughter as they were recalled. Warm friendly hugs filled the room as old friends reunited after so many years apart. It was as if 50 years had passed only yesterday.

Where had they been and what had all these people been doing since graduation? The committee had requested that those attending and unable to attend write a one-page summary of their lives after graduation.

Mine read as follows:

What I Have Done Since Graduation

With ambition soaring after graduation from Central, I would go to college, become a lawyer, settle down in Cape Girardeau and live in a house on Sunset. I look back today and say, "Well, fulfilling one out of four ain't bad."

With an offer of a basketball scholarship to Missouri University, I forsook Cape State and figured that All-American recognition was a virtual cinch. A year later, with my dream quashed with the reality that I ain't even good enough to make the traveling squad, I transferred back to Cape, spent three years on Houck Field House's bench, got an accounting degree (I was honored in 1998 to receive the Southeast Missouri State University's Alumni Merit Award—College of Business) and once again dreamed of becoming a tax attorney, settling down in Cape and so on. Reality once again reared its ugly head.

Shell Oil Co. entered the picture, and their offer of $376 a month to become a Treasury Management Trainee swelled my head with visions of really becoming rich. Alas, my student deferment was lost, and the U.S. Army wanted my body. With a quick right turn, I joined the U.S. Navy, went to OCS, spent three years on a LMD (large mahogany desk) in Norfolk, VA, and in 1960 returned to Shell in St. Louis.

With neither desire nor interest, I got out of accounting, joined Shell's sales force in 1961 and spent more than 14 years persuading dealers to clean their rest rooms, leasing and purchasing service station sites, and spending time in Des Moines, St. Louis, New York City, Chicago, and Houston. My retail career continued to skyrocket laterally and somewhat downward until Shell wisely or unwisely transferred me into public relations in 1975. Eureka! I finally found something that I could really screw up. On the other hand, how could anybody screw up Big Oil? They're masters at it!

My last 11 years with Shell (Manager, Public Affairs—1980-1991) was spent on the West Coast where I attempted to convince the public that pollution from oil refineries, chemical plants and pipelines was good for one's health.

Retiring in 1992, I started a consulting firm in Los Angeles specializing in crisis communications and media training. Leaving the crowded freeways in 1996, I moved to Anacortes, Washington, continued consulting and after a year and a half, shed my raincoat and moved to Flagstaff, Arizona in 1997 where everybody is above average and looks it.

Flagstaff brought me more luck than I deserved. I married Molly, an incredibly fantastic lady, continued consulting, and became a dedicated and passionate volunteer for the American Red Cross. Despite a few aches and pains, my life is very good here in the mountains, a long way from Sunset.

I'm one lucky dude!

Later, reading their life's experiences made me even more proud of my classmates. Alene Sadler, one of our best and finest English teachers, once told me, "Gene, this was the class that the stars shined upon." Miss Sadler's pronouncement was certainly a precursor to so many of those who graduated from Central in 1952 and who later have lived such totally fulfilled professional and personal lives.

We left the reception and joined others (Andy and Jennie Juden nee Hosea, Bill and Dixie Banks nee Bader, Roger and Alice Jean Adams Thweatt nee Porritt, Don & Janey Bruns nee McNeely) for a sumptuous dinner at the Petit N'Orleans, Cape's finest restaurant. Others there must have thought that there was a family reunion going on as continuous laughter filled the room. They were right, we were family!

Calling it a night, we went back to Drury where Molly begged off as John and I sauntered over to Outback restaurant for a nightcap. We had had a lovely evening seeing old friends, and it was only natural to continue our conversation over to our early days on South Middle, riding our bicycles to and from Capaha Park, our early crushes, playing softball and basketball at Lorimier school, being terrified of Coach Muegge and his infamous canvassed-back paddle, setting pins at the Lutheran bowling alley, and all of the youthful things young boys did.

So many years ago. So many memories.

We were the last customers at Outback that evening. Our nervous waiter kept pacing past our table wondering when these two old men were going to leave. We tipped him handsomely as we finally left just after midnight.

Back in our room, Molly was sound asleep. I wasn't sleepy, so I rested there in the dark and reflected on the day, the reunion, and particularly my parents.

Thinking about my father and remembering how he was such a master in the courtroom I wondered if I had missed something by not becoming a lawyer. I think not, and believe he would have been very proud of what my life had become. I only wish that in his waning days before he passed away in 1964, I had told him that I loved him. I shall always regret that.

My thoughts turned to my mother. My being solely raised by her, especially after moving to Cape, brought on a tremendous change in both of our lives. As a single parent, she sacrificed so much for my welfare and happiness, doing without so many things so that I could move into the town without embarrassment or feeling that I didn't belong because I didn't have a father living with us. Thanks to her and my friends' parents, I always felt that I belonged.

Mother never re-married after leaving Dad and to my knowledge, never even dated another man. Instead, she devoted her entire life to me from the seventh grade at Lorimier to my graduation from college in 1956.

Ah, but she did have a sharp tongue that was cutting and many times would go "over the line" with my friends, destroying long-term relationships in a brief moment. A loyal Democrat and a voracious reader, she never suffered fools and sycophants lightly. In 1987, still living in the same apartment on Broadway, after almost 14 years, she fell and broke her hip. For the next five years, she lingered in a nursing home, first in Cape and later in Little Rock. Mother passed away in 1992 at the age of 92. She was one remarkable lady, not without faults, of course. Knowing her childhood, that her mother died at an early age and was followed by a string of step-mothers who would just as soon have had "Little Ruth" out of their lives, her marriage and often stormy relationship with her husband, she was truly amazing. And I loved her deeply and told her often. She will always be my hero, "the wind beneath my wings."

It was nearly 2 am, and I was still wide awake. My sister, Martel, 13 years older, then came into my mind. That age difference essentially eliminated her from my growing up in southeast Missouri. She had married and was out of my life during that time. She had been in a Cincinnati nursing home for the past two years, her health failing; she passed away in December 2002. While living in Little Rock, she was Mother's constant visitor during those nursing home days. I shall forever be indebted to her for her kindness and unselfish devotion to our mother.

Saturday, September 28, dawned bright and clear, a perfect fall day. We drove out Bloomfield Road to see the Juden's new house under construction. My, how that one-lane road's ambience has changed, with its upscale subdivisions now standing proudly among the road's mature oak and maple forests!

For lunch, we went with John out to visit the Hinni family (John and Marie) off Big Bend Road. John Hinni had also been a big part of my early life as a Boy Scout counselor at Camp Lewallen. When I left Cape to work at Shell in St. Louis, he took over my room and became Mother's renter. She loved him as one of her sons, watching him finish at the college and then go on to receive his Ph.D. at Northwestern University. He and I became detached for many years, but were reunited at Mother's funeral in 1992. Since then, we communicate frequently, sharing our similar philosophies and reminiscing over our beloved scouting days. John is my soul mate and brother.

John H. had not seen John B. since scouting days, so their reunion was very special. Sitting out on the porch of the Hinni's pastoral house snuggled amongst an abundance of unspoiled trees and fauna, we laughed unending at our tales of attending and working at the scout camp along the

St. Francis River. We talked about hunting frogs at night bare-assed from a canoe, drinking coffee from a pot that was never cleaned or emptied, and wondering why our girlfriends weren't writing to us.

Broussard's, Cape's Cajun restaurant located on Main Street, later indulged our quasi-youthful and enthusiastic patter as we scoffed down delicious crab cakes, fried oysters and cold beer . . . Budweiser, of course! Another time warp among old friends.   Another magical moment of that weekend.

Saying goodbye to the Hinni's, we sauntered down Main Street, once the scene of our hangin' out on Saturdays as we would wander in and out of stores, seldom buying anything, but hoping we would see our friends and those girls whom we wished were our girlfriends. Again, like magic, we ran into some of the old gang, also eating at one of the street's newest restaurants and taking in the sights and sounds of a street that once bustled with stores and shops serving Cape and the surrounding area. The emergence of Interstate 55 and its surrounding centers of economic activity had changed that. Main Street was no longer the street we remembered, and its time had passed. As some anonymous and wise sage once said, "There is nothing as constant as change."

Returning to the country club that evening for a buffet dinner and dance was a lovely way to end the reunion. Many classmates during the day had visited old friends and relatives and simply drove around town to see the changes over the years. A few had not been back to Cape in many years, so the changes they saw occupied much of the exchanges during the dinner, e.g., "Gosh, the Broadway, Rialto, Esquire, and Orpheum theaters are no more. Where are the movies in town? Did you see that big bridge that they're building across the river? What are they going to do with the old one? Have you seen how the college has grown? What in the world has happened to our Central High School? It's no longer on Pacific Street . . . where is it now?"

We ate, danced to the swinging music of Jerry Ford's three-piece combo (I had been his scoutmaster with Centenary Methodist Church's Troop 3) and continued to gather with our classmates and their spouses, hearing complaints about their aches and pains, about their next planned vacation, extolling their work as volunteers in their communities and so on. Despite some there who had had most impressive careers, there was no braggadocio directed toward that subject. Those conversations were focused on others, their lives, what were they doing now. There was no "look at me and how important I am" in the room!

Calling it an evening, we headed back to Drury with a short stop at the Petit. There, John gave the bartender a rather definitive lecture on the importance of having fresh beer on hand for the customer. Molly and I beamed at John's suave approach to bringing the young man into the 21st Century with a tutorial on why beer needs to be fresh. Anheuser-Busch would have been proud of John, too!

Finally calling it a day, we bade farewell to John, promising to join him and Martha at their house in Idaho, or wherever they decided to live in the future. He promised to do the same, to visit us in Flagstaff. It had been too long since I had seen John, an absence that will not be repeated in our future.

Driving back to St. Louis the next morning, I didn't have a lot to say to Molly. My thoughts focused on those classmates still with us, and those who had gone to the "Big Tiger in the sky," old departed friends like: Ranny Young and Don Rasche (classmates of mine at U.S. Navy OCS in 1957), Don Stehr (fellow high school and college's Benton Society member, who I would always get together with when he was in Los Angeles on business with IBM), Jo Donna Crenshaw nee Day (Central's best dancer, one who I was always too shy to even ask to dance), and so many more.

I also was saddened that despite seeing all of those classmates at the reunion, those who were such a huge part of my early days, my roots, those for whom I would forever have great love and appreciation for were absent. Would I ever see them again?

Back in Flagstaff, I sent the following letter to the *Southeast Missourian* commenting on our reunion:

October 2, 2002
To: Editor, Southeast Missourian

Having attended Central High School's 1952 class reunion recently, I was so grateful for the experience and the opportunity to renew those special friendships from our salad days. Those who planned the reunion deserve our entire classmates' appreciation and thanks for a job well done.

The only regret for my 50th is that, for the most part, I probably will never see many of these friends ever again. However, the joy of seeing them even for the last time will remain with me always.

There are undoubtedly many former high school graduates who, for whatever reason, decline to attend their school's reunion. Whatever the reason, make every effort to do so in the future. It's well worth it.

Gene Munger
Flagstaff, Arizona

Later in 2002, I received a letter from Ann Smirl nee Keim who acknowledged that she had received my letter to the *Missourian* from her sister, Sue. The last words of her letter so captured my thoughts about the reunion, life without parents, family and loved ones. Ann wrote, "It isn't the aches and pains that hurt so much, it's the goodbyes."

Reunion of the 50s

For many years, Central High School alums have held a reunion every five years at Cape's Arena Park.

On the weekend of July 11-12, 2008, more than 700 alums from the graduating classes of the 1950s and their spouses filled the Arena and during those two days, joined together as if "nothing had changed over the years." Indeed we all were in a wonderful time warp.

It was truly one of the most gratifying experiences of my life being able to see, visit and reminisce with our classmates of more than 50 years ago, many, I suspect will not be with us five years from now.

As I would relate the reunion's happenings to my Flagstaff friends, they responded almost incredulously. "Why would you want to go back there and do that? Was Central High School that important in your early life that you would want to travel all the way to southeast Missouri to be reunited with those classmates?"

"No," I answered. "It's a Central High School thing. You wouldn't understand."

I was so proud to be at that reunion. It was so special and will always be remembered with the fondest of memories.

Tiger's forever!

Gene Munger '52, Jim Miller '53, Mike Zadick '53, and John Brussman '52 catching up during the Reunion of the 50s in July of 2008.

■ ■ ■ ■ ■

Looking Back

As I reflect on the many stories written about my growin' up in southeast Missouri during the 40s and 50s, my thoughts return to going to the Navy's Officer Candidate School in January 1957.

Ranny Young, Don Rasche and I, all 1956 Southeast Missouri State College graduates, arrived in Newport, Rhode Island on that cold, windy January day. Along with a bus load of Ivy School graduates, from Yale, Harvard, Tufts, etc., we prepared to spend four months in the Navy's attempt to make officers and gentlemen out of us.

None there had ever heard of the college or even Cape Girardeau. Some even sneered at the sight of us "farm boys" who thought they could get through the courses and become officers. For us, we never gave it a second thought. We knew we could.

In a short time, their attitude changed as we adjusted quickly to the routine of going to classes, being tested every day, and remaining cool during the stresses and strains brought on by the daily demands of Navy life. In May, we were commissioned, each ranking in the upper middle of the class and enjoying the total respect of all our peers.

Perhaps, we were too dense to be awed and intimidated by the changes brought on by existing in a military environment or just maybe, each of our southeast Missouri backgrounds made us better prepared to integrate successfully into a different culture whatever the need or task.

My long-time friend, John Brussman, now a retired executive with Anheuser-Busch, explained it very well, "We didn't know how lucky we were! Anyone not attending school in Benton and Cape during the 40s and 50s could never relate."

His thoughts ring so true. Indeed, we didn't know how lucky we were! Was luck involved in our attending schools there? No, it wasn't luck. It was simply the opportunity of having excellent teachers and friends who stood by and supported us regardless of economic and social circumstances, and communities where moral values were present and brought home in every phase of our lives.

These are a few examples of the many people and institutions that influenced me greatly:

Our teachers always dressed appropriately and as professionals. They were treated with respect. We addressed them as "Mr., Mrs., Miss, and Dr." We responded, "Yes Sir, No Sir, Yes Ma'am, No Ma'am." Their influence on us was lasting. To them we shall always be grateful.

Benton School's Oneida Daniels: Miss Daniels was one of my grade school teachers. We would have spelling contests with two teams of students being challenged to spell words provided by her. As you would imagine, the poor spellers were dismissed first, the better lasting until they were eliminated, and the winning team taunting the losing team.

At the time, it always bothered me to see my friends being humiliated by being eliminated. I talked to Miss Daniels and expressed my feelings.

I shall never forget what she told me, "Gene, those who aren't such good spellers must work to improve themselves, and when they do, they and their team will be the ultimate winner. They must not feel like they're losers. They will now work harder to be the best speller and be on the winning team. We can't all be winners, but we can always strive to do the best we can."

Lorimier School's librarian, Edith Lightfoot: Miss Lightfoot would read to us and stop now and then to ask us the meaning of a word in her reading. When we would give the meaning, she would mark a plus in her grade book, a minus when we couldn't. Because of her, I began to appreciate the value of a vocabulary, as well as the importance and joy of reading.

Central High School's English teacher, Alene Sadler: In high school, I continued to remain so naïve about life—why people, my friends, and classmates did what they did and so on.

As my English class finished reading *Death of a Salesman*, I asked Miss Sadler, "Why would anyone kill himself by driving a car into a tree?" My classmates laughed at the question.

Sadly, she looked at me and the rest of the class and said, "Sometimes, life becomes too difficult for us, and we take measures that go beyond anything any of you can imagine. Someday, you'll understand that."   I now know how prophetic her response was.

She will always remain my most favorite high school teacher. This book is dedicated to her memory.

Southeast Missouri State College's Dr. Harold Grauel: Dr. Grauel's College Grammar class was a hoot, and one of my college's most enjoyable classes. He was a perfectionist, e.g., classroom chairs were positioned precisely on marks on the floor and when in even a little bit of disarray, there was hell to pay.

From his class, I learned to really appreciate the importance of good grammar, in both speech and in writing. For that experience in his classroom, I shall always be grateful.

Scouting: Another great influence was scouting.   In those days, scouting was really the only game in town. We couldn't wait to join the Boy Scouts, and even at 11 years old, I wished the rules would change so I could be one.

Through scouting, I learned discipline, the agony of failure, and the need to assess that failure to make the necessary changes needed for success.

Learning camping skills, becoming comfortable in forests and streams, and developing leadership among my peers and my scout troop were all the result of my scouting experience.

For a young man whose parents were separated, scouting, in my mother's words, "kept me off the streets" and helped make a man out of me.

Were we, as young people, so out of control that we sometimes did things that would embarrass our parents, even ourselves?

Was swimming buck naked in the Mississippi River without our parent's knowledge and permission dangerous?

Was taking young Tenderfoot scouts on snipe hunts so shameful as to destroy one's self esteem? Was stealing apples in Och's Orchard and then throwing them off of Fort A's cliff onto cars traveling on Main Street irresponsible and dangerous?

Was slipping our dates through Leming Hall's side windows past curfew so bad?

Was sneaking down to the Blue Hole and drinking a beer during basketball season breaking training?

Did obtaining a previous copy of Dr. Doherty's European History test hoping he would give it again a breakdown in our moral principles?

Perhaps. But, hopefully we learned from our youthful indiscretions and became honest, law abiding, and responsible citizens.

Living in Flagstaff, Arizona today, my friends are amazed how I can recall my experiences of the 40s and 50s, as well as the boyhood and college relationships that have endured for now more than 50 years.

What is it about southeast Missouri that makes this happen? Is it the grade schools, high schools and college? Why does Sue and Bill Roussel's *Tiger Update,* their weekly e-mail that brings messages and remembrances, obituaries, etc. from nearly 1,000 former Central High School graduates of the 40s and 50s reflect such passion and enjoyment?

Is this unique among other places? Are we an elite group that stands above all others, having such special relationships and memories of our salad days?

I have no answer for that. John Brussman is probably right, "Anyone not attending school in Cape and Benton in the 40s and 50s could never relate."

The Munger Family in 2003 in Flagstaff, Arizona.
Pictured from left to right are stepson David Carder;
David's wife, Rory; Gene; Molly; and stepdaughter
Casey Shimpuku.

About Gene Munger

A native Missourian, Gene grew up in southeast Missouri, attended Chaffee, Sikeston, Benton, and Cape Girardeau schools. He graduated from Southeast Missouri State College in 1956 with a B.S. in Accounting.

He then joined Shell Oil Company in St. Louis in its accounting department. Entering the U.S. Navy's Officer Candidate School in January 1957, he was commissioned an ensign and served on the staff of the Supreme Allied Commander Atlantic. In 1960, he returned to Shell with assignments in retailing, real estate, and public relations. He stayed with it until his retirement in 1991 as Shell's West Coast's Public Affairs Manager for refining and marketing operations, a position he held for eleven years.

After retirement, he established Munger & Associates, a public affairs consulting firm specializing in crisis communications, media relations, emergency response plans and community relations, all areas in which he became nationally recognized.

Since 1997, he has lived in Flagstaff, Arizona. His volunteer activities include Northern Arizona University's Athletic Department, American Red Cross, Big Brothers/Big Sisters and the Coconino County Literacy Volunteers.

In 1998, Southeast Missouri University presented Munger with its Alumni Merit Award for the College of Business.

He assumed the role as the Executive Director of the Flagstaff Arizona Symphony Orchestra in 2005. After more than a decade of deficits, he restored operations to "in the black" and out of debt. He retired in April 2007.

His current hobbies include creative writing, fishing, hiking and traveling.

His wife, Molly, is the current Director of Community Relations, Northern Arizona University and was recently selected as the 2007 *Arizona Daily Sun* female Citizen of the Year.

Gene and Molly served as the co-chairs of the 2008 Coconino County United Way Campaign.